Southern
ELEGANCE

A Collection of the Best of Carolina Cuisine

Junior League of Gaston County, North Carolina

The Junior League of Gaston County, North Carolina is a non-profit service organization chartered in 1959. Its purpose is exclusively educational and charitable and is to promote voluntarism and to improve the community through the effective action and leadership of trained volunteers.

The profit realized by the Junior League of Gaston County from the sale of **Southern Elegance** will be used to support community projects that we undertake in the Gaston County area. Projects supported in the past include Teen Outreach, Family Approach to Childhood Development and the funding and building of a Habitat for Humanity House.

Additional copies may be obtained by sending $15.95 per book plus $2.50 per book for postage and handling. (North Carolina residents add $ .96 per book for sales tax.)

Junior League of Gaston County, N.C.
P.O. Box 3684
Gastonia, North Carolina 28053

First Printing	November 1987	7,000
Second Printing	November 1988	10,000
Third Printing	July 1990	10,000
Fourth Printing	April 1992	10,000
Fifth Printing	March 1993	10,000
Sixth Printing	March 1995	10,000

Printed in the USA by

WIMMER
The Wimmer Companies, Inc.
Memphis • Dallas

INTRODUCTION

Lying between the peaks of the Blue Ridge Mountains and the flatlands of the Coastal Plains, the Piedmont Plateau of North Carolina enjoys a way of life that reflects our southern heritage.

We came from the North and from the mountains to the west to find a better life in this gently rolling countryside with its warm climate and rich soil. Here we built vital, growing cities that embody our faith in the potential of our future. Our lives are at once as fast-paced as our industry, as we craft our textiles with pride, and as slow and easy as a sleepy summer afternoon and the smell of freshly cut grass.

In this region where natural resources abound, we hunt in the mountains and coastal marshes and fish in our lakes and rivers and ocean. We are nurtured by the land which provides us with the game and fowl, the seafood and bountiful harvests for our tables.

Our cuisine is more than the mere preparation of food. It is a way of life. It is relaxed, gracious entertaining and an expression of love and caring and celebration for family and friends.

The legacy of our southern heritage and the pace of our contemporary lifestyles are woven together to create our own special kind of "Southern Elegance."

Cookbook Committee

Original Committee

Patti Hunter *Chairman*
Paulette Elmore *Co-Chairman*
Peggy Cooke
Sharron Davis
Connie Gibbons
Elizabeth Goble
Cathy McCosh
Suzanne McLean
Roseanne Nichols
Allison Sonier

Holt Harris *Artist*
Original watercolor for cover by Scott Barnes reproduced by permission

In Memoriam
Mary Scott Alford Barnes
December 13, 1987

Her artistic talent enriched this book.
Her life was her greatest work of art.

*We thank all of the Junior League members
who shared recipes with us.*

Contents

Y'all Come
Menus

ACC Party
Buffalo Meal

Buffalo Wings
Bleu Cheese Dip
Carrots
Celery
German Potato Salad
Beer, Wine, Soft Drinks
Strudel with Whipped Cream

Art and History Museum Open House

Beef Tenderloin
Herb Butter and Horseradish Cream
Fresh Shrimp Mold
Deviled Eggs with Caviar and Chopped Herbs
Ham and Cheese Pastries
Roquefort Grapes
Almond Stuffed Dates with Bacon
Linzer Heart Cookies
Pressed Mints
Fruit Punch
Red and White Wine

After Theatre Supper

Sangria Blanc
Caviar Mold
Artichoke and Shrimp Casserole in Patty Shells
Tomato Aspic
Coffee Liqueur Bar

Bridal Brunch

Bride's Bowl
Screwdrivers or Wine Coolers
Pea Pods Stuffed with Herbed Cream Cheese
Cold Sliced Ham
Cherry Tomatoes with Farm Cheese
Blanched Green Beans with Vegetable Dip
Charleston Cottage Cheese Cake
Minted Iced Tea
Melon Balls
Assorted Cookies in Baskets

Dance Club Breakfast

Orange Juice with Bananas
Fresh Fruit Bowl with Tarragon Dressing
Grits Casserole
Country Ham
Scrambled Eggs
Coffee Cake
Coffee

Easter Egg Hunt

Girl Scout Punch
Lemon or Coconut Cookies
Make Your Own Sundae with Cinnamon-Blueberry Sauce,
Hot Fudge Sauce, or Granola Ice Cream Topping

Funeral Luncheon
For Out of Town Family Attending a Funeral

Biscuits
Deli Tray - Assorted Cold Meats and Cheeses
Horseradish Sauce, Mayonnaise, and Dijon Mustard
Vegetable Sandwiches
Chicken Salad Sandwiches
Deviled Eggs
Cup of Hot Soup
Brownies
Green Grapes
Iced Tea, Coffee, and Lemonade

Peach Harvest Celebration

Fuzzy Navels
Cold Peach Soup
Ham with Peach Glaze
Baked Rice
Fresh Asparagus for a Crowd
Sour Cream Rolls with Peach Preserves
Peach Ginger Crunch
Coffee with Peach Brandy and Whipped Cream

Scotch Foursome

Layered Salad
Seafood Casserole
Marinated Shrimp
Sourdough Bread
Chocolate Layered Dessert
Beer, Wine, and Iced Tea

July 4th River Picnic

Smoked Barbeque Picnic and Sauce
Potato Salad
Marinated Slaw
Baked Beans
Sourdough Rolls
Perfect Chocolate Cake
Beer
For the Children:
Hot Dogs
Chips
Pickles
Soft Drinks

Halloween Supper

Hot Mulled Wine
Pumpkin Crisp
Russian Rye Bread and Dip
Make Your Own Open-Faced Sandwiches
Creamy "Philly" Soup
Potato Salad
For the Children:
Fried Chicken
Apples in a Dish
Apple Cider
Rebecca's Refrigerator Cookies - Decorate Your Own

Octoberfest

Sauerbraten with Gingersnap Gravy
Red Cabbage with Apples
Cucumber Salad
Fresh Apple Cake

Open Season Feast

Georgia Quail or Dove
Wild Rice Pilaf
Citrus Honey Carrots
James Forney's Spinach Timbales
Cheese Biscuits
Lane Cake

Oyster Roast

Roasted Select Oysters
Boiled Jumbo Shrimp
Cocktail Sauce
Drawn Butter
Assorted Fruits and Cheeses
Mock Crab Spread
Cole Slaw
Baked Beans
White Wine
Hot Apple Crisp
Irish Coffee

Tailgate Picnic

Cheese Ball
Evelyn's Ham Biscuits
Raw Vegetables Marinated in Italian Dressing
Chicken Livers and Wings
Thermos Jug Soup
Pickled Peaches
Chocolate Chip Pie
Bloody Marys
Chilled Wine

Traditional Thanksgiving Day Dinner

Whiskey Sours
Turkey
Oyster Casserole
Dressing
Giblet Gravy
Sweet Potato Casserole
Raw Cranberry Salad
Green Beans with Almonds
Fresh Coconut Cake
Chocolate Pecan Pie
Ambrosia
Tea
Coffee

Traditional Christmas Brunch

Fresh Squeezed Orange Juice for the Children
Mimosas with Fresh Squeezed Orange Juice for the Adults
Do-ahead Broiled Bacon for a Crowd
Grilled Link Sausage
Swedish Pancakes (Platter) with Lingonberries and Sour
Cream
Eggs for a Crowd with Blender Hollandaise Sauce
OR
French Scrambled Eggs
Fresh Fruit Cup (Diced and Sliced Seasonal Fruit)
Cream Cheese Braids
Vort Limpe (Traditional Swedish Bread) Toast
Coffee with Cinnamon and Real Cream

New Year's Eve Champagne Fling

Crab Dip with Sesame Crackers
Mushrooms in Wine
Cornish Hen
Saffron Rice
Spinach and Artichoke Casserole
Yeast Rolls
Praline Cheese Cake
Swedish Cream
Irish Coffee
Champagne

New Year's Day

Hair of the Dog Bloody Marys
Black-Eyed Peas with Rice (Hoppin' John)
Turnip Greens with Pepper Vinegar
Glorified Onions
Country Ham
Cornbread
Sour Cherry Salad
Fruit Cobbler
Coffee

Cookbook Kickoff Cocktail Party

Mushroom Croustades
Roquefort Mousse
Cold Grilled Steak with Mustard Sauce
Icy Pickled Shrimp
Vegetable Tray with Beau Monde Dip
Chafing Dish Crab Spread
Pate de Joie de Volaille
Sugar and Spice Pecans
Frosted Grapes
Chatham Artillery Punch

Winter Fireside Supper

Lasagna
Spinach Salad with Homemade Croutons
Garlic Bread
Charlotte Russe

York-Chester Road Race

Baked Cheese and Crackers
Blondies Carbonara
Caesar Salad
Parmesan Toasts
Fresh Fruit with Whipped Cream
Beer

Super Bowl Party

Keg of Beer
Margaritas
Tex Mex Dip and Chips
Guacamole
Mexican Cornbread
McCosh's Texas Chili
Sliced Vegetable Tray
Hundred Dollar Brownies

Supper Club Dinner

California Shrimp and Avocado Salad
Marinated Beef Tenderloin
with Bernaise Sauce or Mushrooms and Onions
Parslied Rice
Broiled Herbed Tomatoes
Sally Lunn Bread
Red or Rosé Wine
Fresh Berries in Cointreau with Whipped Cream
Brandy Alexanders
Coffee

Down Home Cookin'
Good Ole Southern Recipes

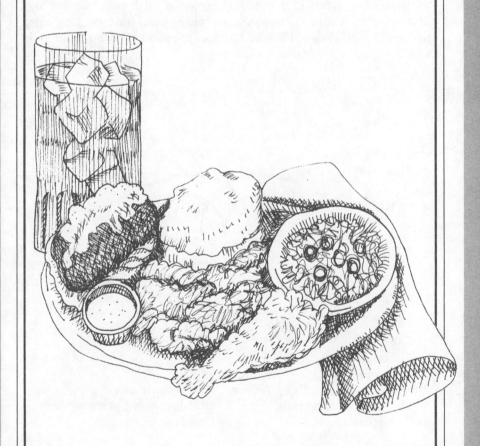

Quick Oyster Stew

Serve immediately   Serves 4

½ pint oysters   ¾ teaspoon garlic salt
1 stick butter   1 quart of whole milk
1 small onion, grated   Fresh ground pepper to taste
¾ teaspoon salt

Pick oysters for bits of shell. Place in collander and rinse with cold water. In a skillet saute onion in 2 tablespoons butter until onions are transparent. Add the rest of the butter, salts, pepper, and oysters; heat until edges of oysters curl. Pour into large pan with milk that has been heated but not boiled. Simmer to near boiling point. Add more fresh pepper and pour into soup bowls. More salt, pepper, and butter may be added for individual taste.

Sharron Davis

Tomato and Okra Gumbo

Serve immediately   Serves 8

2 pounds okra, fresh or frozen   ½ teaspoon salt
1 No. 2 can of tomatoes   1 tablespoon butter
  (2½ cups)   1 tablespoon sugar

Cut okra in ½-inch pieces. Pour tomatoes in saucepan. Add okra along with all other seasonings and cover. Cook on medium heat for 20 minutes.

Cookbook Committee

Cheese Grits

Serve immediately   Serves 6-8

1 cup grits
4 cups water
1 teaspoon salt
1-6 ounce package sharp
  Cheddar cheese

¼ cup butter
2 egg yolks, well beaten
2 egg whites, stiffly beaten
Cracker or dry bread crumbs

Cook grits, butter, and cheese in salted water until done. Add egg yolks. Fold in egg whites. Put in greased casserole. Sprinkle top with crumbs. Bake at 350 degrees for 45 minutes.

Cookbook Committee

Simplest Brunswick Stew

Serve immediately   Makes 2 quarts

2 pounds pork or chicken,
  cooked and chopped
1 teaspoon fresh ground pepper
3 teaspoons Worcestershire
  sauce
⅓ cup bacon drippings
½ cup barbeque sauce

1½ cups catsup
2 cups cooked potatoes,
  diced
3-17 ounce cans cream style
  corn
1-16 ounce can baby lima beans

Place all ingredients in saucepan, cover and heat slowly. Salt and more hot sauce may be needed according to taste preferred.

Sharron Davis

Barbequed Spareribs

Serve immediately   Serves 4

4 pounds of lean pork   **Your favorite barbeque**
** spareribs**   **sauce**

Wash ribs and sprinkle generously with salt and pepper. Place in roaster and seal with foil. Cook in oven at 350 degrees for about 30 minutes. Remove foil. Drain liquid from roaster. Pour barbeque sauce generously over ribs. Return to oven and bake at 350 degrees until ribs are brown and tender.

Cookbook Committee

Barbequed Chicken

Serve immediately   Serves 4

1-2 pound fryer, cut into   **2 tablespoons butter**
** 4 parts**   **2 cups barbeque sauce**
1 cup flour

Flour chicken lightly and brown quickly in butter. Place chicken on hot barbeque grill, cover and cook until tender, turning every 15 minutes. About 10 minutes before chicken is completely done, brush generously with barbeque sauce.

Cookbook Committee

Chicken and Dumplings

Serve immediately   Serves 8

1-2½ pound chicken, disjointed   **1 teaspoon salt**
and ready to cook   **1 teaspoon pepper**

Cover chicken with water in a large pot, and add salt and pepper. Boil over medium heat for 30 minutes. Pour off broth and save to use for dumplings. Remove chicken from bones.

Dumplings:
2 cups flour   **½ cup buttermilk**
½ cup milk

Mix in bowl and knead into another bowl of flour until dough is firm. Mash flat on floured surface. Let stand about 10 minutes. Roll out with rolling pin until knife-blade thin. Cut into 2-inch squares. Drop into boiling broth. Cook about 10 minutes on high heat. Reduce heat to low and return chicken to pot. Pour in 1½ cups milk. Remove from heat. Add salt and pepper if needed.

Cookbook Committee

Favorite Chicken Pie

Serve immediately   Serves 6

1-6 pound hen, cooked   **1 stick butter, melted**
1½ cups chicken broth   **½ teaspoon salt**
1-10¾ ounce can cream of   **Dash of pepper**
chicken soup   **1 cup buttermilk**
1 cup self-rising flour

Cut chicken into bite-size pieces and place in greased 9 x 13-inch dish. Mix broth and soup and bring to a boil. Pour over chicken. Combine flour, butter, salt, pepper, and buttermilk. Spoon over chicken slowly. Bake at 425 degrees for 30 minutes.

Beverly Poag

Cole Slaw

This is better if prepared ahead.

May prepare ahead   Serves 10-12

1 large head cabbage	1 to 2 carrots, grated
½ cup sugar	(optional)
½ cup vinegar	½ cup red cabbage, grated
¼ cup milk	(optional)
1 to 2 cups mayonnaise	1 green pepper, grated
Salt and pepper to taste	(optional)
1 small onion, grated	
(optional)	

Wash and grate cabbage or chop finely in food processor. Add sugar, vinegar, milk, and salt and pepper to taste. Add enough mayonnaise for the desired consistency. You may also add the onion, carrots, green pepper, or red cabbage as an option. Refrigerate until ready to serve.

Cookbook Committee

Turnip Greens

You may cook collards or mustard greens this way except for the roots.

Serve immediately   Serves 6

1 large bunch fresh turnip	2 cups water
greens with roots	1 teaspoon salt
1 medium-size piece salt pork	

Strip stems from leaves (unless very tender) and wash thoroughly. Place in covered saucepan; add meat, water, and salt. Cook for 45 minutes on medium heat or until tender. Remove meat; drain greens in collander. Place in pan and chop scissor-like with two knives. Depending on taste, you may want to add more salt. Keep hot and add 2 tablespoons of bacon drippings and butter or margarine.

Cookbook Committee

Fried Okra

Serve immediately   Serves 4

1 pound fresh okra   **Salt and pepper to taste**
½ cup white cornmeal

Wash okra and slice into ½-inch rounds. Toss okra in plastic bag with cornmeal seasoned with salt and pepper. Fry in hot oil in skillet, turning often and sprinkling with salt and pepper as needed. When lightly browned, remove with slotted spoon and drain on paper towels.

Variation: For a thicker crust, dip in beaten egg before rolling in cornmeal.

Cookbook Committee

Creamed Corn

Serve immediately   Serves 6

1 dozen medium ears sweet   **1 teaspoon pepper, freshly**
corn, cut off cob   **ground**
½ cup butter or bacon   **1 cup milk**
drippings   **2 tablespoons flour**
¾ tablespoon salt
2 tablespoons sugar

Cook corn in heavy open boiler with other ingredients, except milk and flour, over low heat for 15 minutes. Stir with wooden ladle often to make sure corn does not stick. Stir in milk thickened with flour. Let simmer for a few minutes and remove from heat. If not thick enough, simmer longer. If too thick, add water.

Cookbook Committee

Stewed Squash Casserole

Serve immediately   Serves 6

4 pounds yellow squash
1 medium onion
1 tablespoon salt
Freshly ground pepper

½ cup water
½ stick butter
1 can cream of mushroom soup
1 cup sharp Cheddar cheese, grated

Slice squash and onion in saucepan. Cook in water over medium heat about 20 minutes. Drain. Mash and add other ingredients. Place in baking dish and cover top with cheese. Bake for 20 minutes, or until bubbly.

Cookbook Committee

Black-Eyed Peas

Serve immediately   Serves 4

1 cup dried black-eyed peas
6 cups hot water
2 slices salt pork

1 medium onion, chopped
2 teaspoons salt

Wash peas. Place in large pot with hot water and rest of ingredients. Cover, bring to a boil slowly, and simmer over low heat for 2½ hours or until tender. Drain before serving.

Serve in individual bowls and crumble cornbread on top. Top with raw chopped onion or diced cucumber and tomato that have been marinated in vinegar.

Cookbook Committee

Hint: To clean aluminum pots when they become stained dark, boil with a little cream of tarter, vinegar or acid foods.

Old Fashioned Fried Potatoes

Serve immediately   Serves 4

¼ cup bacon fat   2 teaspoons salt
1 large onion, sliced   ½ teaspoon pepper
4 cups pared potatoes, sliced

Heat bacon fat in a large skillet. Add onions and potatoes in layers.
Sprinkle with salt and pepper. Saute, covered, over low heat for 15 minutes.
Then, uncover, turn heat up, and saute for 10 minutes, or until golden
brown and crispy on underside. Do not stir. Fold in half like an omelet.

Cookbook Committee

Cornbread Muffins, Squares or Cracklin' Bread

Serve immediately   12 muffins or squares

1¼ cups corn meal   ⅓ cup salad oil
¾ cup flour, sifted   1 egg
1 teaspoon salt   1 teaspoon baking powder
⅔ cup milk

Mix liquid and dry ingredients separately. Pour mixed liquid into
mixed dry ingredients. Stir with spoon until well mixed. Fill 12 greased
muffin tins about ⅔-full. Bake in preheated oven for 25 minutes at 425
degrees. For squares, bake same recipe in a 8 x 8-inch pan. For cracklin'
bread add 1 cup of pork fat cracklins to same basic recipe.

Cookbook Committee

Homemade Biscuit Mix

May prepare ahead   Yields: 6 pounds mix

3¾ cups shortening (butter   5 pounds self-rising flour
   flavored is best)

Cut shortening into flour. Store in closed cannister. Use for biscuits, coffee
cakes, quick bread, pancakes, muffins, or any recipe calling for commer-
cial biscuit mix.

Sharron Davis

Biscuits From Homemade Mix

Serve immediately   Makes 1 dozen

**2 cups Homemade Biscuit Mix   ½ teaspoon baking soda
½ cup buttermilk**

Preheat oven to 450 degrees. Mix ingredients together and turn out on a lightly floured surface. Knead a few times, then roll out to ½-inch thickness. Cut with biscuit cutter and place on greased baking sheet. Bake for 10 minutes.

Sharron Davis

Cinnamon Rolls From Homemade Mix

Serve immediately   Makes 10 to 12 rolls

**2 cups Homemade Mix   ½ cup nuts, chopped
½ cup buttermilk   1 tablespoon cinnamon
½ teaspoon baking soda   2 tablespoons sugar
½ cup raisins   ½ stick butter, melted**

Preheat oven to 450 degrees. Mix first three ingredients together and turn out on a lightly floured surface. Knead a few times, then roll out into a rectangular shape approximately ½-inch thickness. Brush with melted butter. Mix cinnamon and sugar and sprinkle over buttered dough. Sprinkle nuts and raisins over all. Starting at closest end, begin rolling dough until large roll is formed. With sharp knife slice into 1-inch slices. Bake for 10 minutes. While still warm, glaze with a mixture of softened butter and powdered sugar.

Sharron Davis

Heavenly Biscuits

Serve immediately   Yields: 1 dozen

1¾ cups Homemade Biscuit Mix   1 cup heavy cream

Preheat oven to 450 degrees. Stir cream lightly into biscuit mix. Turn out on a lightly floured surface. Turn gently to coat in enough flour so dough will not be sticky, kneading a little but not much, as you turn it. Pat out to 1-inch thickness and cut with biscuit cutter. Place biscuits on greased baking sheet and bake for 10 to 12 minutes.

Sharron Davis

Southern Style Biscuits

Serve immediately   Makes 16 biscuits

2 cups self-rising flour   2 tablespoons margarine
½ teaspoon baking powder   ⅓ cup buttermilk
1 tablespoon butter-flavored   ⅓ cup whole milk
** Crisco**

Sift flour and baking powder into bowl. Cut in Crisco and margarine until mixture resembles coarse cornmeal. Fill measuring cup with buttermilk, whole milk and enough water to make ¾ cup. Make well in center of dry flour, pour in liquid. With hands mix lightly and quickly to form dough, moist enough to leave sides of bowl. Turn on lightly floured surface. Knead dough gently turning 6 or 7 times. Work dough into large ball while kneading. Keep finger dry by dipping into dry flour frequently. Refrigerate for 20 minutes before rolling out. Roll out about 1-inch thick on floured surface. Cut with biscuit cutter. Brush with melted butter (optional). Bake in preheated oven at 450 degrees for 12 to 15 minutes.

Cookbook Committee

Old Time Pound Cake

May prepare ahead   Makes 1 cake

1 pound butter   4 cups cake flour, sifted
2 cups sugar   twice
10 or 12 eggs   1 teaspoon flavoring

Cream butter and add sugar a little at a time. Add eggs one at a time, beating well after each. Sift flour twice and add a little at a time, scraping sides of the bowl and beaters, if necessary. Add flavoring (try liquid cinnamon from your pharmacist for a different taste). Put batter into a 10-inch tube pan that has been greased and floured (or try Baker's Joy). Cook for 1 hour at 300 degrees and increase to 325 degrees for the next 30 minutes. Cool in pan for 5 to 10 minutes.

Mary Margaret S. Hunter

Old Fashioned Pound Cake

May prepare ahead   Serves 20

1 pound butter   ½ teaspoon salt
2 cups sugar   1½ teaspoons vanilla
6 eggs, separated   1 cup nuts, chopped
3 cups cake flour, sifted

Cream butter and sugar until fluffy. Add yolks and continue to cream for 5 minutes. Add flour gradually and beat for 5 more minutes. Add unbeaten egg whites, vanilla, and salt. Beat at high speed for 15 minutes. Fold in nuts. Pour into greased and floured tube pan. Put in cold oven and bake at 325 degrees for 1½ hours.

Cookbook Committee

Fresh Coconut Cake

*This recipe is from my grandmother and is well worth the extra effort.
Our family always had this for Easter dinner and
there was never a crumb left over.*

May prepare ahead   Serves 8-10

3 eggs, separated
1½ cups sugar
½ teaspoon vanilla
2¼ cups cake flour, sifted
¾ cup butter

2¼ teaspoons baking
  powder
Milk
1 large coconut, grated
Milk from coconut
½ teaspoon salt

Beat egg whites to soft peaks; gradually add ½ cup sugar. Beat egg yolks until thick. Cream butter with vanilla and beat in remaining sugar. Stir in egg yolks and cream well. Sift flour, baking powder and salt together 3 times. Add enough milk to reserved coconut milk to make 1 cup liquid; alternate adding to butter mixture with flour mixture. Blend in ¼ cup coconut and beat well. Fold in egg whites and pour into 2-9 inch or 3-8 inch layer pans. Bake at 350 degrees for 25 to 30 minutes. Frost with White Mountain Frosting. Sprinkle with remaining coconut.

White Mountain Frosting:
2 egg whites
¾ cup sugar
1 teaspoon vanilla

3 tablespoons water
⅓ cup light corn syrup

Beat egg whites until peaks form. Mix sugar, water, and syrup in a saucepan, cover, and bring to a boil. Remove cover and cook until syrup spins a thread 6 to 8 inches. Pour hot syrup slowly over egg whites, beating constantly and continue until frosting holds a peak. Add vanilla. Frost coconut cake.

Sharron Davis

Hint: To keep icings moist and to prevent cracking, add a pinch of baking soda to the icing.

Southern Strawberry Shortcake

May prepare ahead   Serves 6-8

1 cup flour, sifted
1 teaspoon baking powder
¼ teaspoon salt
2 eggs
1 cup sugar
2 tablespoons butter

½ cup hot milk
1 teaspoon vanilla
4 to 5 cups strawberries,
   sliced and sugared
Fresh whipped cream

Sift together flour, baking powder, and salt. Beat eggs until thick and lemon colored. Gradually add sugar, beating constantly. Quickly fold dry ingredients into egg mixture. Add butter to hot milk; stir with vanilla into batter, and blend well. Pour into well greased 8 x 8-inch baking pan. Bake at 350 degrees for 25 to 30 minutes. Remove from pan when cool and cut into squares. Top with berries and whipped cream.

Cookbook Committee

Lane Cake

Lane Cake, which originated in Alabama, is one of the South's most outstanding cakes.

Must prepare ahead   Makes one 3-layer cake

1 cup butter or margaine,
   softened
2 cups sugar
3¼ cups cake flour, sifted
2 teaspoons baking powder

Pinch of salt
1 cup milk
2 teaspoons vanilla extract
8 egg whites (reserve yolks
   for filling)

Cream butter; gradually add sugar, beating until light and fluffy. Combine dry ingredients. Add flour mixture to creamed mixture alternately with milk, beginning and ending with flour mixture. Stir in vanilla. Beat egg whites (at room temperature) until stiff peaks form; fold into batter. Pour batter into 3 greased and floured 9-inch round cakepans. Bake at 375 degrees for 20 minutes or until a wooden pick inserted in center comes out clean. Cool in pans for 10 minutes; remove from pans, and let cool completely. Spread filling between layers of cake; spread top and sides of cake with frosting.

Filling:

8 egg yolks
1 cup sugar
½ cup butter or margarine
1 cup maraschino cherries, finely chopped
1 cup pecans, finely chopped

¾ cup raisins, finely chopped
¾ cup grated coconut
2 tablespoons bourbon whiskey or brandy

Combine egg yolks, sugar, and butter in a 2-quart saucepan. Cook over medium heat, stirring constantly about 20 minutes or until thickened. Remove from heat and stir in remaining ingredients. Let cool before spreading on cake.

Frosting:

½ cup sugar
¼ cup light corn syrup
2 tablespoons water

⅛ teaspoon salt
2 egg whites
½ teaspoon vanilla

Combine sugar, syrup, water, and salt in a heavy saucepan. Cook over medium heat, stirring constantly, until mixture is clear. Cook, stirring frequently, until mixture reaches firm ball stage (242 degrees). Beat egg whites (at room temperature) until soft peaks form; continue beating egg whites while slowly adding syrup mixture. Add vanilla; continue beating until stiff peaks form and frosting is thick enough to spread.

Cookbook Committee

Blackberry Cobbler

May prepare ahead   Serves 4

2 cups blackberries
1 cup flour
1 cup sugar

½ cup butter, softened
Dash of salt

Preheat oven to 350 degrees. Wash berries and drain well. Put berries in a buttered 1-quart baking dish. Mix all remaining ingredients and crumble over berries. Bake uncovered for 40 to 45 minutes or until crust is light brown.

Cookbook Committee

Anne Byrd's Strawberry Cobbler

May prepare ahead   Serves 6-8

6 to 8 cups whole strawberries   ½ teaspoon baking soda
⅓ cup sugar   ½ teaspoon salt
2 cups flour, plus ¼ cup if   1½ sticks butter, cut
  using frozen strawberries   into pieces
⅔ cup sugar   1 cup buttermilk
2 teaspoons baking powder

Preheat oven to 400 degrees. Place the strawberries in a greased
9 x 13-inch shallow baking dish. Sprinkle ⅓ cup of sugar on top. Sift
the flour into a bowl. Add ⅔ cups sugar, baking powder, baking soda,
and salt. Mix together. Cut the butter into the flour mixture until it
is coarse and crumbly. Add the buttermilk and stir until blended. Beat
with a spoon for about 30 seconds or until the dough sticks together.
Spread the dough on top of the strawberries. Don't worry if there are
holes because they will fill as the cobbler bakes. Bake for 30 to
40 minutes or until golden brown.

Roseanne Nichols

Persimmon Pudding

Must prepare ahead   Serves 8

2½ quarts persimmons   1½ sticks butter, melted
1½ cups flour   4 eggs
1½ cups sugar   2 cups buttermilk
2 teaspoons soda   Dash of nutmeg
½ teaspoon salt

Strain the persimmons through a sieve. This should leave you with
approximately 1 quart of persimmon pulp. Mix persimmon pulp with
the rest of the ingredients and pour into a shallow baking dish. Place
in a 275-degree oven. Stir every time the pudding puffs, approximately
every 10 to 15 minutes. The pudding will gradually shrink and turn a
dark reddish brown. It will be done in about 1 hour and 20 minutes.
Serve hot with a generous serving of whipped cream. Pudding gets
better each time you warm it over.

Dr. E. S. Whitesides

Banana Pudding

May prepare ahead   Serves 8

¾ cup sugar   2 cups whole milk
3 tablespoons flour   ½ teaspoon vanilla
Dash of salt   1 box vanilla wafers
4 eggs   6 ripe, medium-size bananas

Combine ½ cup sugar, 3 tablespoons flour, and salt in the top of a double boiler. Mix in 1 whole egg and 3 egg yolks, reserving egg whites. Stir in milk and cook uncovered over boiling water, stirring constantly until thickened. Remove from heat. Add vanilla.

Spread a small amount on the bottom of a 1½-quart casserole. Cover with a layer of vanilla wafers. Top with a layer of sliced bananas. Pour about ½ of custard over the bananas. Continue to layer wafers, bananas and custard to make 3 layers of each ending with custard.

Beat the remaining 3 egg whites stiff, but not dry. Gradually add remaining ¼ cup sugar and beat until mixture forms stiff peaks. Pile on top of pudding, covering the entire surface. Bake in a preheated 425-degree oven for 5 minutes, or until delicately browned.

Sharron Davis

Hard Sauce

This is wonderful served over any warm fruit pie or fruit cake.

Serve immediately   Yields: 1 pint

½ cup butter, softened   3 tablespoons brandy
2 cups powdered sugar   1 tablespoon vanilla
¼ teaspoon salt

Cream butter and sugar thoroughly. Add remaining ingredients and mix well.

Cookbook Committee

Sweet Potato Pie

May prepare ahead   Serves 8

1 cup brown sugar	2 eggs
1½ teaspoons cinnamon	1½ cups evaporated milk
½ teaspoon cloves	1½ cups boiled, peeled
½ teaspoon nutmeg	sweet potatoes beaten
¼ teaspoon salt	with mixer

Blend sugar, spices, and salt together. Beat eggs with milk and combine with rest of ingredients until smooth. Heat in saucepan until almost boiling and pour into unbaked Never Fail Pie Crust with pecans. Bake at 425 degrees for 15 minutes, reduce heat to 350 degrees and continue to bake until knife comes out clean. Best served with Hard Sauce or lots of whipped cream.

Sharron Davis

Buttermilk Pie

May prepare ahead   Serves 8-10

3 eggs, beaten	1 teaspoon vanilla
½ cup butter, melted	1 cup buttermilk
2 cups sugar	1-10 inch deep dish pie
3 tablespoons flour	shell, unbaked

Preheat oven to 350 degrees. Blend together filling ingredients and pour into pie shell. Bake until custard is set, approximately 40 to 45 minutes.

Cookbook Committee

Pocketbook Stickies
or York County Stickies

May prepare ahead   Makes 48

4 cups Red Band flour	1½ cups milk
4 teaspoons Rumford baking	1 pound butter
powder	1½ cups sugar
½ teaspoon salt	Additional flour for
¾ cup Crisco	kneading

Sift flour, baking powder, and salt. Work in Crisco. Add milk. The dough will be very moist. Turn onto floured board and knead at least 100 times (this requires a lot of added flour). Divide dough in half, then divide each half into 6 pieces. Roll these pieces, one at a time, into squares approximately 8" x 8". Cut into four squares (4" x 4"). On each square put 1/12 stick of butter and 1½ teaspoons of sugar. Fold opposite corners and pinch dough to seal. Arrange these squares in a greased 9 x 13-inch pan—4 across and 6 down. This will fill two pans. Bake at 425 degrees for 10 minutes, then turn oven down to 350 degrees until they turn a soft golden brown (about 15 more minutes). Remove from pan while warm as they become sticky.

Mrs. Giles Beal (Martha)

Grannie's Lemon Butter

May prepare ahead   Makes less than a quart

1 stick butter	2 cups sugar
4 eggs	Juice of 3 lemons
Pinch of salt	Rind of 3 lemons, grated fine

Melt butter in double boiler. Break eggs in bowl. Add a pinch of salt to eggs and beat. Beat in sugar, juice of lemons, and finely grated lemon rinds. Stir this mixture into the melted butter in double boiler. Continue cooking and stirring until mixture thickens. Pour into jars and refrigerate.

Mrs. T. Dale Ward (Ann)

Chunky Barbeque Sauce

May prepare ahead   Makes 1½ quarts

2 cups vinegar
Juice of 3 lemons
2 cloves garlic, crushed
1 small onion, grated
½ cup brown sugar
¼ cup honey
4 cups catsup

2 tablespoons salt
½ tablespoon cayenne
  pepper
1 tablespoon freshly ground
  black pepper
4 tablespoon Gulden's
  mustard

Boil vinegar, lemon juice, garlic, onion, sugar, and honey together. Mix other ingredients and boil about 5 minutes. If the sauce is not as hot as desired, add Tabasco sauce to taste preferred.

Cookbook Committee

Lemon Barbeque Sauce

May prepare ahead   Yields: 2 cups

1 cup butter
1 clove garlic, minced
4 teaspoons flour
⅔ cups water
1 tablespoon sugar

4 teaspoons salt
¼ teaspoon pepper
6 tablespoons lemon juice
¼ teaspoon Tabasco sauce
½ teaspoon dried thyme

Sauté garlic in hot butter in a saucepan for a few minutes. Stir in flour, then rest of ingredients. Cook stirring until slightly thickened. Cool.

Cookbook Committee

Milk Gravy

Great with rice or mashed potatoes.

Serve immediately   Makes 2 cups

3 tablespoons chicken, pork   **1 cup milk**
  chop, or bacon drippings   **Dash of salt and pepper**
3 tablespoons flour

After frying chicken, chops, or bacon, pour off excess grease, leaving about 3 tablespoons of fat with crumbs. Add flour to pan and stir while it browns. Slowly add milk as it thickens. Add hot water if too thick. Add salt and pepper to taste.

Cookbook Committee

Crisp Cucumber Pickles

May prepare ahead   Makes 4 jars

1 gallon small cucumbers   **5 cups white vinegar**
8 small onions   **1 teaspoon turmeric**
½ cup salt   **1 tablespoon pickle spice**
5 cups sugar

Mix salt, onions, and cut-up cucumbers. Put in ice cubes. Let stand 3 hours. Bring sugar and vinegar to a boil. Pour in drained cucumbers and onions and add spices. When the mixture comes to a boil, pour into sterilized jars and seal.

Cookbook Committee

Quick Pickled Peaches

May prepare ahead   Serves 8

1-24 ounce can peach halves,   ½ cup vinegar
  drained   ½ stick cinnamon
Whole cloves   ½ cup granulated sugar
1 cup peach syrup, drained
  from peaches

Stud each peach half with 3 or 4 cloves. Simmer with rest of ingredients for 3 to 4 minutes. Cool and refrigerate.

Cookbook Committee

Greatest Garlic Pickles

Must prepare 4 or 5 days ahead   Yields: 2 quarts

½ gallon Kosher dill pickles   2 tablespoons pickling
4 cups sugar   spices
15 cloves garlic   1½ cups vinegar

Slice pickles in ½-inch rounds and place in large bowl. Add sugar, garlic, and spices. In saucepan bring vinegar to a boil and pour over pickle spices. Cover and let stand for 4 or 5 days, stirring each day to keep seasoning well mixed. Transfer to sterilized jars and refrigerate.

Mrs. Robert Leeth Davis

Bread and Butter Pickles I

Must prepare ahead   Yields: 7 pints

1 gallon cucumbers   **½ cup salt**
8 small white onions

Syrup:
5 cups sugar   **1 teaspoon celery seed**
1½ teaspoons turmeric   **2 tablespoons mustard seed**
½ teaspoon ground cloves   **5 cups vinegar**

Slice cucumbers and onions paper thin. Mix salt with cucumbers and
onions in a large bowl and bury pieces of cracked ice in mixture. Cover
with weighted lid or plate and let sit for 3 hours. Drain well. Place over
low heat in syrup and heat to scalding but not boiling, stirring occasionally. Pour into hot jars and seal.

Peggy Cooke

Bread and Butter Pickles II

Must prepare ahead   Makes 5 pints

8 cups cucumbers, sliced   **3 cups sugar**
2 cups onions, sliced   **2 teaspoons celery seeds**
4 tablespoons salt   **2 teaspoons turmeric**
2 cups cider vinegar   **2 sticks cinnamon**

Place cucumbers and onions in large colander. Sprinkle with salt and
let stand for 1 hour. Rinse well with cold water and drain thoroughly.
In large pot place cucumber and onions and add remaining ingredients.
Bring to a boil and cook about 5 minutes. Ladle into hot sterilized jars
and seal.

Note: Jars are easily sterilized in dishwasher on hottest setting.

Cookbook Committee

Chow-Chow

*This is my Grandmother Spurrier's recipe. My mother and I always make
this each fall. It takes 2 days to make but it is well worth the effort.
It will keep for a year if not given away for gifts.*

Must prepare 2 days ahead   Makes 6-8 quarts

3 quarts green tomatoes   3 quarts onions
3 quarts green peppers   1 large cauliflower
3 quarts red peppers   1 small bunch celery hearts
3 quarts cabbage   1 cup salt

Sauce:
3 quarts vinegar   3 tablespoons turmeric
1 pound light brown sugar   1 handful cloves, tied
3 pounds white sugar   in bag
1 cup flour   3 to 4 sticks cinnamon
3 tablespoons dry mustard   ½ box white mustard seed

Cut and chop all vegetables into small pieces. Be sure to string celery
when chopping it. Mix all together in a large bowl and pour 1 cup salt
on top. Cover with cloth and let stand overnight in refrigerator. The next
day, squeeze juice out of vegetables. Make sauce by mixing all dry ingredients well. Add vinegar to dry ingredients and bring sauce to a boil. Put
drained vegetables in sauce and bring to a boil slowly. Put the hot mixture into sterilized jars and seal. No processing is necessary when the
sauce and jars are hot. Refrigerate after opening.

Mrs. Mary Lewis Bryant

Tasties
Appetizers

Almond-Stuffed Dates With Bacon

May prepare ahead   Makes 60

1 pound pitted dates   **1 pound bacon**
1-4 ounce package blanched
 whole almonds

Stuff each date with an almond. Cut bacon strips into thirds and wrap
a piece around each date. Secure with a round wooden toothpick. Put the
dates on a foil-lined baking sheet and bake in a preheated 400-degree oven
until the bacon is crisp about 12 to 15 minutes. Do not overcook. The dates
burn easily. Drain on paper towels. Serve warm.

Prepared dates can be frozen in advance and baked unthawed in a
preheated 400-degree oven until crisp. Dates can also be stuffed with
walnuts or pecans.

Jennifer Davis

Peach Almond Sandwiches

My mother-in-law, Lois McCosh, won 1st prize at the
Georgia Peach Festival with this original recipe.

May prepare ahead   Serves 8-10

1-3 ounce package cream   **2 tablespoons crystalized**
 cheese   **ginger, chopped**
2 tablespoons brown sugar   **Bread rounds**
3 tablespoons mashed peaches   **Peach pieces to garnish**
3 tablespoons toasted almonds **Parsley to garnish**

Blend cream cheese and brown sugar. Add other ingredients and mix
well. Spread on small bread rounds and top with another round. Garnish
with a small piece of a fresh peach and parsley.

Cathy McCosh

Hot Asparagus Canapes

*This may be used as an appetizer or left whole to be
served as a vegetable with a meal.*

May prepare ahead   Serves 30 people
Freezes well

20 slices white bread   1 egg
1-8 ounce package cream   20 asparagus spears, cooked
  cheese, softened   2 sticks butter, melted
1-3 ounce package Bleu
  cheese, softened

Trim crusts from bread and use rolling pin to flatten slices of bread.
Blend cheeses and egg to workable consistency and spread evenly on
each slice. Roll one asparagus in each slice; use toothpicks to fasten and
dip in melted butter (or brush generously). Place rolls on cookie sheet
and freeze. When frozen firmly, slice into sections. When ready to use,
bake at 400 degrees for 15 minutes or until lightly browned.

Kathy Linker Jenkins

Bacon Roll-Ups

May prepare ahead   Serves as many as desired
Freezes well before cooking

Bread slices   Onions
Cream cheese   Bacon
Chives

Remove crust from bread. Spread cream cheese, chives, and onions on
bread; then cut the bread in half. Take a half of a slice of uncooked bacon
and roll the bread with the bacon on the outside of the bread and the
cream cheese on the inside of roll. Use a toothpick to secure the roll.
Place roll-ups on cookie sheet and cook at 325 degrees for 25 minutes.
Turn roll-ups after cooking for ½ of the time. Serve warm.

Mrs. Pamela Mayo

Smoked Catfish Log

Lasts in refrigerator for 3 to 5 days.

Must prepare ahead   Serves 4-6

6 catfish fillets, smoked   1 teaspoon horseradish
2-8 ounce packages cream   Tabasco sauce
  cheese   Salt and pepper to taste
1 onion, chopped   Garlic powder to taste
2 tablespoons   Pecans and parsley to coat
  Worcestershire sauce
1 tablespoon lemon juice

Put everything in processor except seasonings, pecans, and parsley. Add seasonings after ingredients are blended. Roll into log adding chopped pecans and parsley as a coating. Chill overnight.

Carolyn Sumner

Caviar Pie

May prepare ahead   Serves 16

9 hard-boiled eggs, separated   1 cup sour cream
4 tablespoons butter, melted   Red caviar
4 tablespoons mayonnaise   Black caviar
2 tablespoons onion, minced

Set aside 3 cooked yolks. Place remaining eggs in a processor. Add butter and mayonnaise and process until smooth. Add onion. Place this mixture evenly in a pie-shaped dish. Spread sour cream evenly. Dice the 3 yolks which have been set aside. Spread a ring of red caviar around edge of plate. Then spread a ring of black caviar, then a ring with the diced yolks. Serve with crackers or cut into wedges as a first course.

Sara Stowe

Caviar Mousse

I got this recipe from Mrs. George Gray (Ellen) when we served it at a wedding party. Everyone just loved it.

Must prepare ahead   Serves 10-12

1 envelope unflavored gelatin
2 tablespoons cold water
½ cup boiling water
1-3½ ounce jar black or red caviar

2-8 ounce cartons sour cream
2 tablespoons mayonnaise
2 tablespoons lemon juice
Dash of hot sauce

Soften gelatin in cold water. Add boiling water; stir until gelatin is dissolved. Stir in remaining ingredients. Spoon into a 4-cup mold lightly oiled or sprayed with Pam. Cover with Saran Wrap and chill for several hours. Serve with wheat or sesame crackers. (This recipe may be doubled or tripled for a larger crowd.)

Cathy McCosh

Caviar Mold

Must prepare ahead   Serves 8-10

1 dozen hard-boiled eggs, chopped fine
1 medium onion, chopped fine
Salt and pepper to taste

Juice of 1 lemon
2 tablespoons mayonnaise
1 stick butter
Sour cream
Black caviar

Line a mold with Saran Wrap; mix first six ingredients and chill in mold. To serve, turn out and cover with layer of sour cream. Serve with separate bowl of black caviar and Bremner wafers.

Lin Lineberger

Baked Cheese

Serve immediately   Serves 8-10

1-6 ounce wheel Gouda cheese   **1 egg white**
1 can Pillsbury crescent rolls   **Poppy seeds**
1 teaspoon Gray Poupon
  mustard

Paint top of cheese with Gray Poupon mustard. Carefully wrap cheese
with the unfolded crescent roll dough, being sure to seal all seams. Brush
with egg white. Sprinkle the top with poppy seeds and bake according
to crescent roll directions.

Cookbook Committee

Beau Monde Dip

May prepare ahead   Serves 8-10

1⅓ cups sour cream   **⅓ cup mayonnaise**
2 teaspoons Beau Monde   **2 teaspoons dill seed**
2 teaspoons parsley flakes **2 teaspoons onion flakes**

Mix all ingredients together to make dip. Hollow out middle of round
loaf of French or sourdough bread and fill with dip. Use extra bread as
dip pieces.

Marsha Jones

Bleu Cheese Dip

This is excellent as a dip for Buffalo Wings or fresh vegetables.

Must prepare 1 hour ahead   Makes 3 cups

1 cup mayonnaise   **1 clove garlic, finely**
4 to 6 tablespoons bleu   **minced**
  cheese, crumbled   **½ teaspoon black pepper**
½ cup plain yogurt   **2 tablespoons lemon juice**
2 green onions, finely chopped   **¼ to ½ cup parsley,**
  (both white and green parts)   **minced**

Mix all the ingredients together. Refrigerate at least one hour before
serving. Garnish with additional parsley.

Allison Decker Sonier

Buffalo Wings

My husband grew up in Buffalo, New York, so he is used to the original Buffalo Wings found at Frank and Teresa's Anchor Bar. This great recipe was invented back in the 1960's. The wings are served mild, medium, or hot - it all depends on your taste buds. Bleu Cheese Dip, carrots, and celery are always served with Buffalo Wings.

May prepare ahead   Makes 12 to 15 servings
Reheat to serve

2½ pounds chicken wings
½ cup butter or margarine,
  melted
¼ cup RedHot* (or more to
  taste)

Enough tomato paste to
  thicken the sauce so it
  will cling to the wings

Split the wings at each joint and discard tips; pat dry. Deep fry in butter or margarine at 400 degrees (high) for 12 minutes or until completely cooked and crispy; drain. OR bake at 425 degrees for 1 hour, turning halfway through cooking time.

Mix together RedHot and tomato paste. Put the wings into a covered container a few at a time. Add the sauce. Cover and shake until coated well. Repeat until all wings have been covered. Serve with Bleu Cheese Dip, carrots, and celery.

*May substitute any hot sauce. This particular brand is very difficult to find here.

Allison Decker Sonier

Dried Beef Party Sandwiches

This also works well as a spread for crackers.

May prepare ahead   Serves 8
Freezes well

½ cup dried beef, finely
  shredded (about 1 package)
1-3 ounce package cream
  cheese, softened

1 tablespoon horseradish
1 tablespoon mayonnaise
1 tablespoon onion, minced
Bread with crust removed

Mix together all ingredients. Spread on bread (cut into desired shapes) to make sandwiches.

Kathy Linker Jenkins

Memaw's Cheese Straws

This is an original recipe of my mother-in-law's,
Lois McCosh, from Columbus, Georgia.

May prepare ahead   Makes 3-4 dozen
Freezes well

13 ounces extra sharp   Dash of salt
  Cheddar cheese (Cracker   Cayenne pepper to taste
  Barrel, red wrapping)   3 cups flour, sifted
1 stick butter (Land 'O Lakes)
1 stick corn oil margarine
  and sweet cream butter
  (Country Morning Blend)

Grate cheese and mix with softened butter, softened Country Morning
Blend, salt, and pepper until doughy. Add flour. Squeeze batter and flour
with hands until all of it is mixed. Put dough into cookie press and press
out on ungreased cookie sheet about 1 inch apart as they will grow as
they cook. Bake at 375 degrees for 15 minutes. Be careful not to overcook as cheese burns easily. Alternative: This batter may be formed
around pecan halves or whole dates and baked at 375 degrees for 15
minutes to add a different flavor to plain cheese straws. These can be
frozen after cooking or you may store in an airtight container for 2 to
3 weeks. They are great served hot or at room temperature.

Cathy McCosh

Special Cheese Rounds

Must prepare day before   Makes 2-3 dozen
Serve immediately after cooking

1 cup sharp Cheddar cheese,   4 spring onions, grated
  grated   ½ cup mayonnaise
½ cup mozzarella cheese, grated ⅛ teaspoon Beau Monde
¼ cup Parmesan cheese, grated   seasoning
¼ teaspoon garlic powder

Combine all ingredients together and mix well. Refrigerate overnight,
if possible. Spread on French sourdough rolls, sliced thinly; or on Triscuit
wafers and put under broiler until bubbly.

Mrs. Kay Stevenson
by Debbie Brake

Cheese Puffs

May prepare ahead   Makes 2-3 dozen

1 loaf white unsliced bread	**2-3 ounce packages cream**
4 egg whites, beaten stiff	**cheese**
1 cup butter	**½ pound sharp Cheddar**
	cheese

Remove crust and cut bread into 1-inch cubes. Beat egg whites. Melt together over medium heat butter, cream cheese, and Cheddar cheese. Stir constantly until well mixed. Remove from heat and fold in egg whites. Dip bread into mixture until well-coated. Place on well-oiled cookie sheet and freeze. When frozen, remove and freeze in bags. DO NOT DEFROST before baking. Bake at 400 degrees for 12 to 15 minutes on greased cookie sheet. These are wonderful served hot.

Mrs. J. Wylie Goble

Cheese Ring

This is great for a party!

Must prepare ahead   Serves a crowd

1 pound sharp Cheddar	**1 cup pecans, chopped**
cheese, grated	**1 medium onion, grated**
¾ cup mayonnaise	**½ teaspoon Tabasco sauce**
1 clove garlic, pressed	**1 cup strawberry preserves**
through a garlic press	**1 stick butter or margarine**

Combine all ingredients except the preserves and mix well. Press into a ring-shaped mold which is lined with Saran Wrap (this makes unmolding much easier). Refrigerate for at least several hours.

When ready to serve unmold on a platter and fill the center with the preserves. Serve with your favorite crackers.

Mrs. Tami T. Pearson

Cheese Pastry for Dates or Olives

May prepare ahead   Makes 2 dozen
Freezes well

1 cup sharp Cheddar cheese,   **¼ teaspoon salt**
  grated   **½ teaspoon paprika (use**
3 tablespoons butter   **for olives not dates)**
½ cup flour

Blend cheese and butter; add other ingredients. Wrap a small amount
around the date or olive. Can freeze at this point. Place on ungreased
cookie sheet and bake at 400 degrees for 10 to 15 minutes or until lightly
browned. Serve hot.

Martha Beal

Cheese and Pickle Sandwiches

Serve immediately   Serves a crowd

Loaf bread   **Claussen whole Kosher dill**
Mayonnaise   **pickles**
                                        American cheese slices

Remove crust and spread bread slices with mayonnaise; cut into fourths.
Place one thin "round" of dill pickle on each piece of bread and top with
slice of cheese. Broil on cookie sheet until cheese melts.

Patti Hunter

Boursin Cheese

May prepare ahead   Yields: 2½ cups

2 cloves garlic   **¼ teaspoon pepper**
2-8 ounce packages cream   **½ teaspoon oregano**
  cheese   **¼ teaspoon thyme**
8 ounces butter   **¼ teaspoon dill**
¼ teaspoon marjoram
¼ teaspoon basil

Chop garlic in food processor. Add cheese and butter a few chunks at
a time. Add herbs and blend; refrigerate. Remove from refrigerator 1 hour
before serving. Serve with Stone Wheat Thins or with a toasted split
bagel.

Mrs. J. T. Comer, III

Pate De Foie De Volaille

May prepare ahead   Serves a crowd

1 medium onion
½ pound butter (unsalted)
½ pound chicken livers
3 ounces baked ham (fat
    included)
¼ teaspoon nutmeg
1 teaspoon dry mustard
Pinch of ground cloves

Pinch of coriander
Pinch of cayenne pepper
2 teaspoons Cognac
1 clove garlic
½ teaspoon salt (omit if
    using salted butter)

Use the fine slicing disc on your food processor to slice onions; sauté in melted butter until transparent. Add drained chicken livers and continue cooking until firm.

Use the steel blade on your food processor and with machine running, drop garlic through the feed tube and mince. Add ham to bowl, and chop finely. Add remaining ingredients. Process until blended. Add cooked onions and livers to the bowl and process until smoothly blended. Pour into a ceramic crock and refrigerate. Stir frequently to blend butter well into mixture as it cools. It is best served the following day. Serve with toast points and cornichon pickles.

Note: The paté may be sealed with clarified butter if not being used the next day. This recipe may easily be doubled in the food processor.

Lin Lineberger

Chicken Livers

*These are excellent in a chafing dish for cocktail
parties or as something different for picnics.*

Must prepare ahead   Serves 10-12

3 dozen chicken livers
2 to 3 cups soy sauce

2 pounds bacon

Marinate the chicken livers in soy sauce overnight. Wrap each liver with ½ slice of bacon and anchor with toothpick. Put on cookie sheet and broil, turning once, until livers and bacon are done, approximately 5 minutes per side. This recipe may be doubled or tripled easily for large parties.

Patti Hunter

Calvert's Chicken Pate

*My friend, Rita Calvert Cameron, is an accomplished restauranteur,
manufacturer of mustards and condiments, and cookbook author. This
was my first ever attempt at a "paté" and was so
successful that I serve it again and again.*

Must prepare ahead   Serves a crowd

3½ pounds chicken breasts   Juice of one lemon
  and thighs   2 cloves garlic, pressed
2 medium onion, diced and   8 ounces whipping cream
  sautéed in butter until   Salt and pepper to taste
  transluscent   ½ teaspoon thyme, fresh
2 tablespoons butter   if possible
3 eggs
2 tablespoons mustard

Bake chicken for 40 minutes in a 400-degree oven. While baking, prepare
onions as listed above. Skin and bone chicken and place chicken meat
in food processor. Place remaining ingredients in food processor and process until smooth. Pour this mixture into greased bread loaf pan or mold.
Place loaf pan in a larger deep pan and fill larger pan with hot water
until water reaches one-half the height of the loaf pan. Bake at 375
degrees for 1 hour or until firm. Cool and chill in refrigerator. When
ready to serve, loosen edges of pate by running a knife around the sides
of the pan. Invert onto a platter and unmold. Garnish with fresh thyme.

Mrs. H. Garrett Rhyne

Chicken Liver Pate

Must prepare ahead   Serves 8-10

1 pound chicken livers   2 tablespoons lemon juice
4 large onions   4 hard-boiled eggs, chopped
2 teaspoons salt   ½ cup butter, melted
¼ teaspoon black pepper   Parsley, chopped

Cook livers for 5 minutes in water; drain. Grate and drain onions. Add
salt, pepper, lemon juice, and eggs (can use blender very carefully). Add
butter and mix well. Chill at least overnight. Form into desired shape
and roll in parsley. Serve with wheat crackers.

Martha Beal

Chicken Snowballs

These are a unique and delicious appetizer.

May prepare ahead   Yields: 2 dozen

1 cup cooked chicken,
  chopped (white meat)
2 tablespoons chopped pimento
½ cup plus 1 tablespoon
  Miracle Whip salad dressing
1 teaspoon Tabasco sauce

2 tablespoons onion, finely
  chopped
1 cup pecans, chopped
Grated coconut
Parsley flakes

Combine all ingredients except parsley flakes and coconut, mixing well. Chill at least 3 hours and shape into 1-inch balls. Roll in parsley flakes and coconut.

Sharron Davis

Clam or Crab Dip (Hot)

May prepare ahead   Serves a crowd

2-8 ounce packages cream
  cheese
2½ tablespoons parsley flakes,
  dried
1 small onion, very finely
  chopped

1 tablespoon dry Vermouth
2-6½ ounce cans of clams or
  crab, drained
  (reserve juice)
1 teaspoon Tabasco sauce

Combine all ingredients in a double boiler. Heat and stir until cheese is melted. If the mixture becomes too thick, use reserved juice to thin it out. Serve hot with Triscuits or your favorite cracker.

Pat McCloskey

Crab Dip

May prepare ahead   Serves 8

1 cup sour cream
½ pound crab meat, fresh or
  frozen (Delicaseas' frozen
  seafood blend of fish and
  crab meat may be substituted)
Lawry's seasoned salt to taste
¼ cup mayonnaise
1 tablespoon onion, grated

1 tablespoon lemon juice
½ teaspoon Worcestershire
  sauce
Pepper to taste
Round loaf of pumpernickel
  or sour dough bread
Crackers (optional)
Parsley (optional)

Combine all ingredients except bread, crackers, and parsley; mix thoroughly. Chill thoroughly before serving. Cut out section in top of bread to put serving bowl. Place serving bowl in bread. Use bread and crackers for dipping. Garnish with parsley.

Mrs. Larry Stiles (Janie)

Hot Crab Spread

May prepare ahead and refrigerate   Serves 8-10
until ready to cook

1-8 ounce package cream
  cheese, softened
1 cup crab meat (8 ounce can
  or fresh)
1-2 ounce package almonds,
  chopped

1 tablespoon milk
2 tablespoons onion,
  chopped
½ teaspoon horseradish
Salt and pepper to taste

Blend all ingredients together. Bake in a round Pyrex dish at 350 degrees for 20 minutes. Serve hot with your favorite crackers. May be doubled and baked in a 9 x 13-inch casserole.

Mrs. William L. Beam (Anne)

Mock Crab Spread

Serve immediately   Serves 12

1-14 ounce can artichoke   1 cup Parmesan cheese
  hearts, finely cut   Sliced almonds
1 cup Hellman's mayonnaise   Paprika
Dash of garlic powder

Mix together artichoke hearts, mayonnaise, garlic powder, and Parmesan cheese. Smooth evenly in an 8 x 8 x 2-inch Pyrex or CorningWare dish. Sprinkle with almonds and paprika. Bake at 350 degrees for about 30 minutes until golden brown on top. Serve with Ritz crackers or Triscuits.

Microwave directions: Microwave at full power for 5 minutes turning once.

Mrs. John B. Garrett, Jr. (Nancy)

Crab Pizza

May prepare ahead   Serves 8-10

12 ounces cream cheese,   Dash garlic powder
  softened   Approximately ½ bottle
2 tablespoons Worcestershire   chili sauce
  sauce   1-6½ ounce can crab meat
1 tablespoon lemon juice   2 tablespoons fresh parsley,
2 tablespoons mayonnaise   chopped
1 small onion, grated

Mix cream cheese, Worcestershire sauce, lemon juice, mayonnaise, onion, and garlic powder and spread on a flat dinner plate. Cover cream cheese mixture with chili sauce; then sprinkle with the crab meat. Sprinkle chopped parsley on top and refrigerate at least 2 hours before serving with your favorite crackers.

Mrs. Mona L. Fulton

Crab Wedges

Must prepare ahead   Makes 48 wedges
Freezes well

1 stick butter
1 jar Old English Cheese
  Spread
1 teaspoon seasoning salt
2 teaspoons mayonniase

1 teaspoon garlic salt
1 can crab meat, drained
6 English muffins, split

Soften butter and cheese to room temperature. Add rest of ingredients and spread on muffins and freeze. Cut into 8 wedges when ready to serve and broil until bubbly.

Mrs. Frank P. Cooke, Jr.

Trawler's Famous Crab Dip

May prepare ahead   Yields: 3 cups

1¼ cups mayonnaise
4 tablespoons French
  dressing
1 teaspoon horseradish

1 cup crab meat
½ cup Cheddar cheese,
  grated fine

Mix all of the above ingredients and serve with crackers. If you prefer a little extra tang, don't be afraid to add more horseradish or French dressing to suit your taste.

Mrs. Davis Patton

Crab Meat Spread

May prepare ahead   Serves 4-6

1 can crab meat, drained
½ cup mayonnaise
2 tablespoons celery flakes
2 teaspoons instant minced
  onion

¼ teaspoon salt
Dash paprika
½ to 1 cup Cheddar cheese,
  grated
1 tablespoon lemon juice

Mix all ingredients and serve with a buttery cracker (Club crackers are great).

Mrs. Monica Cain

Egg Salad Mold

Use red caviar for the holidays.

Must prepare ahead   Serves 10

10 to 12 hard-boiled eggs   **2 drops hot sauce**
1 teaspoon dry beef bouillon   **½ cup mayonnaise**
1 tablespoon Dijon mustard   **2 cups sour cream**
1 teaspoon garlic salt   **Black or red caviar**

Put eggs in food processor and add other ingredients except sour cream
and caviar and mix completely. Put in a well oiled 1-quart mold and
refrigerate overnight. Unmold (go around the edges with a knife by dipping in warm water). Turn out on a glass plate. Cover the outside of the
molded eggs with the sour cream that has been whipped. Fill the center
with caviar (that has had a little lemon juice squeezed over it, if desired).
Serve with rye crackers.

Martha Beal

English Muffin Goodies

Must prepare ahead   Makes 48

1½ cups extra sharp Cheddar   **1 cup black olives, chopped**
  cheese, grated   **(1 can pitted olives)**
1 cup mayonnaise   **¼ teaspoon curry powder**
½ cup scallions, chopped   **6 English muffins, split**
½ teaspoon salt
¼ teaspoon Worcestershire
  sauce

Add all ingredients together and spread on English muffin halves. Freeze
on cookie sheet (put in plastic bag with waxed paper between them to
save). When ready to serve, cook at 350 degrees for 10 to 15 minutes
or until bubbly. Cut into quarters and serve hot. For 6 times this recipe
use: 5 packs shredded cheese (9 cups), 6 cups mayonnaise, 6 cups olives
(6 cans), 2 cups scallions (2 bunches), 3 teaspoons salt, 1½ teaspoons curry
powder, and 1½ teaspoons Worcestershire sauce.

Lin Lineberger

Scotch Eggs

When I was in England and Scotland a few years ago, I found all the pubs serve these. I brought the recipe back with me and they always make a hit, especially with men.

May prepare ahead   Makes 32

1 pound bulk sausage   **2 eggs, beaten**
8 hard-boiled eggs, medium   **Bread crumbs (7 to 8 slices**
¼ cup flour   **in blender)**

Divide sausage into 8 slices. Flatten 1 slice between 2 squares of plastic wrap. Remove top plastic wrap. Roll 1 egg in flour. Wrap sausage around egg, enclosing the egg completely in the meat. Remove the plastic wrap. Continue until all the eggs are wrapped in the meat. Roll eggs once more in flour, lightly, dip into beaten egg batter and then roll in bread crumbs. (You may refrigerate at this stage and fry later.)

Fry in an electric skillet in deep oil at 350 degrees. Keep turning until eggs are golden brown. Drain on paper towels. These may be served hot or cold. Cut each in half or quarters to serve as a finger food.

You may also serve with the following mustard sauce:

½ cup mayonnaise   **½ cup prepared mustard**
2 tablespoons bottled steak   **8 drops Tabasco sauce**
sauce
1 tablespoon lemon juice

Mrs. Virginia Avery

Jezebel Sauce

This keeps indefinitely in the refrigerator in a covered container.

May prepare ahead   Serves 15

1-10 ounce jar pineapple   **1-5 ounce jar horseradish**
preserves   **1-8 ounce package cream**
1-10 ounce jar apple jelly   **cheese**
1½ ounces dry mustard

Mix together preserves, jelly, mustard, and horseradish and spread this over the block of cream cheese. Serve with crackers.

Patti Hunter

Ham and Cheese Pastries

May prepare ahead   Serves 10-12

⅔ pound well-chilled Saga
  Bleu cheese, rind removed
2 tablespoons plus 1½
  teaspoons dry sherry
1 package frozen Puff Pastry
  sheets

⅓ pound paper-thin slices
  baked ham
2 egg whites, beaten to
  blend (glaze)

With electric mixer beat cheese until light. Mix in sherry. Working with one sheet of dough at a time, roll out on lightly-floured surface to a 12 x 10-inch rectangle. Spread ½ of cheese mixture evenly over, leaving ½-inch border. Cover cheese with half of ham. Starting at one long side, roll dough up very tightly, jelly-roll fashion. Repeat with remaining dough, cheese, and ham. Place rolls on baking sheet and freeze until firm, at least 45 minutes. (Can be prepared to this point up to 1 week ahead. Wrap lightly. Soften slightly in refrigerator before continuing.)

Preheat oven to 400 degrees. Lightly grease baking sheets. Cut dough into ½-inch thick slices. Arrange cut-side down on prepared sheets. Brush with glaze. Bake for 20 to 25 minutes or until lightly browned.

Jennifer Davis

Roquefort Grapes

Must prepare ahead   Makes 50

1-10 ounce package almonds,
  pecans, or walnuts, toasted
1-8 ounce package cream cheese
¼ pound Roquefort cheese

2 tablespoons heavy cream
1 pound seedless grapes, red
  or green, washed and
  dried

To toast nuts, preheat oven to 275 degrees. Spread the nuts on a baking sheet and bake until lightly toasted. Chop nuts coarsely in food processor or by hand. Spread on a platter.

In bowl of an electric mixer combine the cream cheese, Roquefort, and cream; beat until smooth. Drop clean, dry grapes into the cheese mixture and gently stir by hand to coat. Then roll the coated grapes in the toasted nuts one at a time and put on a tray lined with waxed paper. Chill until ready to serve.

Jennifer Davis

Anne Byrd's Guacamole

May prepare ahead   Serves 6-8

4 large ripe avocados
1 medium onion, finely chopped
1 clove garlic, finely minced
2 teaspoons coriander

¼ cup lemon juice
Salt and freshly ground
  black pepper

Peel the avocados and reserve the seeds. Mash the avocado pulp and combine it in a bowl with the onion, garlic, coriander, lemon juice, salt, and pepper to taste. Blend well and place the avocado seeds on top of the mixture. This will prevent the guacamole from darkening as it stands; remove the seeds before serving.

Roseanne Nichols

Evelyn's Ham Biscuits

May freeze before cooking   Makes 20 tiny sandwiches

¼ pound butter, at room
  temperature
2 teaspoons prepared mustard
2 tablespoons poppy seeds
2 teaspoons Worcestershire
  sauce
1 small onion, grated

1 package (20) party rolls
1-4 or 5 ounce package
  sliced, cooked ham
1-4 ounce package sliced
  Swiss cheese

Mix together butter, mustard, poppy seeds, Worcestershire sauce, and onion. Use tiny day-old party rolls. Open them and spread mixture on both sides of roll, and top each half with a small piece of ham. Put a small piece of Swiss cheese between halves before closing. Heat in a 350-degree oven until cheese is melted.

Lin Lineberger
Holt Harris

Marie's Mushroom Dip

May prepare ahead   Serves a crowd

12 ounces mushrooms   Salt to taste
Butter, not margarine   Pinch nutmeg
Flour   Garlic salt to taste
1-8 ounce carton sour cream   Wheat Toast crackers

Chop mushrooms in fourths or finer if desired and cook in butter. Sprinkle with flour and add sour cream and all spices, and cook over low heat. (Add enough flour to thicken.) Serve hot on Wheat Toast crackers.

Mrs. Ann Massey

Mushroom Croustades

May prepare ahead   Makes 24
Freezes well

Butter, not margarine   ⅛ teaspoon cayenne pepper
24 slices bread   ½ teaspoon lemon juice
4 tablespoons butter   ½ teaspoon salt
3 tablespoons green onions,   1 tablespoon parsley
  finely chopped   1½ tablespoons chives,
½ pound fresh mushrooms,   chopped
  chopped   2 tablespoons Parmesan
2 tablespoons flour   cheese
1 cup whipping cream

With pastry brush heavily coat 24 small muffin tins with butter. Cut 3-inch rounds from bread. Carefully press the bread into the tins to form cups. Bake at 400 degrees for 10 to 12 minutes. Set aside and cool.

Melt 4 tablespoons butter and stir in onions and mushrooms. Cook 10 to 15 minutes until moisture evaporates. Sprinkle flour over and stir until dissolved. Pour in cream and bring to boil. Cook until thick stirring frequently. Remove from heat and stir in remaining ingredients except Parmesan cheese. Let cool. Fill croustades and sprinkle with Parmesan cheese. Bake for 10 minutes at 325 degrees. Broil briefly to brown if desired.

Mrs. Frank P. Cooke, Jr.
Mrs. Charles T. Stowe, Jr. (Sara)

Oyster Cracker Snack

Better when prepared ahead   Serves a crowd

1 small or medium package
  dry ranch dressing
¼ teaspoon garlic powder
⅓ teaspoon dillweed
¼ teaspoon lemon pepper
  (optional)

½ cup oil
1-11 ounce box Sunshine
  oyster/soup crackers
Parmesan cheese, grated

Combine dressing, spices, and oil; mix well. Add crackers to mixture. Stir until oil is absorbed, and sprinkle with Parmesan cheese.

Mrs. Holt Harris

Oyster Roll

Must prepare ahead   Serves 16

2-8 ounce packages cream
  cheese
2 to 3 tablespoons mayonnaise
2 teaspoons Worcestershire
  sauce
½ onion, pressed

Garlic, pressed (1 large or
  2 small cloves)
At least ⅛ teaspoon salt
2 cans smoked oysters

Cream enough mayonnaise into cheese to hold it together. Add Worcestershire sauce, pressed garlic, onion, and salt. Combine well. Spread about ½-inch thick on waxed paper. Chop oysters and spread them on top of cheese mixture. Roll as you would a jelly roll, using a knife to start it. Chill for 24 hours. Serve with toast rounds or crackers.

Sara Stowe

Sugar 'N Spice Pecans

May prepare ahead   Makes 5 cups nuts

2 cups sugar   ¾ cup milk
2 teaspoons cinnamon   2 teaspoons vanilla
½ teaspoon salt   4 cups pecan halves

Mix sugar, cinnamon, salt, and milk together in a saucepan. Boil to soft ball stage (240 degrees on candy thermometer or 8 minutes at a hard boil over high heat). Remove from heat. Add vanilla and nuts. Stir until mixture is grainy. Turn out on waxed paper. Separate nuts and when cool, store in airtight container.

Connie Gibbons

Glazed Pecans (Microwave)

May prepare ahead   Yields: 2 cups

2 cups pecans   ¼ cup orange juice
1 cup sugar

Mix together pecans, sugar, and orange juice and pour into microwave dish. Microwave for 6 minutes on 70 percent power. Remove and mix together. Then microwave for another 3 to 4 minutes. Remove from microwave and pour onto buttered foil. Separate and let harden.

Mrs. Linda T. Ratchford

Luscious Pecans

This is another original recipe from Jim's mother, Lois McCosh.

¼ cup sugar   ¼ cup butter
1 teaspoon lemon or orange   ¼ teaspoon cinnamon
  juice   ⅛ teaspoon nutmeg
1 teaspoon orange or lemon   1 cup pecan halves
  rind, grated

Bring all ingredients except pecan halves to a boil. Boil for 3 minutes and add pecans. Stir until well coated. Spread on waxed paper and cool. Roll in powdered or granulated sugar and serve as a great pick-up for any type party.

Cathy McCosh

Perfect Puffs

May prepare ahead   Makes as many as needed

Premium saltine crackers   **Seasoning salt or garlic**
  with salted tops (single   **salt**
  squares)   **Parmesan or Romano cheese**
Ice water
Melted butter

Preheat oven to 450 degrees. Grease baking sheet. Fill large bowl with ice water and immerse 3 or 4 crackers at a time for 30 to 45 seconds. Remove with slotted spatula to baking sheet (these will puff, so do not crowd). Lightly drizzle butter over crackers. Sprinkle with garlic or seasoning salt and cheese. Reduce heat to 400 degrees and bake for 15 minutes. Further reduce heat to 300 degrees and bake for 25 minutes until golden brown. Store in an airtight container. Option: I like to sprinkle these with seasoning salt or garlic salt, and Parmesan or Romano cheese.

Sharron Davis

Potato Skin Appetizers

Serve immediately   Makes as many as needed

Potatoes   **Cheddar cheese**
1 pound bacon, cooked and   **Garlic salt**
  crumbled   **1-8 ounce carton sour**
Spring onions   **cream, or more**

Bake potatoes; cut them into thick strips, and slice off top layer of potato. Mix together cooked crumbled bacon, spring onions, cheese, garlic salt, and sour cream. Butter potato strips and add sour cream mixture. Reserve some bacon to put on top. Bake at 400 degrees for 10 minutes.

Mrs. Ann Massey

Roquefort Mousse

Must prepare ahead   Serves 10-12

4 tablespoons butter
4 ounces cream cheese
1 egg, separated
½ pound Roquefort cheese

1 tablespoon unflavored
  gelatin
1 teaspoon Dijon mustard
½ cup whipping cream

Allow cheese and butter to come to room temperature. Whip cream and set aside. Beat egg white until stiff and also set aside. In a large bowl beat yolk, add Roquefort and beat until smooth. Add cream cheese and butter; continue beating until smooth. Dissolve gelatin in cold water. Add gelatin and mustard to cheese mixture. Fold in egg white and then whipped cream. Pour into greased mold. Chill overnight and serve with fruit and crackers.

Pat McCloskey

Russian Rye Bread and Dip

Must prepare 24 hours ahead   Serves a crowd

3 packages Buddig's chipped
  beef
1½ pints mayonnaise (NOT
  salad dressing)
2 teaspoons Beau Monde
  seasoning
2 teaspoons dried dill weed

1½ pints sour cream
3 tablespoons dried parsley
2 tablespoons fresh onion,
  finely chopped
1 round Russian rye bread

To prepare dip: Chop chipped beef into little slivers. In a large bowl mix together all ingredients except bread. Store in an airtight container in the refrigerator for 24 hours. At least twice during this time, stir well. Cut out top of bread and pull bread apart in bite-size pieces. The center of the bread should be hollow so that you can put the dip in it. Use the bite-sized pieces of bread to eat dip.

*Dabney Vigor's recipe
by Katherine Currence*

St. Charles Dip

May prepare ahead   Serves a crowd

½ avocado, mashed   ½ tomato, mashed
1 tablespoon mayonnaise   Juice of ½ lemon
½ pint sour cream   1 package Good Seasons
Dash Tabasco   Italian dressing

Mix all above ingredients together and chill. Serve with corn chips or
Doritos.

Mrs. Robert Poovey (Marsha)

Salmon Spread

This has been one of my most complimented appetizers.

May prepare ahead   Serves a crowd

1-16 ounce can red salmon   ¾ cup mayonnaise
4 tablespoons dill pickle   Dash seasoned salt
  cubes, drained   1 teaspoon dried parsley
1 small onion, grated   2 tablespoons lemon juice

Drain salmon, remove large bones and skin; chill. Combine remaining
ingredients and refrigerate. Right before serving place salmon on a
shallow plate on a bed of lettuce. Pour mixture over salmon. Serve with
Triscuits or bagel crisps.

Mrs. Charles Gray, III (Sara)

Glorified Onions

May prepare ahead   Serves 10-12

5 to 6 medium onions, sliced   1 teaspoon celery seed
  thin   (optional)
1 cup sugar   ½ cup vinegar
2 cups water   1 teaspoon celery salt
½ cup mayonnaise   (optional)

Soak onions in vinegar, sugar, and water in refrigerator for 2 to 4 hours.
Drain well and toss with mayonnaise and seasonings. Serve with your
favorite crackers.

Peggy Cooke

Sausage-Onion Snack

May prepare ahead   Makes 32 appetizers

1 pound bulk pork sausage
1 large onion, chopped
2 cups Bisquick baking mix
¾ cup milk
2 eggs

1 tablespoon caraway or
  poppy seed
1½ cups sour cream
¼ teaspoon salt
Paprika

Preheat oven to 350 degrees and grease a 13 x 9 x 2-inch baking pan. Cook and stir sausage and onion over medium heat until sausage is browned; drain. Mix Bisquick, milk and 1 egg. Spread in pan. Sprinkle with caraway seed. Top with sausage and onions. Mix sour cream, salt, and remaining egg; pour evenly over sausage. Sprinkle with paprika. Bake uncovered until set, 25 to 30 minutes. Cut into rectangles, about 2 x 1½-inches, to serve.

Cathy McCosh

Swedish Pickled Shrimp

A traditional Christmas day first course at our home. This recipe comes from a family friend, Janice Raper, who always contributed it to the Christmas lunch when I was growing up.

Must prepare ahead   Serves 6-8

2 to 2½ pounds shrimp, in
  shell
½ cup celery tops
¼ cup mixed pickling spices

1 teaspoon salt
2 cups onion, sliced
7 or 8 bay leaves

Marinade:
1⅓ cups salad oil
3 tablespoons capers plus juice
1½ teaspoons salt

¾ cup white vinegar
2½ teaspoons celery seed
Dash Tabasco sauce

Cover shrimp with boiling water; add celery tops, pickling spices, and salt. Cover and simmer for 5 minutes. Drain, peel and devein shrimp. Alternate shrimp, onion, and bay leaves in shallow dish. Mix the ingredients for the marinade and pour over the shrimp. Cover; chill 24 hours, spooning marinade over shrimp occasionally. Will stay in refrigerator for one week. Serve as an appetizer with toothpicks. Pretty in a clear glass bowl.

Mrs. Joseph S. Stowe (Janice)

Shrimp Mold

Must prepare ahead   Yields: 1 mold

2 envelopes Knox gelatin,   2 cans shrimp, flake with
  softened in ¼ cup cold   fingers and save juice
  water   1 medium onion, grated
1 cup mayonnaise   2 tablespoons capers,
1 teaspoon Tabasco sauce   (I use one bottle)
2 teaspoons Worcestershire   2 hard-boiled eggs, finely
  sauce   chopped
Few drops red food coloring

Add softened gelatin to boiling lemon water (make by adding juice of
1 lemon, juice from shrimp and water to make one cup). Remove from
heat when gelatin is well dissolved. Stir in mayonnaise, then add Tabasco
sauce, Worcestershire sauce, and a few drops of red food coloring; then
add solid ingredients. Mold and serve with crackers.

Lin Lineberger

Fresh Shrimp Mold

Must prepare 1 day ahead   Serves 6-8

3 cups shrimp, boiled and   ¼ cup parsley, coarsely
  cleaned   chopped
¾ cup Miracle Whip salad   4 hard-boiled eggs, grated
  dressing   2 tablespoons onion, grated
¼ cup mayonnaise   1 tablespoon lemon juice
1 package unflavored gelatin   ½ teaspoon Worcestershire
¼ cup cold water   sauce
1 cup celery, coarsely   Salt and pepper to taste
  chopped

Boil, shell and devein shrimp; chop. Heat Miracle Whip and mayonnaise
in double boiler over hot water. Dissolve gelatin in ¼ cup cold water and
add to the mayonnaise and Miracle Whip. Mix all ingredients and pour
into a greased mold. This must be done the day before serving. Unmold
and garnish with parsley. Serve with crackers. Use glass or plastic mold,
not metal. Mayonnaise/seafood dishes will discolor in a metal container.

Jennifer Davis

Chelsea House Party Shrimp

Each fall and again each spring the company where I work has parties in our
High Point Showroom for the Southern Furniture Market. Over the past
several years I have acquired a number of cocktail party food recipes.
I can't claim credit for these because some have been given us by
friends and customers from all over the country.

Must prepare ahead   Serves a crowd

1-10 ounce can tomato soup   1 cup mayonnaise
1-8 ounce package cream   1 small onion, grated
  cheese   1 cup celery, diced
½ envelope Knox gelatin   2 cups shrimp, chopped
¾ cup water

Heat the soup and put in blender with cream cheese. Add ½ envelope
of gelatin that has been softened in ¾ cup cold water to 1 cup mayonnaise. Add onion, celery, and shrimp to soup mixture. Add gelatin and
mayonnaise. Pour in greased mold and refrigerate overnight. Serve with
a butter cracker.

Martha Beal

Shrimp Toast

Serve immediately   Serves 4-6

1 pound uncooked shrimp   Dash of pepper
4 tablespoons onions, finely   1 egg white, unbeaten
  chopped   1 teaspoon cornstarch
1 tablespoon wine   THIN slices of bread
1 teaspoon salt

Chop uncooked shrimp very fine and add to onions, wine, salt, and pepper.
Next add egg white and cornstarch. Mix everything until well blended.
Spread on thin slices of bread and fry in deep oil until golden brown.
Watch carefully so that bread does not burn. Cut into small bite size
pieces.

Note: The bread can be prepared beforehand and put into refrigerator, but cooking
must be right before serving.

Lee Matheny

Icy Pickled Shrimp

This is a family favorite for a Christmas Eve appetizer or Easter dinner.

Must prepare 2 days ahead   Serves 12

2 pounds unpeeled fresh shrimp	⅓ cup catsup
1-3 ounce package seafood boil	1¼ cups vegetable oil
1 teaspoon salt	⅓ cup vinegar
2 garlic cloves, crushed	2 teaspoons sugar
2 teaspoons Worcestershire	1½ teaspoons dry mustard
sauce	1 large onion, sliced
¼ teaspoon pepper	4 bay leaves
⅛ teaspoon hot sauce	

Boil shrimp in seafood boil and salt according to directions on package. Drain and cool. Peel and devein shrimp. Combine next 9 ingredients in blender. Blend until smooth.

Layer half of shrimp, onion slices, and bay leaves in large glass bowl. Repeat layering with last half of ingredients. Pour sauce over all and refrigerate for 2 days. Serve with crackers.

Serve icy cold in glass container. Do not allow sauce to come in contact with silver or other metals, as the acid will react with the metal. Garnish with sprigs of fresh parsley and lemon swirls.

Mrs. John Bridgeman (Nan)

Shrimp Ball

May prepare ahead   Yields: 1 large ball

2 cans shrimp	Worcestershire sauce
1 onion	Kraft Miracle Whip salad
2 eggs, hard-boiled	dressing
Tabasco sauce	Paprika

Rinse shrimp, drain, and crumble with fingers. Very finely chop or grate onion and eggs. Mix shrimp, onion, and eggs together with a generous shake or two of Tabasco sauce and Worcestershire sauce.. Put enough Miracle Whip with these ingredients to hold together. Shape into a ball. Sprinkle with paprika and serve with crackers of your choice.

Suzanne Butler McLean

Pickled Shrimp

This is a traditional Christmas Day pick-up for our family.

Must prepare 24 hours ahead   Serves 8-10

1 layer of sliced onions   1 layer of sliced lemons
1 layer of cooked shrimp   1 layer of bay leaves
  (small)

Sauce:
1-10 ounce can tomato soup   ¼ cup vinegar
¾ cup salad oil   2 tablespoons sugar
1 teaspoon onion, minced   1 teaspoon paprika
1 teaspoon salt

In medium to large salad bowl alternate layers of onions, lemons, bay leaves, and shrimp. Mix ingredients for sauce until blended well (I double the sauce recipe for 2 to 3 pounds of shrimp). Pour sauce over shrimp layers. Cover and refrigerate for at least 24 hours before serving. Serve the shrimp on toothpicks.

Mrs. Mary Lewis Bryant

Blanche's Shrimp Balls

*This recipe came to me from Mrs. Dean French and I have
never seen it in print anywhere else.*

Must prepare 1 day ahead   Makes 30 balls

1 pound cooked shrimp   3 tablespoons cream cheese
1 tablespoon chili sauce   2 teaspoons horseradish
  (from a jar)   ¼ cup celery, chopped
1 hard-boiled egg, chopped   1 tablespoon onion, grated
Salt and pepper to taste   Parsley, finely chopped

Finely chop cooked shrimp. Blend together remaining ingredients and add to shrimp. Form into small balls. Roll these balls in fresh chopped parsley and chill. Serve with crackers.

Mrs. Ralph S. Robinson, Jr.

Spinach Brownies

This tastes like bite size quiche and can be used as an appetizer or as a vegetable.

May prepare ahead   Serves 10-12

1 cup flour
½ teaspoon salt
1 teaspoon soda
1 cup milk
2 eggs

½ cup onion, chopped
¾ to 1 pound Cheddar
  cheese
1 package frozen chopped
  spinach, thawed*

Mix flour, salt, soda, milk, and eggs with a fork; fold in onion, grated cheese, and thawed, drained spinach. Bake in a greased 12 x 8 x 2-inch pan at 350 degrees for 30 to 35 minutes. Let cool slightly before slicing into brownie-size squares. This makes approximately 30 pick-up bite-size squares. *You can substitute broccoli for spinach, if desired.

Martha E. Williard

Steak Tartare

Must prepare ahead   Serves 8-10

4 mashed anchovies
½ cup onion, finely chopped
Capers to taste
Olive oil
2 raw egg yolks

2 pounds ground round,
  ground twice
Worcestershire sauce to
  taste
Parsley, chopped, to taste

In a wooden bowl mash anchovies, onion, and capers with olive oil. Add raw egg yolks and beat slightly. Add ground round, Worcestershire sauce, and chopped parsley. Mix well. Chill in decorative mold. Serve on platter garnished with parsley or watercress and crackers.

Lin Lineberger

Tex-Mex Dip

Must prepare ahead   Serves 6-8

3 medium ripe avocados or   2 cans jalapeno bean dip
  1-6 ounce carton avocado dip   1 cup green onions, chopped
2 tablespoons lemon juice   2 to 3 medium tomatoes,
Salt and pepper to taste   chopped
1 cup sour cream   2 small cans ripe olives,
½ cup mayonnaise   chopped
1 package taco seasoning mix   8 ounces Cheddar cheese,
                                     shredded

Mash avocados with lemon juice, salt, and pepper. Combine sour cream
with mayonnaise and taco seasoning in separate bowl. Spread bean dip
in shallow platter (quiche dish is good). Top with avocado mixture. Layer
with sour cream mixture, green onions, tomatoes, and olives. Cover with
cheese, and chill at least 1 hour. Serve with round tortilla chips.

Julie Solomon

Marinated Vegetables

Must prepare ahead   Serves 10-12

1 pound carrots, sliced   1 onion, sliced
1 bunch broccoli, cut into   1 bottle of your favorite
  bite-size pieces   Italian dressing
1 head cauliflour, cut into
  bite-size pieces

Mix all ingredients and marinate for several hours in the refrigerator.

Roseanne Nichols

Vera's Dip

This also makes a delicious vegetable dish so you have a choice.

May prepare ahead   Serves 6-8
Freezes well before cooking

⅓ cup olive oil
3 cups eggplant, peeled and
  cubed
⅓ cup green pepper, chopped
1 onion, chopped
1-4 ounce can sliced
  mushrooms
2 or more cloves garlic,
  crushed
1-6 ounce can tomato paste

¾ cup green olives,
  chopped
½ teaspoon oregano
½ teaspoon pepper
2 tablespoons wine vinegar
1½ teaspoons sugar
1 teaspoon salt
Tabasco sauce to taste

Heat oil; add eggplant, green pepper, onion, mushrooms, and garlic. Cover
and cook for 10 minutes; stir. Add remaining ingredients and simmer
for 30 to 40 minutes. Serve hot with Fritos or your favorite crackers.

Ginny Ratchford

Water Chestnut Appetizer

Serve immediately   Serves 4-6

1 can water chestnuts, whole
¼ cup soy sauce

2 tablespoons sugar
1 pound bacon

Marinate water chestnuts in mixture of soy sauce and sugar for 30
minutes. Cut bacon strips in half and wrap each water chestnut with
bacon and fasten with wooden toothpicks. Bake at 350 degrees for 30
minutes.

Penny White

Toddies
Beverages

Amaretto Liqueur

Must prepare 2 weeks ahead   Yields: 6 quarts

4 quarts water
7 cups sugar
1 cup dark corn syrup
2 tablespoons freeze-dried
  coffee

2 ounces vanilla extract
6 ounces almond extract
1 fifth of Golden Grain
  alcohol (190 proof)

Combine water, sugar, and syrup in a large Dutch oven or heavy pan.
Bring to a boil. Boil hard for 50 minutes uncovered. Remove from heat,
and cool slightly. Add 2 tablespoons freeze-dried coffee and stir until completely dissolved. Cool to room temperature. Add vanilla extract, almond
extract, and alcohol. Stir well. Let age for 2 weeks. This can be put in
small bottles to give as gifts.

Marsha Jones

Between the Sheets

Serve immediately   Makes 1 drink

1½ ounces rum
½ ounce brandy

½ ounce Triple Sec
1 ounce lemon juice

Shake well with cracked ice and strain into a cocktail glass.

Cookbook Committee

Bunches of Bloodys

May prepare ahead   Serves 25

1-46 ounce can V-8 juice
1-10 ounce can beef broth or
  bouillon
5 ounces Dr Tillit Suit's
  Bloody Mary Seasoning
1-32 ounce can tomato juice

32 ounces vodka or gin
½ cup fresh squeezed
  lemon juice
Lots of crushed ice
Lime wedges
Fresh ground pepper

Pour all ingredients into a 1-gallon container. Stir to mix. Serve over
lots of crushed ice. Garnish with lime wedges and fresh ground pepper.

Sharron Davis

Brandy Alexander

Serve immediately   Makes 1 drink

1 ounce brandy   1 ounce Creme de Cacao
1 ounce heavy cream

Shake well with cracked ice, and strain into a cocktail glass.

Cookbook Committee

Bride's Bowl

Must prepare ahead   Serves 12-16

Half of a fresh pineapple   1½ bottles of 750 ml.
⅓ cup sugar   Gold Label rum
1 cup lemon juice   1 pint strawberries
2 cups unsweetened   2 quarts soda
   pineapple juice

Peel and slice pineapple into wedge-shaped pieces, discarding core, and
put in large pitcher with sugar, lemon juice, pineapple juice, and rum.
Chill for 2 hours. Put block of ice in a punch bowl and pour rum-pineapple
mix over ice. Just before serving, add sliced strawberries and soda.

Cookbook Committee

Chambord Hot-Buttered Brandy

Rich and creamy-and absolutely delicious!

Serve immediately   Makes 4 drinks

1 tablespoon unsalted butter,   ¼ cup vanilla ice cream,
   room temperature   softened
¼ cup powdered sugar   1⅓ cups boiling water
¼ teaspoon grated lemon peel   ⅓ cup Chambord
                                  ⅓ cup brandy

Cream together butter, sugar, and lemon peel in a medium bowl. Stir
in ice cream until thoroughly blended. Add remaining ingredients and
serve.

Cookbook Committee

Chambord Frappe

Serve immediately   Serves 4

8 scoops or 1 quart Breyer's   **6 ounces Chambord**
  vanilla ice cream   **(raspberry) liqueur**

Put ice cream in blender. Add liqueur. Blend until smooth. Serve in stemmed glasses. (Amaretto may be substituted for amaretto frappes.)

Connie Gibbons

Grand Cappucino

This is a wonderful after-dinner drink, or dessert.

Serve immediately   Serves 8-10

3 ounces Kahlua   **8 cups freshly made,**
2 ounces brandy   **strong, hot expresso**
2 ounces Grand Marnier   **2 cups heavy cream**
2 heaping tablespoons dark
  brown sugar

Heat Kahlua, brandy, Grand Marnier, and brown sugar in a saucepan. Add hot coffee and warm cream, stirring constantly until heated thoroughly.

Mrs. Robert Leeth Davis

Cafe Au Lait Mix

*This mix makes a great gift but be sure to include the
directions for serving with your gift.*

May be prepared ahead   Yields: 2 cups mix

1-6 ounce jar instant   **¼ cup instant coffee**
  non-dairy creamer (1½ cups)   **crystals**
¼ cup packed brown sugar   **Dash of salt**

Thoroughly mix all ingredients together. Store in airtight container. When ready to serve, mix ¼ cup mix with ⅔ cup boiling water.

Cookbook Committee

Chatham Artillery Punch

Must prepare at least
2 weeks ahead

Makes 12 gallons
or serves 200

1 pound green tea
2 gallons water
Juice of 3 dozen oranges
Juice of 3 dozen lemons
5 pounds brown sugar
1 gallon brandy

1 gallon rye whiskey
1 gallon gin
1 gallon rum, light or dark
12 quarts champagne
2 quarts cherries, chopped

Soak green tea in 2 gallons of cold water for 24 hours and then strain.
Mix strained tea and juices together first, preferably in a cedar tub, but
a milk can will do. Add sugar and stir thoroughly. Add liquors, stir, and
let stock set covered for at least 2 weeks. When ready to serve, add ice,
12 quarts (15 fifths) of champagne and cherries. The stock and finished
punch should both be stirred well.

Mrs. Tom Hunter (Patti)

Spiced Cider

Serve immediately

Yields: 5 quarts

1 gallon apple cider
6 cloves

3 sticks whole cinnamon
1 bottle scuppernong wine

Just heat cider with spices; add scuppernong wine, and serve.

*Note: If this mixture is heated thoroughly, the alcohol evaporates from the wine.
The enchanting flavor of the scuppernong remains, but the beverage becomes tame
enough for a Sunday School social.*

Mrs. Kay Kincaid Moss

Coco Blizzard

Serve immediately

Serves 2

½ cup pineapple or orange juice
½ cup Cream of Coconut

4 ounces plain yogurt
8 ounces club soda

Place juice, yogurt, and Cream of Coconut in blender. Blend for
30 seconds. Add club soda and serve over cracked ice.

Cookbook Committee

Cooling Cinnamon Water

I discovered this wonderful party beverage in an old book,
Valuable Secrets in Arts and Trades (1816).

May be prepared ahead   Yields: 1 quart
Freezes well

1 quart water   1 to 2 cups sugar
3 cloves   Additional water to dilute
½ ounce whole cinnamon,
   broken

To make concentrate: Bring to boil 1 quart of water. Put in 3 cloves and
½ ounce whole cinnamon. Set off heat. Allow spices to steep until cold.
Strain. Add 1 to 2 cups sugar depending upon desired sweetness.

To dilute: 1 cup concentrate in 2 quarts water OR 1 quart concentrate
in 2 gallons of water. Serve iced. It is so refreshing on a hot summer's day.

Mrs. Kay Kincaid Moss

Basic Fruit Cordial

Must prepare 8 weeks ahead   Makes 3 pints

½ cup water   2½ cups fresh fruit
1 cup sugar   4 cups vodka

Mix water and sugar in a saucepan. Bring to a boil, reduce the heat,
and cook for 5 minutes or until the sugar dissolves. Remove from heat
and cool. Slice fruit and place in a wide-mouth, 2-quart glass jar. Add
the sugar syrup and vodka. Stir gently. Store in a cool, dark place. Allow
the cordial to mature for 8 weeks, inverting the jar carefully once a week.
Strain the cordial mixture through a cheesecloth or paper coffee filter
and pour into a glass bottle. Cap or cork the container and store in a
cool, dark place.

Variation: Pears, blueberries, or oranges may be used.

Cookbook Committee

Coffee Bar

This is a wonderful ending to a brunch or dinner.

Several pots of gourmet
  roast coffee
Amaretto
Kahlua
Brandy

Irish Whiskey
Irish cream
Grand Marnier
Raw sugar
Cream

Garnishes:
Cherries
Cinnamon sticks
Shaved chocolate

Ground cinnamon
Ground nutmeg
Lots of fresh whipped cream

Fill coffee cups ⅔ full and allow each person to add his own liqueur and garnishes.

Sharron Davis

Coffee Cognac

Serve immediately   Serves 1

2 large scoops coffee ice cream   Instant coffee as garnish
2 tablespoons Cognac
  (Optional)

Process ice cream and cognac in a blender. Pour into a large chilled wine glass. Garnish with sprinkling of instant coffee.

Note: This is a thick drink perfect for dessert and should be served with a straw or spoon.

Cookbook Committee

Irish Coffee

Serve immediately   Serves 1

Hot coffee
1 jigger (ounce) Old Bushmill
  Irish Whiskey in Irish
  coffee glass

½ teaspoon sugar, or to
  taste
3 tablespoons Cognac
Whipping cream, prepared

Fill glass ¾-full with hot coffee. Add Irish whiskey, sugar to taste, cognac and stir. Top with whipping cream. Delicious!

Cookbook Committee

Hot Southern Comfort Nog

You'll taste down-home Southern hospitality in every sip of this delicious nog.

Serve immediately   Serves 4

1 cup light cream or half-n-half	1 cup Southern Comfort
3 cups milk	1 cup bourbon
4 eggs, lightly beaten	Fresh grated nutmeg
2 tablespoons sugar	

Heat milk and cream in a medium saucepan over low heat until bubbles appear around the edges. Remove from heat and set aside. Whisk together eggs and sugar in a small bowl until thick and light yellow. Stir in Southern Comfort and bourbon. Divide among four 12-ounce mugs. Add about 1 cup hot milk mixture to each mug and sprinkle with nutmeg.

Cookbook Committee

Mrs. Bauer's Egg Nog

May prepare 1 day ahead   Yields: 8 large mugs or
                                                              12-14 punch cups

6 eggs, separated	1 pint vanilla ice cream
6 tablespoons sugar, divided	1/2 pint whipping cream
12 tablespoons bourbon	Nutmeg (optional)

Beat egg yolks until thick. Add 4 tablespoons sugar gradually. Add bourbon a little at a time. Beat well each time. At serving time, add softened ice cream and whipped cream. Beat egg whites and the 2 tablespoons of sugar until stiff. Fold into other mixture.

Janice Stowe

Fish House Punch

Tastes deceptively benign. BEWARE!

May prepare ahead without club soda   Serves 20

1¼ cups simple syrup   2 cups water
  (boil together with 1   ½ cup peach brandy
  cup water and 1 cup   ½ cup Jamaican rum
  sugar for 5 minutes)   1 cup brandy
1¼ cups fresh lemon juice   3 cups club soda

Combine all ingredients except club soda. Chill. Before serving, add club soda. Serve in a punch bowl with cracked ice.

Connie Gibbons

Frozen Daiquiri Punch

Freezes well   Serves 6

1-6 ounce can frozen limeade   5-6 ounce cans water
2-6 ounce cans frozen   1 pint white rum
  lemonade

Mix all ingredients and freeze in large container. Put in punch bowl before guests arrive and allow to become "slushy".

Cookbook Committee

Fuzzy Navel

Serve immediately   Serves 1

1 ounce peach schnapps   1 ounce vodka
2 ounces orange juice   Orange slice

Mix all ingredients. Serve in stemmed glass over cracked ice. Garnish with orange slice.

Connie Gibbons

Fruit Punch

*This punch is a light, refreshing, and delightful
punch recipe. Easy, too!*

Must prepare ahead   Serves 20-25

**1-24 ounce bottle white   2-28 ounce bottles
  grape juice   ginger ale**

Chill white grape juice and ginger ale until very cold. Pour into a punch
bowl together to mix. Make ice rings from another recipe of punch
adding fresh berries and fresh mint leaves. Freeze until firm; keep frozen
until ready to serve. Unmold and add to punch at serving time.

*Variation: ½ can pineapple juice can be added for each recipe for a little different
flavor.*

Jennifer Davis

Girl Scout Punch

*I used this green punch when I was a Girl Scout leader. This is also good
for St. Patrick's Day and Christmas when a non- alcoholic punch is needed.*

Must prepare ahead   Serves 18

**2 cups boiling water   1-12 ounce can frozen
½ cup sugar   lemonade
2-3 ounce packages lime Jello   1-46 ounce can pineapple
1 cup cold water   juice
1-12 ounce can frozen orange   1-28 ounce bottle ginger ale
  juice**

Mix together boiling water, sugar, and Jello. Stir until sugar and Jello
dissolve. Add cold water and fruit juices. Chill. When ready to serve, add
ginger ale.

Connie Gibbons

Hot Buttered Rum

This is a must for after-skiing gatherings.

May prepare ahead   Yields: 1 gallon of butter base

1 pound powdered sugar   ½ gallon Breyer's vanilla
1 pound brown sugar   bean ice cream,
1 heaping tablespoon cinnamon   softened
1 heaping tablespoon nutmeg   Rum
1 pound butter, softened   Boiling water

Mix together sugars, spices, butter, and ice cream. This butter base will keep for several weeks in the refrigerator.

To serve, spoon 2 tablespoons of the base into a large warmed mug. Add 2 ounces of rum and boiling water to fill mug. Stir until blended.

Mrs. Robert Leeth Davis

Hot Mulled Wine

Serve immediately   Yields: 2 liters

1 cup sugar   18 whole cloves
3 cups water   1 stick cinnamon
Peel of ½ lemon   2 bottles Rosé wine

Boil together sugar, water, lemon peel, cloves, and cinnamon stick. Simmer for 15 minutes and strain. Add wine and heat gently. DO NOT BOIL!

Mrs. Donald D. Howe

Irish Lullaby

This recipe is served at the Tremont Hotel in Chicago, Illinois.

Serve immediately   Serves 1

½ cup vanilla ice cream   1 ounce Chambord liqueur
1 ounce Bailey's Irish Cream   Raspberries to garnish

Blend all ingredients except raspberries in blender. Serve in stemmed glass. Garnish with a raspberry or two.

Connie Gibbons

Mint Cup

May prepare ahead   Serves 6

Leaves from 4 sprigs of mint   **¼ teaspoon salt**
2 cups sugar   **Dash green food coloring**
2 cups water   **1 quart ginger ale**
2 cups fresh lemon juice

Boil mint, sugar, and water for 5 minutes. Strain the syrup. Add the
lemon juice, salt, and food coloring. Chill well. Add ginger ale before
serving.

Connie Gibbons

Mint Julep

Serve immediately   Serves as many as wanted

Water   **Wild Turkey 101-proof**
Sugar   **bourbon**
Fresh mint   **Silver beakers**
                                     Crushed ice

To each jigger of water, add 1 teaspoon sugar. Dissolve. Crush a good
deal of mint into this. Add approximately 4 to 5 jiggers
bourbon. Fill the beakers with crushed ice, pour in mixture, let ice sub-
side. By this time the beakers should be covered with frost, so never touch
the beaker during preparation. Add more ice, place a sprig of mint at
the side and serve with pleasure to your guest.

Paulette Elmore

Mocha Punch

Serve immediately   Serves 8-10

4 heaping teaspoons instant   **4 cups strong, cold coffee**
  cocoa mix   **1 gallon vanilla ice cream,**
2 cups whole milk   **softened**

Stir cocoa mix into milk. Add coffee and stir. To serve, pour mocha mixture into pitchers or a punch bowl and stir in softened ice cream.

Cookbook Committee

Lemonade Iced Tea

Can be prepared ahead   Yields: 1 gallon

3 family-sized tea bags   **1 small can frozen lemonade**

Prepare tea according to directions. Stir in lemonade until dissolved.
Serve with slices of lemon.

Sharron Davis

Lemonade

May prepare ahead   Serves 4

4 cups water   **½ cup fresh lemon juice**
1 cup sugar syrup (boil together   **1 lemon, sliced thinly**
  1 cup sugar and 1 cup water   **Ice cubes**
  until sugar dissolves)

In a pitcher combine all ingredients and add ice cubes. Serve in tall
glasses with lemon slices and sprigs of mint.

Cookbook Committee

Marvelous Mochas

Use for, or instead of, dessert.

Serve immediately   Serves 10-12

½ gallon good quality chocolate   **1½ cups Kahlua**
  ice cream   **½ cup strong, cold coffee**
½ cup creme de cacao   **Chocolate shavings**

Combine in blender half the ice cream, half the Cream de Cacao, half
the Kahlua and half the coffee. Repeat process. Serve in chilled, stemmed
glasses; garnish with chocolate shavings

Cookbook Committee

Margarita

Serve immediately   Serves 1

1 fresh lemon
Salt
1 ounce tequila
1 ounce triple sec liqueur

1 ounce Rose's lime juice or
  fresh lime juice
Crushed ice

Rub edge of glass with fresh lemon and dip edge in salt. Mix all ingredients and serve in salt-rimmed glass over crushed ice.

Cookbook Committee

Old Fashioned

A favorite of The Drake Hotel, in Chicago.

Serve immediately   Makes 1 drink

2 to 3 dashes Angostura
  bitters
Splash of club soda
1 teaspoon very fine
  granulated sugar

1½ ounces blended
  whiskey, bourbon, or
  scotch
Cherries
Orange slices

Shake Angostura bitters and club soda on sugar. Muddle. Add two ice cubes. Pour in liquor. Garnish with cherry and orange slice. Stir and serve.

Cookbook Committee

Percolator Punch

May prepare ahead   Serves 6-8

2¼ cups pineapple juice
2 cups cranberry juice
1¾ cups water
½ tablespoon allspice

1 tablespoon whole cloves
3 sticks cinnamon
¼ teaspoon salt
⅓ cup sugar (brown or
  white)

Put liquids in an 8-cup percolator. Put spices and sugar in basket; perk. Serve hot in mugs or coffee cups.

Mrs. Pamela P. Glenn

Polynesian Punch

Must prepare ahead   Serves 20

6 to 7 bananas
1-12 ounce can frozen orange juice
1-6 ounce can frozen lemonade
1-46 ounce can pineapple juice

3 cups water
1 cup sugar
4 quarts ginger ale, chilled

Mash bananas in blender or food processor with 1/4 cup orange juice. In a large mixing bowl, combine all ingredients except ginger ale. Pour into molds and freeze. Two hours before serving, put frozen molds in punch bowl and add ginger ale.

Cookbook Committee

Whiskey Sour Punch

Must prepare ahead   Serves 18
Freezes well

1-12 ounce can frozen lemonade
⅕ gallon bourbon (24 ounces)
4½ cups water

6 tablespoons orange juice concentrate
1-12 ounce can ginger ale

Mix together lemonade, bourbon, water, and orange juice and freeze for at least 2 days in advance of serving. Take out of freezer 1 hour before serving and allow to partially thaw. Put into punch bowl and add ginger ale.

Mrs. John Dalton

Red Citrus Punch

May prepare ahead   Serves 10

1-6 ounce can frozen juice
¼ cup frozen limeade
4 cups water

¼ cup frozen lemonade
2 cups cranberry juice
2 cups ginger ale

Combine all ingredients except ginger ale and chill. When ready to serve, add ginger ale. Serve over decorative ice ring in punch bowl.

Cookbook Committee

Rusty Scupper

Serve immediately   Makes 4 drinks

8 ounces Amaretto   8 ounces orange juice
16 ounces vanilla ice cream

Mix in blender with about 6 ice cubes. This is excellent as a drink or
a dessert with a small cookie.

Cookbook Committee

Sangria

May prepare ahead   Serves 8

1 quart red wine   1 cup brandy
1 cup fruit brandy   1-12 ounce bottle club soda
2 oranges, thinly sliced   2 lemons, thinly sliced

Mix all ingredients in large glass pitcher. Chill and serve.

Cookbook Committee

Sangria Blanc

May prepare ahead   Serves 6

½ lemon, sliced   ¼ cup brandy
½ orange, sliced   1 tablespoon sugar
½ apple, sliced   1-12 ounce can carbonated
3 cups dry white wine   lemon-lime soft drink

Thinly slice fruits and place in a 1-quart container. Add wine, brandy,
and sugar. Stir to dissolve sugar. Chill thoroughly. Add lemon-lime soft
drink just before serving.

Cookbook Committee

Strawberry Sparkle

Serve immediately   Yields: 1 pitcher

¾ cup mashed strawberries   1 cup whole strawberries
1 bottle champagne or   Fresh mint sprigs (optional)
  sparkling wine

Place mashed strawberries in bottom of glass pitcher, pour bottle of champagne in. Float in whole strawberries. Pour in frosted champagne glasses and float mint sprig on top as garnish if desired.

Sharron Davis

Syllabub

Serve immediately   Serves 4-6

4 cups whipping cream (use   1 cup sugar
  half-n-half for a lower calorie ¼ cup sherry or whiskey
  version)   1 cup milk
1 teaspoon vanilla extract

Combine all ingredients in a large bowl. Beat at medium speed of an electric mixer until foamy.

Cookbook Committee

Tea Punch

Can prepare up to a week ahead   Yields: 2½ gallons

20 regular tea bags   1-12 ounce can frozen
20 cups hot water   orange juice
6 cups sugar   concentrate, thawed
1 cup fresh lemon juice   1-46 ounce can unsweetened
                                   pineapple juice

Steep tea in hot water for 20 minutes. Discard tea bags. Add sugar while mixture is still warm. Let cool. Add remaining ingredients and stir well. Store in a sealed container in the refrigerator.

Mrs. Robert L. Davis

Velvet Hammer

Serve immediately   Serves 4

1 quart vanilla ice cream   2 jiggers brandy
2 jiggers Cointreau   2 jiggers creme de cacao

Put all in blender and mix.

Peggy Cooke

Wassail

May prepare ahead   Makes 4½ quarts

1 gallon apple cider   3 small oranges
1 quart unsweetened tea   1½ teaspoons whole cloves
¼ cup sugar

Combine cider, tea, and sugar in a large, deep pan. Stud oranges with cloves and add to cider mixture. Bring mixture to a boil. Reduce heat and simmer, uncovered, for 1 hour. Serve hot.

Cookbook Committee

Wassail-Crowd Size

Serve immediately   Serves 50-75 cups

2 gallons apple cider   2 quarts orange juice

Pour these two ingredients into a large coffee pot.

2 cups brown sugar   4 teaspoons whole allspice
4 sticks cinnamon   Dash of nutmeg
4 teaspoons whole cloves

Mix the above ingredients and place in perk basket. Let coffee pot perk as it would for coffee. You may half ingredients for home 30-cup coffee maker.

Cookbook Committee

Soups and Stews

Easy Oven Beef Stew

Serve immediately   Serves 8-10

2 pounds stew beef	4 small onions, quartered
2 tablespoons flour	4 small carrots, cut in
1 teaspoon salt	1-inch slices
¼ teaspoon pepper	4 small potatoes, quartered
⅛ teaspoon paprika	1 cup celery, sliced
2 tablespoons vegetable oil	1 cup water
2-8 ounce cans tomato sauce	Salt and pepper to taste

Combine flour, salt, pepper, and paprika. Roll beef in seasoned flour. Toss with oil in large casserole dish. Bake beef uncovered at 400 degrees for 30 minutes stirring once.

While baking beef, place vegetables, water, tomato sauce, salt, and pepper in a large bowl. Stir well. Add vegetable mixture to meat, mixing them well. Cover and bake 1 hour and 45 minutes at 350 degrees.

Jennie Stultz

Barbequed Beef Stew

Prepare same day   Serves 6-8
Freezes well

2 pounds lean stew beef	⅛ teaspoon pepper
2 tablespoons cooking oil	2 cups beef stock or 1 can
1 cup onions, sliced	beef broth
½ cup green peppers, diced	⅔ cup water
1 large clove garlic, halved	1-8 ounce can tomato juice
⅓ cup barbeque sauce	½ teaspoon salt

Thickening:

2 tablespoons cornstarch	¼ cup water

Brown stew beef in 2 tablespoons cooking oil. Combine other ingredients with browned beef in a Dutch oven or a slow cooker, covered. Cook 3 or 4 hours slowly. Thicken stew with thickening ingredients mixed together well. Serve over rice, if desired.

Mrs. Richard Akers (Gretchen)

Borsch

My mother makes this on hot summer days and keeps it in the refrigerator in a big pitcher. Very refreshing!

May prepare ahead   Serves 6-8

1 No. 2 can beets (2½ cups)   1 tablespoon lemon juice
1 can bouillon   ½ teaspoon salt (optional)
1 cup cold water   ¼ cup sour cream
1 teaspoon onion, minced

Finely chop drained beets, but reserve the juice. Combine with beet juice, bouillon, water, and minced onion. Heat thoroughly but do not boil. Add salt and lemon juice. Serve hot or cold topped with sour cream.

Peggy Cooke

Cream of Broccoli Soup I

Delicious and pretty served at Christmas or Thanksgiving meals.

May prepare ahead   Serves 6

1 bunch fresh broccoli or   5 tablespoons flour
  2-10 ounce packages   Half-n-half
  frozen broccoli   Salt to taste
½ onion, chopped   White pepper to taste
3 cups (2 cans) chicken   Garnishes: paprika,
  consomme   croutons, and parsley
4 tablespoons butter

Cook broccoli in stock with onion until soft. Place in blender and blend quickly. Leave small pieces of broccoli. Make a roux by constantly stirring flour in butter until it browns. Add broccoli and stock to roux. To avoid lumps, stir constantly until thick. Thin to preferred consistency with half-n-half. Add salt and white pepper to taste. Serve hot and garnish with cheese croutons, paprika, and parsley.

Mrs. Charles C. Elliott (Carol)
Mrs. Mona L. Fulton

Cream of Broccoli Soup II

May prepare ahead   Serves 6

1 can cream of potato soup
1 can cream of celery soup
1¼ cups milk
1-10 ounce package frozen
  chopped broccoli
¼ teaspoon dry mustard

¼ teaspoon dry whole basil
1 teaspoon Dijon mustard
½ teaspoon dried whole
  thyme
½ cup sharp Cheddar
  cheese, grated

Combine all the ingredients except the cheese in a 2-quart saucepan. Cook over low heat for 40 minutes. Stir occasionally. Top with sharp grated Cheddar cheese.

Mrs. Terry Ratchford (Trish)

Broccoli and Cauliflower Soup

Well worth the preparation time   Serves 4-6

1-8 ounce package frozen
  cauliflower
1-10¾ ounce can condensed
  chicken broth
½ teaspoon mace
⅓ cup onion, finely chopped
¼ cup butter
2 tablespoons flour

½ teaspoon salt
½ teaspoon pepper
3½ cups milk
1-10 ounce package frozen
  broccoli
½ teaspoon dill
½ teaspoon mustard
1 cup Swiss cheese, shredded

In a 3-quart pan cook cauliflower covered in half the broth for 5 to 8 minutes. Place in blender with mace and blend until smooth. Set aside.

Sauté onion in butter until tender. Stir in flour, salt, and pepper. Add all milk and cook, stirring constantly, until thickened. Meanwhile, cook broccoli in rest of broth with rest of seasonings for 5 to 8 minutes. Then stir sauce, cauliflower mixture, and cheese into broccoli. Heat thoroughly until cheese melts. Garnish with broccoli.

Peggy Cooke

"Soup Avgolemono" - Chicken Egg Lemon Soup

*This Greek soup is a favorite in our home. It is made with poultry
and is gently boiled with rice. The distinctive difference is in the blending
of an Avgolemono Sauce (egg-lemon) which gives the soup a frothy,
pale yellow appearance and a tart flavor hard to equal.*

May prepare ahead   Serves 8

1-3 to 4 pound hen, cut-up
2 medium-size carrots
2 celery stalks and leaves
3 whole green or 1 small onion
1 bay leaf
Salt to taste

1 teaspoon black pepper
1 quart water
¾ cup long grain rice
 or 1 cup Orzo (manestra)
5 eggs
Juice of 1½ lemons

Cover the hen, vegetables, and seasoning with water. Bring to a boil.
Skim off fat. Reduce heat and cook for 1½ to 2 hours until hen is tender.
Remove hen from broth. Debone hen and set aside. Strain broth into a
saucepan, discarding vegetables. If too much fat has settled on top, skim
some off and add ½ stick butter. Bring broth to a boil and add rice. Reduce
heat and cook covered until rice is tender. Blend hot soup with
Avgolemono sauce.

Avgolemono sauce (egg-lemon sauce): With electric mixer, beat 5 eggs
until light and fluffy. SLOWLY add the lemon juice of 1½ lemons while
beating constantly with electric mixer. Add broth (not the rice) very
slowly into the egg mixture until all the broth or most of the broth has
been added. Pour sauce into the pot with the remaining soup while stirring vigorously over very low heat until thickened (1 to 2 minutes). DO
NOT BOIL as it will curdle. Serve hot.

Mrs. Tami T. Pearson

Eastern North Carolina Brunswick Stew

Freezes well   Serves 15-20

1-5 pound hen
1 large cabbage, chopped finely
4 or 5 onions, chopped
2 large cans tomatoes
2 cans tomato soup
2 cans corn
2 cans butter beans

2 cans green beans
2 tablespoons Worcestershire
  sauce
Salt and pepper to taste
Instant potato flakes,
  enough to thicken stew
  OR 6 or 7 potatoes,
  peeled and diced

Use a large pot (I use my canner pot or two 3-quart pots.) to boil hen until tender. Remove from water to cool. Add cabbage and onion to chicken broth; cook until translucent (1 to 2 hours). While the broth is cooking, skin and debone hen. Drop meat into the broth; add tomatoes and soup. Boil slowly for several hours. Add corn, butter beans, green beans, and spices. To thicken, add instant potatoes. Serve with fried corn bread.

Ginny Hall (Mrs. Alex)

Hint: Never put a cover on anything that contains milk unless you want to spend hours cleaning up the stove when it boils over.

Quickest Clam Chowder

The main thing is to have plenty of clams and to season well.

Serve immediately   Serves 4

1 large onion, chopped
4 tablespoons butter
1-10½ ounce can New England
  clam chowder

1 large can clams, minced
1 to 2 cups milk
Salt and pepper to taste
Worcestershire sauce to taste

In a saucepan saute the onion in 2 tablespoons butter. Add the clam chowder and the clams in their juice. Mix well and add milk, salt, pepper, 2 tablespoons butter, and Worcestershire sauce. Heat thoroughly and serve with your favorite cracker.

Sharron Davis

Doris' Crab Soup

May prepare ahead   Serves 6

4 tablespoons butter
½ cup onion, chopped
1 small clove garlic, minced
½ cup peeled apple, finely
  diced
½ tablespoon curry
3 tablespoons flour
½ cup tomato, finely chopped

3 cups chicken broth
Salt and pepper to taste
½ pound backfin crabmeat
½ cup heavy cream
Tabasco to taste
Fresh parsley (optional)

Melt butter and saute onion. Add garlic and apple. Then sprinkle with curry and flour. Add tomato and broth. Stir until thick and smooth. Add salt and pepper. Add crab. Simmer 10 minutes. Add cream and Tabasco sauce. Serve with chopped parsley.

Ginny Ratchford

She Crab Soup

A true delicacy. The eggs add a special flavor to the soup.

Serve immediately   Serves 4-6

1 tablespoon butter
1 teaspoon flour
1 quart milk
2 cups white crabmeat and
  crab eggs
¼ to ½ teaspoon salt
½ teaspoon Worcestershire
  sauce

Few drops onion juice
⅛ teaspoon mace
⅛ teaspoon pepper
4 tablespoons dry sherry
¼ pint cream, whipped

Melt butter in top of double boiler and blend in flour until smooth. Add the milk gradually, stirring constantly. To this add crabmeat and eggs and all seasonings except sherry. Cook slowly over hot water for 20 minutes. To serve, place one tablespoon of warmed sherry in individual soup bowls. Add soup and top with whipped cream. Sprinkle with paprika or finely chopped parsley. If unable to obtain "she-crabs", crumble the yolk of a hard-boiled egg in the bottom of the soup bowl.

Cookbook Committee

Simple Crab Stew

May prepare ahead   Serves 6

4 tablespoons flour
1 teaspoon salt
¼ teaspoon white pepper
1 quart whole milk
1 tablespoon butter
¼ teaspoon Tabasco sauce

2 tablespoons white wine
Worcestershire sauce
1 tablespoon fresh lemon
  juice
½ cup crabmeat
¼ cup sherry (not cooking
  sherry)

Combine flour, salt, pepper, and milk in a heavy saucepan over medium heat. Add butter and stir until smooth and slightly thickened. Add Tabasco sauce, white wine, Worcestershire sauce, and lemon juice. Heat until bubbling. Just before serving add crabmeat and warm sherry.

Sharron Davis

Creamy "Philly" Soup

Serve immediately   Serves 4

⅓ cup celery, chopped
¼ cup onion, chopped
2 tablespoons butter
1-8 ounce package Philadelphia
  cream cheese
1 cup milk
1 chicken bouillon cube

1 cup boiling water
1-16 ounce can cream style
  corn
Dash of pepper
½ teaspoon salt
Dash of chives and chervil

Sauté celery and onion in medium saucepan. Add cream cheese and milk. Cook over low heat, stirring until smooth. Dissolve bouillon cube in boiling water; stir into cream cheese mixture. Add remaining ingredients. Heat.

Becca Mitchell

Fiesta Cod Soup

May prepare ahead   Serves 6

1 pound frozen cod, perch, or
  sole fillets, thawed
1-12 ounce can vegetable juice
  cocktail
½ can (10½ ounce size)
  condensed beef bouillon
1-13¾ ounce can Mexicorn*
¾ teaspoon salt
1-16 ounce can stewed
  tomatoes

Dash of hot pepper sauce
½ cup pitted black olives,
  sliced
½ can (4 ounce size)
  chopped green chilies
½ package garlic salad
  dressing mix (shake or
  stir before measuring)

Put all ingredients in slow cooker and cook on high 1 hour. Turn to low
and cook 3 to 4 hours longer. OR cook on low heat 5 to 6 hours. Garnish
with parsley. Serve with hot crusty French bread.

*Note: If Mexicorn is not available, plain whole-kernel corn can be used. Whole
green chilies can be drained and chopped if chopped chilies are not available.*

Mrs. Paulette H. Elmore

French Onion Soup I

May prepare ahead   Serves 6-8

4 tablespoons butter
2 tablespoons oil
2 pounds onion, thinly sliced
2 tablespoons flour
2 quarts fresh or canned
  beef stock

Salt and pepper to taste
French bread, thick sliced
Swiss cheese, grated
Parmesan cheese, grated

In soup pot sauté onions in butter and oil until soft and browned (about
20 minutes). Sprinkle in flour and stir until golden. Add boiling beef
stock; salt and pepper to taste. Simmer 30 minutes.

Toast thick slices of French bread brushed with butter in 350- degree
oven. Rub with garlic clove. Put piece of toast in soup dish and top with
grated Swiss and Parmesan chesses. Ladle hot soup over this and serve.

Mrs. Thomas L. McCarter (Karen)

French Onion Soup II

May prepare ahead   Serves 4

3 onions, chopped
¼ cup butter or margarine
2-10½ ounce cans consomme
  soup (or beef bouillon)
1 tablespoon sugar

3 dashes nutmeg
Salt to taste
French bread, sliced,
  buttered and toasted
Mozzarella cheese slices

Sauté onion in butter. Prepare soup according to directions. Add sugar, nutmeg, and salt. Add onion. Bring to a boil. Let simmer 20 minutes. Pour into soup crocks or oven-proof bowls. Top each with a slice of French bread and a slice of cheese. Heat in a 350-degree oven for 5 to 10 minutes, or until cheese melts.

Mrs. Dan Page (Ibby)

Sausage / Duck Stew

Serve immediately   Serves 6

3 large onions, sliced
3 large green peppers, cut into
  narrow strips
½ stick margarine
2 to 3 packages Polish or
  smoked sausage (packages
  usually contain two large
  pieces per 1-pound package)
12 duck breasts, cut into
  strips (can use goose breasts
  or a combination)

1-16 ounce can stewed
  tomatoes
2 small cans mushrooms
2 cans Mexican style corn
1 cup water
6 potatoes, diced
4 packages Lipton Cup-a-
  Soup "Spring Vegetable";
  or use 3 to 4 packages
  Lipton dried tomato/onion
  soup
Pepper to taste

Sauté onions and green peppers in margarine using a heavy Dutch oven. "Chunk" cut the sausage and add to above onions and peppers. Add duck and/or goose strips. Sauté until meat begins to cook and browns, stirring occasionally.

Add stewed tomatoes, mushrooms (including liquid), corn (including liquid), water, potatoes, and soup mix. Simmer 1½ hours, stirring occasionally. Serve with crusty bread and a beverage.

Lin Lineberger

Henderson House Cold Peach Soup

This special recipe is from the Henderson House in New Bern, North Carolina. On our way to Camp Seafarer and Sea Gull each summer, we visit the Henderson House for its Cold Peach Soup.

May prepare ahead   Serves 4

3 cups peaches, sliced   ¼ to ½ teaspoon almond
1 cup sour cream   extract

Peel peaches and slice. Place peaches with sour cream and extract into blender. Blend until pureed. Serve chilled.

Mrs. Carl Ellis Fisher

Hint: If soup tastes too salty, add a raw piece of potato in the pot and it will absorb the salty taste.

Potato Soup

Serve immediately   Yields: 10 cups

2 stalks celery, sliced   ¾ teaspoon seasoned salt
1 medium onion, chopped   ¼ teaspoon ground thyme
2 tablespoons margarine, melted   ½ teaspoon rosemary,
6 medium potatoes, cubed   crushed
2 carrots, sliced   Dash of garlic powder
3 cups water   Dash of pepper
5 chicken-flavored bouillon   2 cups milk
   cubes   1 cup Longhorn Cheddar
                                         cheese, shredded

Sauté celery and onion in margarine in a large Dutch oven until tender. Add next 9 ingredients; cover and simmer about 20 minutes or until vegetables are tender.

Remove from heat, and mash vegetables with a potato masher. Add milk and cheese; cook, stirring constantly, until cheese is melted. Great with green salad and French bread.

Mrs. Ann R. Cline

Seafood and Sausage Gumbo

Even though this recipe is involved, it is worth every second.
When I lived in New Orleans, I collected several versions of this
and this is a combination of them all.

May prepare up to 2 days ahead   Serves 20

1 cup vegetable oil
1 cup flour
3 large onions, chopped
8 celery stalks, chopped
1 large bell pepper, chopped
½ cup fresh parsley, minced
6 garlic cloves, minced
2 tablespoons shortening
1 pound okra, cut crosswise
2 teaspoons red wine vinegar
4 pounds uncooked shrimp, unshelled
4 quarts chicken stock
1 pound spicy sausage, cut into ½-inch round and sauteed quickly on both sides

½ cup Worcestershire sauce
½ cup catsup
1 large tomato, chopped
1 teaspoon cayenne pepper
1 teaspoon thyme
¼ teaspoon rosemary
2 bay leaves
1 pound lump crabmeat
1 quart shucked oysters, drained
2 cups cooked chicken, chopped
¾ cup light brown sugar
2 tablespoons lemon juice
Salt and pepper to taste

Heat oil in heavy large pot over very low heat. Gradually add flour and stir with wooden spoon until roux is nicely browned, about 30 minutes. Increase heat to medium. Add onions, celery, bell pepper, parsley, and garlic to roux and cook until vegetables are soft, stirring often, about 45 minutes.

Melt shortening in heavy large skillet over medium-low heat. Add okra and vinegar and cook until okra is no longer stringy, stirring occasionally, 25 to 30 minutes. Add to onion mixture.

Meanwhile, poach shrimp in boiling water to cover until pink. Drain, reserving liquid. Shell shrimp.

Add reserved shrimp liquid, stock, sausage, Worcestershire sauce, catsup, tomato, cayenne, thyme, rosemary, and bay leaves to okra mixture and simmer until very thick, stirring occasionally, about 3 hours. (Can be prepared 2 days ahead. Cool completely, cover and refrigerate. Bring to a simmer before continuing with recipe.)

Add shrimp, crabmeat, oysters and chicken to gumbo and cook until edges of oysters begin to curl, about 5 minutes. Stir in brown sugar and lemon juice. Add salt and pepper to taste. Remove gumbo from heat.

Serve with lots of freshly cooked brown or white rice. To serve, spoon rice into large soup bowls. Ladle gumbo over the rice.

This makes a great complete meal or you can serve wtih a green salad or slaw and a hot French bread or cornbread.

Sharron Davis

Thermos Jug Soup

This recipe is perfect for a picnic but is so good that you will want to serve it at home, too.

May prepare ahead   Yields: 10 cups

2-10¾ ounce cans condensed tomato soup
1-10½ ounce can condensed onion soup
1-10¾ ounce can condensed chicken broth

4 cups water
½ cup dry sherry or additional water
1 tablespoon Worcestershire sauce
1 teaspoon dried basil
Dash of hot pepper

Place tomato soup and onion soup in blender container. Cover and blend until onions are finely chopped. In a large saucepan combine soup mixture, chicken broth, water, sherry or additional water, Worcestershire sauce, basil, and hot pepper. Heat over medium heat until boiling, stirring occasionally. Reduce heat. Simmer 15 minutes. Pour into three 1-quart thermos bottles or one 1-gallon thermos.

Mrs. Greg Bobo (Lou)

Quick Fix Soup

May prepare ahead   Serves 25-30

3 cans cream of potato soup   1 can tomatoes
2 cans Swanson's clear   2 cans Snow Crab soup
  chicken broth   2-8 ounce cartons sour cream
1 can cream of celery soup   1 pint milk
1 can cream of mushroom soup   Pepper to taste

Mix all ingredients together thoroughly, heat, and stir. Serve hot with
your favorite crackers or cornbread.

Cookbook Committee

Gazpacho

Must prepare ahead   Serves 4

1-10 to 12 ounce can tomatoes,   1 small onion, finely
  strain and save juice   chopped
1 green pepper, finely minced   2 to 3 cups tomato juice
2 tablespoons olive oil   1 to 2 teaspoons Lea &
Salt and pepper to taste   Perrin steak sauce
Sugar to taste

Combine all ingredients and chill. Serve cold.

Ann Cain

Salmon Soup

Serve immediately   Serves 4

1½ sticks butter   1½ pints whole milk
1 small onion, finely chopped   Salt and pepper to taste
1 small can pink salmon   Dash of Tabasco sauce

Sauté onion in ½ stick of butter until onions are soft and translucent.
Place salmon in heavy sauce pan. Bring to a boil in remaining butter.
Pour in milk and onion mixture and simmer while stirring to near boiling. Add salt, pepper, and Tabasco sauce. Heat all ingredients and serve
hot with crackers or croutons.

Cookbook Committee

Delicious Vegetable Soup

May prepare ahead   Serves 6-8
Freezes well

1 pound ground chuck
3 tablespoons rice, uncooked
3 tablespoons elbow
  macaroni, uncooked
3 potatoes, diced
3 carrots, chopped
1 large onion, chopped

½ pound beef stew, cooked
1 can succotash
3 large cans tomato sauce
½ teaspoon thyme
1 tablespoon Worcestershire
  sauce
Salt and pepper to taste

Cook ground chuck for 60 minutes in 3 quarts of water. Add rest of ingredients and simmer for 1 hour.

Beverly Poag

Hearty Vegetable Bean Soup

May prepare ahead   Serves 8

½ cup green pepper, chopped
¼ cup onion, chopped
1 small clove garlic, crushed
1 tablespoon vegetable oil
1-20 ounce package frozen corn
1-13¾ ounce can single
  strength beef broth
1-12 ounce can tomato juice
1 teaspoon cumin

2-15 ounce cans red kidney
  beans, drained
1-20 ounce can tomatoes,
  undrained and cut in
  pieces
1 tablespoon chili powder
1 tablespoon sugar or 3
  packages of Sweet'N Low
1 cup Cheddar cheese,
  shredded

In a 4-quart pan sauté green pepper, onion, and garlic in oil 5 to 7 minutes or until tender. Add remaining ingredients except the cheese. Bring to a boil over medium to high heat. Reduce heat and simmer for 10 minutes, stirring occasionally. Sprinkle each serving with 2 tablespoons of cheese.

Ginny Ratchford

Kay's Mock Vichyssoise

Wonderful for bridge lunch with fruit salad and hot salad.

May prepare ahead   Serves 4-5

1 can Campbell's potato soup	1 can Swanson's clear
1-8 ounce carton sour cream	chicken broth
2 tablespoons onion, grated	Chopped chives

Mix together in blender or food processor. Chill and serve with generous sprinklings of chopped chives.

Additional Use:
This recipe can be doubled and then the following is to be added to feed a larger crowd:

1 pound fresh crabmeat	Dash of lemon juice
1½ pounds fresh shrimp,	Dash of Tabasco sauce
cooked and peeled	

Serve hot as chowder and even more delicious left over COLD the next day.

Mrs. Walter Carroll, Jr. (Billie May)

Cold Zucchini Soup

Must prepare ahead   Serves 4
Freezes well

2 large zucchini, sliced (reserve 4 slices for garnish)	1 cup sour cream
1 green pepper, chopped	1 tablespoon fresh parsley, chopped
½ cup onion, chopped	½ teaspoon dill, chopped
3 cups chicken stock	Salt and pepper to taste

Place vegetables and stock in saucepan and simmer covered for 20 minutes. Place sour cream, parsley, and dill in blender. Add vegetables and liquify. Add stock a little at a time to blend. Salt and pepper soup to taste. Chill several hours.

Serving: Garnish by floating one reserved zucchini slice in each bowl of soup. It looks especially pretty served in clear glass goblets or bowls. Served with tortellini salad this makes a cool summer lunch or light supper.

Mrs. Barbara McCarthy

Greens and Fixin's
Salads and Dressings

Asparagus-Grapefruit Vinaigrette

May prepare ahead   Serves 8

3-10 ounce packages frozen
asparagus tips (cooked) or
2-15 ounce cans asparagus
tips
2-14 ounce cans grapefruit
slices
Italian dressing
½ cup vinegar

½ teaspoon sugar
½ teaspoon salt
Grated onion
⅛ teaspoon tarragon
½ cup olive oil
Pimento

Marinate asparagus in Italian dressing several hours or make sauce with the above ingredients of vinegar, sugar, salt, onion, tarragon, and olive oil.

Before serving drain asparagus. Place lettuce on salad plate. Add about 4 pieces grapefruit. Place asparagus slices on grapefruit (4 or 5 pieces). Place a few slices of pimento across asparagus for effect. Sprinkle a little marinade over all or serve separately.

Mrs. Paulette H. Elmore

Beet Salad Mold

Must prepare ahead   Serves 6

1-16 ounce can diced beets
1-3 ounce package lemon Jello
¼ cup sugar
¼ cup vinegar

1½ cups celery, finely
chopped
1 tablespoon horseradish

Drain beets and reserve liquid. Add enough water to liquid to make 1½ cups. Bring to a boil. Add Jello, sugar, and vinegar and stir until dissolved. Chill until consistency of unbeaten egg whites. Stir in beets, celery, horseradish. Put in oiled 4-cup mold. Chill.

Mrs. Carolyn Sumner

Beef Salad Vinaigrette

Must prepare ahead   Serves 6

Salad:
1 flank steak (about 2 pounds)
1 medium garlic clove, cut in
   half
2 tablespoons olive oil
Salt and freshly ground pepper
   to taste
1 head of oak leaf lettuce
1 small bunch of arugula
   (optional)
1½ teaspoons sweet gherkins,
   finely chopped

1 hard cooked egg, finely
   chopped
¼ cup parsley, finely
   chopped
1 small red onion, cut into
   thin rings
5 tomatoes, sliced
1 European seedless
   cucumber, thinly sliced

Vinaigrette:
1½ tablespoons red wine
   vinegar
1 tablespoon fresh lemon
   juice
¼ teaspoon powdered English
   mustard, such as Coleman's

⅓ cup olive oil
½ teaspoon salt
⅛ teaspoon freshly ground
   pepper

Rub both sides of steak with garlic clove and brush with olive oil. Broil in preheated broiler about 4 inches from heat for 4 to 5 minutes on each side for medium-rare. Season with salt and pepper and let rest for 5 minutes. Slice thin crosswise on the diagonal. Arrange beef in center of bed of lettuce and arugula and sprinkle with capers, gherkins, egg, and parsley. Scatter red onion rings on top and surround with tomatoes and cucumber. In a small bowl, whisk together vinaigrette ingredients until blended. Spoon over salad before serving.

Mrs. H. Garrett Rhyne

Favorite Marinated Salad

Must prepare ahead   Serves 12

2 heads cauliflower   2 bunches broccoli
1 medium red onion

Celery Seed Dressing:
½ cup sugar   1 teaspoon mustard
1 teaspoon salt   2 teaspoons celery seed
⅓ cup vinegar   5 teaspoons horseradish
½ cup olive oil   1 cup mayonnaise

Cut up vegetables, place in a 9 x 13-inch container with tight-fitting cover. Mix together all dressing ingredients, blending well. Pour over vegetables and let stand overnight. Shake container several times before serving.

Mrs. Joanna Woods Owen

Sweet and Sour Broccoli Salad

Must prepare ahead   Serves 4-6

2 bunches fresh broccoli,   1 cup mayonnaise
  chopped   ¼ cup sugar or 4 to 5
1 onion, chopped   envelopes Sweet N Low
⅔ cup Cheddar cheese, grated   2 tablespoons vinegar
4 to 5 pieces bacon, cooked   Salt and pepper to taste
  and crumbled

Mix together all ingredients and chill several hours before serving.

Mrs. William Cain (Monica)

Broccoli-Cauliflower Salad

Must prepare ahead   Serves 12-16

1 bunch broccoli, chopped	½ cup mayonnaise
1 head cauliflower, chopped	2 teaspoons vinegar
½ cup Green Goddess salad	1 teaspoon celery seed
dressing	6 slices bacon, fried crispy

Place broccoli and cauliflower in a large bowl. In a separate bowl combine remaining ingredients. Pour over broccoli-cauliflower mixture and refrigerate overnight. Mix in crumbled bacon before serving.

Mrs. Donald R. Thrower

Jane Hunter's Broccoli Salad

Must prepare ahead   Serves 4-6

1 bunch broccoli	¼ cup or less sugar
½ cup Kraft Miracle Whip	1 tablespoon red wine
salad dressing	vinegar
1 onion, chopped	3 to 6 slices bacon,
1 cup Kraft sharp Cheddar	cooked and crumbled
cheese, shredded	

Peel stems of broccoli and chop with florets. Combine salad dressing, onion, broccoli, cheese, sugar, and wine vinegar. Before serving, add crumbled bacon.

Nancy McLeod Reid

Cucumber-Onion Filled Tomatoes

Must prepare ahead   Serves 4

1 cup cucumbers, finely	Salt and pepper to taste
chopped	4 ripe tomatoes, peeled and
¾ cup onion, finely chopped	hollowed out
Italian dressing	

Finely chop cucumber and onion. Combine with enough Italian dressing to coat thoroughly. Add salt and pepper to taste. Stuff tomatoes with cucumber mixture. Top with mayonnaise.

Mrs. Anne Carriel

115

Capital Broccoli Salad

Must prepare ahead   Serves 4-6

2 bunches broccoli, chopped   ¼ cup of raisins
½ pound bacon, fried &   1 small onion, finely
  crumbled or imitation   chopped
  bacon bits

Dressing: Mix the following ingredients together and blend well.
¼ cup sugar   ¾ cup mayonnaise
2 teaspoons vinegar

Mix together all ingredients. Marinate overnight.

Tami Pearson

Cobb Salad

*This salad was created and was a specialty at the Brown Derby
restaurants in Hollywood.*

Prepare same day   Serves 4-6

½ head of lettuce   6 strips crisp bacon
½ bunch watercress   1 ripe avocado
1 small bunch chicory   3 hard-cooked eggs
½ head romaine lettuce   2 tablespoons chives,
2 medium-size tomatoes,   chopped
  peeled   2 boiled chicken breasts
½ cup Roquefort cheese,   1 cup vinaigrette or your
  finely grated   favorite dressing

Cut FINELY lettuce, watercress, chicory, and romaine; arrange in salad
bowl. Cut tomatoes in half, remove seeds, dice finely, and arrange in
strips across the lettuce. Dice breasts of chicken and arrange over top
of chopped greens. Chop bacon finely and sprinkle over the salad. Cut
avocado in small pieces and arrange around edge of salad. Decorate the
salad by sprinkling over the top the chopped eggs, chopped chives, and
grated cheese. Just before serving, mix the salad thoroughly with the
vinaigrette or your favorite dressing.

Mrs. Robert C. Clements ('Tuga' Wilson)

Caesar Salad

Dressing may be prepared ahead   Serves 8-10

2 heads Romaine lettuce   **1½ cups croutons**
½ cup red onion, thinly sliced

Dressing:
1 egg   **1 teaspoon Worcestershire**
¾ cup oil   **sauce**
¼ cup fresh lemon juice   **¼ cup grated Parmesan**
1 or 2 cloves garlic, pressed   **cheese**
1 or 2 teaspoons dry mustard   **½ teaspoon pepper**
                                     1 teaspoon salt

Put egg in boiling water for one minute ONLY. Crack into blender and whip on high speed until fluffy. Drizzle oil into blender while still on high. Reduce speed and add remaining dressing ingredients. Mix until well blended. Pour dressing over washed and torn lettuce. Toss with croutons and red onion just before serving on chilled plates.

Note: Dressing may be saved in refrigerator in an airtight container for several weeks.

Mrs. John D. Bridgeman (Nan)

Cauliflower Salad

Must prepare ahead   Serves 8

1 small head cauliflower, cut   **1¼ cups radishes, sliced**
into bite-size pieces   **1¼ cups spring onions,**
½ cup celery, chopped   **sliced**

In a small bowl mix the following:
1 cup mayonnaise   **1 cup sour cream**
1 package "Good Seasons"   **1 teaspoon caraway seed**
cheese garlic dressing mix

Pour the above mixture over the vegetables and fold together. Cover and refrigerate overnight.

Mrs. Andrew H. Rutledge, Jr.

Curried Orange Chicken Salad

Prepare same day   Serves 6

3 tablespoons plain yogurt
2 tablespoons mayonnaise
1 small orange, peeled and
  chopped
1 small apple, peeled and
  chopped
2 tablespoons slivered
  almonds

¼ teaspoon curry powder
1 cup cooked chicken, cubed
10 grapes
¼ teaspoon nutmeg
¼ teaspoon dry mustard

Mix all ingredients together and chill before serving.

Mrs. H. Garrett Rhyne

Chicken Salad With Almonds

Must prepare ahead   Serves 4-5

4 cups cooked chicken, finely
  diced
2 cups celery, thinly sliced
1 to 2 tablespoons onion,
  minced
1 tablespoon lemon juice

¾ cup mayonnaise
¼ cup whipping cream
Salt and pepper to taste
¼ to ½ cup almonds, toasted

Toss chicken and celery together. Mix onion, lemon juice, mayonnaise, and cream. Add to chicken mixture and toss until coated. Season with salt and pepper and stir in almonds. Chill and serve on a bed of lettuce.

Mrs. Anne Carriel

Chicken and Fruit Salad

Must prepare ahead   Serves 6

2 cups cooked chicken, diced
1 cup unpeeled red apples,
  cubed
1 cup seedless red grapes
½ cup celery, diced
½ cup pecans, chopped

½ cup sour cream
3 tablespoons mayonnaise
3 tablespoons honey
1 tablespoon lemon juice
⅛ teaspoon salt

Combine chicken, apples, grapes, celery, and pecans; toss gently with a few drops of lemon juice to keep fruit looking fresh. Combine the remaining ingredients and stir until smooth. Pour over chicken mixture and toss gently. Cover and chill for 1 to 2 hours before serving.

Fran Sitton

Chutney Chicken Salad

May prepare ahead   Serves 6

1 cup raisins
¾ cup mayonnaise
1 cup mango chutney
½ cup flaked coconut
2-3 pounds cooked chicken,
  cubed

Salt and pepper to taste
Lemon juice
1 cup salted peanuts
2 bananas, sliced
Lettuce cups

Plump raisins in warm water for 15 minutes. Drain and combine with rest of ingredients and toss lightly. Serve immediately on lettuce. If prepared ahead, store in refrigerator, but leave out peanuts and bananas until the last minute. If you want the salad less sweet, leave out the coconut.

Mrs. Nan Murphy

Cucumber Mousse

Must prepare ahead   Serves 8

1 package lime Jello
1 cup hot water
1 cup onion, finely grated
1 large cucumber, peeled and
  seeded
⅔ cup celery, finely chopped

1 carton cottage cheese
1 teaspoon salt
1 teaspoon Accent
2 teaspoons vinegar
½ cup slivered almonds

Dissolve Jello in hot water; let cool. Chop cucumber and onion in blender. Stir all ingredients into Jello mixture; congeal and serve.

Mrs. Joseph S. Stowe (Janice)

Cucumber Salad

Must prepare ahead   Serves 4-6

3 cucumbers, thinly sliced
2 teaspoons salt
½ cup red wine vinegar

2 tablespoons oil
1 tablespoon dill
½ teaspoon pepper

Place cucumbers in bowl and sprinkle with salt. Refrigerate until chilled. Stir, add ½ cup red wine vinegar and 2 tablespoons oil; mix together. Sprinkle with dill. (Pepper is optional.)

Karen Staker

Cucumber Aspic

Must prepare ahead   Serves 4

1 envelope gelatin
1 cup chicken broth
1 large cucumber, chopped
1 medium onion, chopped
1 teaspoon sugar

3 teaspoons vinegar
1 pinch of salt
Worcestershire sauce, to
  taste
Cayenne pepper, to taste
Black pepper, to taste

Soften gelatin in chicken broth and heat to dissolve. Mix in other ingredients. Pour into a 4-cup mold and chill.

Lin Lineberger

Sugar-Free Blueberry Salad

Must prepare ahead   Serves 8

1-3 ounce package strawberry
   sugar-free Jello
1-3 ounce package raspberry
   sugar-free Jello
2 cups boiling water
1-8 ounce can crushed
   pineapple in own juice

1-12 ounce bag frozen
   blueberries
1-8 ounce package cream
   cheese
1-8 ounce package sour cream
Equal to taste

Dissolve Jello in 2 cups boiling water. Add can of crushed pineapple and package of blueberries. Stir and then chill until set. (Add ice cubes for fast set.) Blend softened cream cheese and sour cream; then add Equal to taste. (Vanilla may also be added, if desired.) Spread mixture over Jello as an icing. Serve on a bed of lettuce, in place of fruit.

Mrs. Eleanor McArver Claiborne

Raw Cranberry Salad

Must prepare ahead   Serves 20

4-3 ounce packages cherry or
   blackberry Jello
2 cups boiling water
½ cup cold water
2 cups fresh cranberries,
   ground (one package)
1 cup pecans, chopped

2 oranges, unpeeled, seeded,
   and chopped
2 apples, unpeeled, cored,
   and chopped
2 cups sugar
1 large can crushed
   pineapple, with juice

Dissolve gelatin in boiling waster. Add cold water and chill until consistency of egg white. Combine cranberries, pecans, oranges, apples, and sugar in food processor. Pulse several times. Fold in gelatin mixture and pineapple. Pour into a 10-cup ring mold (or 2 smaller ones) and chill until set. Unmold onto lettuce leaves.

Patti Hunter

Sour Cherry Salad

Must prepare ahead   Serves 6-8

1-No.2 can sour pie cherries
  (2½ cups)
1 package gelatin softened in
  ¼ cup cold water
1 package lemon Jello

Juice and zest of 1 orange
Juice and zest of 1 lemon
1-No.2 can crushed pineapple
½ cup nuts, if desired

Heat cherry juice to boiling; add gelatin and Jello and stir to dissolve. Remove from heat. Add zest and remaining ingredients and cool. Pour into oiled mold; refrigerate until congealed.

Mary Margaret S. Hunter

Mom's Frozen Fruit Salad

Must prepare ahead   Serves 6-8

1 small can crushed
  pineapple, drained
3 tablespoons cherries,
  chopped
2 cups sour cream
2 tablespoons lemon juice

1 banana, sliced
⅓ cup nuts, chopped
¾ cup sugar
⅛ teaspoon salt

Mix ingredients together. Pour into a 6-cup mold and freeze.

Beverly Poag

Melon Salad

Must prepare ahead   Serves 6

1 honeydew melon
1½ cups green grapes,
  halved
1 cup condensed milk

½ cup butter or margarine
Pinch of salt
½ cup vinegar
1 teaspoon prepared mustard

Dice 1 peeled honeydew melon, add grapes. Let fruits drain in a colander. Prepare dressing by combining rest of ingredients. This sets up very thick when it stands, but the fruits help dilute it. Toss fruit and dressing together. Serve on a lettuce leaf.

Mrs. J. Caswell Taylor, Jr.

Low-Calorie Fruit Salad

May be served as a dessert or for breakfast.

Must prepare ahead   Serves 6-8

4 large apples (or 6 to 7
  medium), shredded (core
  and peel first, use food
  processor to shred, but can
  be done by hand)
½ teaspoon coconut flavoring
1 can Diet 7-Up
1 small can orange juice
  concentrate

2 bananas, sliced
1-16 ounce can pineapple
  chunks in own juice,
  undrained
1 envelope unflavored
  gelatin

Combine all ingredients except gelatin. Sprinkle gelatin on top and mix.
Chill at least 4 hours.

Marsha Jones

Hot Fruit Salad

Great for lunch.

Must prepare ahead   Serves 6

1-16 ounce can peach halves
1-16 ounce can pear halves
1-16 ounce can sliced pineapple
1-16 ounce can apricot halves

1 jar red cherries
1 stick margarine, melted
1 cup dry sherry
½ cup sugar
2 tablespoons flour

Drain fruit well and arrange in a 13 x 9-inch casserole dish. Mix together
in a saucepan: margarine, sherry, sugar, and flour. Bring to a boil and
boil until thick. Pour over fruit and refrigerate overnight. To serve, heat
in a 350-degree oven until hot throughout. Serve hot.

Mrs. Joye S. Rankin

Chunky Gazpacho Salad

Must prepare ahead   Serves 6-8

8 fresh tomatoes   ½ cup white vinegar
4 large cucumbers   ½ cup oil
1 large onion   ¼ cup red wine
½ tablespoon Nature's Season   1 teaspoon salt

Chop vegetables together into a large bowl. Mix seasonings, oil, vinegar, and wine together. Pour over vegetables, mix well and chill. Serve as a salad or side dish. This goes well with light summer menus, fried chicken, BBQ ribs, or steak.

Note: If you have some left over, drain the juice, add 1 teaspoon oregano, and cooked pasta shells for a great pasta salad.

Leslie Dale

Frosted Green Bean Salad

Must prepare ahead   Serves 8

Salad:
2-16 ounce cans cut green beans   ¾ cup oil
6 tablespoons vinegar   1 small onion, sliced
Salt and pepper to taste

Dressing:
8 slices cooked bacon,   4 hard-boiled eggs, diced
  crumbled   2 teaspoons mustard
6 tablespoons mayonnaise   Salt to taste
4 teaspoons vinegar

Six to eight hours before serving, combine salad ingredients, toss, and chill in a 1-quart serving dish. Just before serving, combine dressing ingredients and spoon in cross shape over beans.

Mrs. James Love, III

Green Bean Salad or Scandinavian Salad

Must prepare ahead   Serves 4-6

1-16 ounce can French
  green beans
1-16 ounce can LeSeur
  green peas
1 medium onion, halved and
  sliced

1 cup celery, chopped
1 small jar pimento
1 cup sugar
1 cup oil
½ cup red wine vinegar

Drain green beans and green peas. Mix with onion, celery, and pimento. Mix sugar, oil, and vinegar and pour over vegetables. Refrigerate several hours before serving.

Mrs. Donna Lockett

Cream Cheese Salad

Must prepare ahead   Serves 16

1-4 ounce box lemon Jello
1-4 ounce box lime Jello
1 cup boiling water
1 cup carrots, finely grated
1-8 ounce package cream
  cheese

1-13 to 15 ounce can crushed
  pineapple, with juice
¾ cup mayonnaise
1 cup pecans, chopped

Mix gelatins together and dissolve in boiling water. Add carrots, cream cheese, pineapple with juice, mayonnaise, and pecans - in that order. Mix thoroughly and pour into any 2-quart container, bowl, or Pyrex dish. Refrigerate until congealed. You may serve from container or on a bed of lettuce.

Mrs. John M. Templeton (Beth)

Carol's Pasta Salad

May prepare ahead   Serves 4-6

1 pound Kielbasa smoked
  sausage, peeled
1 tablespoon oil
1-8 ounce can red kidney beans
1 small to medium onion,
  chopped
1 green pepper, diced
8 to 9 ounces rotini pasta
6 tablespoons mayonnaise
3½ tablespoons Dijon mustard

2½ tablespoons cider
  vinegar
½ teaspoon salt
Ground black pepper to taste
1-15 ounce can 3-bean salad,
  Hanover brand
1 tomato, chopped, optional
1 cucumber, chopped and
  peeled, optional

Peel and slice Kielbasa sausage to about ¼-inch thick. Saute in oil, and drain. Drain and rinse red kidney beans. Add green pepper and onion to kidney beans and toss lightly. Cook pasta according to directions on box; drain. Blend mayonnaise and mustard together. Sprinkle cider vinegar, salt, and pepper over cooked pasta; toss lightly. Add red kidney beans, onions, green pepper, Kielbasa sausage, mayonnaise, and mustard mixture, and 3-bean salad; toss lightly. Refrigerate for several hours and serve.

I do not use the tomato and cucumber, but if you do, do not add until just before serving.

Mrs. William B. Shuford, Jr.

Orzo Salad

May prepare ahead   Serves 8-10

1 cup orzo (rice shaped
  macaroni)
1 cup feta cheese, diced
⅓ cup salad oil
3 tablespoons parsley, chopped
3 tablespoons dill, chopped or
  1 tablespoon dried dill

1 large tomato, seeded and
  chopped
¼ cup lemon juice
½ teaspoon salt
¼ teaspoon pepper

Cook orzo according to package directions. Drain and rinse with cold water. Add feta cheese, parsley, dill, and tomato. In a covered jar, combine oil, lemon juice, salt, and pepper; shake well. Pour this mixture over salad and toss. Refrigerate until chilled, and before serving, toss again.

Pat McCloskey

Georgia Peach Salad

Must prepare ahead   Serves 10-12

2 cups orange juice
1-6 ounce package orange Jello
¼ cup plus 2 tablespoons sugar
1 teaspoon lemon zest
2 cups buttermilk

1 cup fresh peaches, finely
** chopped**
1 cup fresh blueberries
Lettuce

Bring 2 cups orange juice to a boil in a medium saucepan. Add Jello, sugar, and lemon zest; stir until Jello is dissolved. Chill until mixture is the consistency of unbeaten egg whites. Gradually add buttermilk and mix well. Fold in peaches and blueberries. Pour mixture into a 6-cup mold and refrigerate until set. Unmold on a lettuce-lined serving plate.

Topping:
¼ cup orange juice   **1 cup sour cream**

Combine sour cream and orange juice and mix well; serve over salad. Garnish with peach slices and blueberries.

Mrs. J. Caswell Taylor, Jr.

Potato Salad I

Must prepare ahead   Serves 6-8

4 cups cooked potatoes,
** diced (red preferred)**
1 cup celery, diced
½ cup or less spring onions,
** sliced**
¼ cup radishes, sliced
2 tablespoons fresh parsley
** or 1 tablespoons dried**
** parsley**

1 cup mayonnaise
2 teaspoons mustard
** (French's)**
⅛ teaspoon pepper
½ teaspoon celery seed
1½ teaspoons salt

Combine potatoes, celery, onion, radishes, and parsley. Mix with other ingredients, which have already been combined. Refrigerate for several hours before serving.

Lin Lineberger

Potato Salad II

May prepare ahead   Serves 6-8

4 hard-boiled eggs, chopped   ½ cup onion, chopped
4 cooked potatoes,   ¼ cup green pepper,
   peeled and diced   chopped

Dressing:
1 cup mayonnaise or   1 tablespoon vinegar
   salad dressing   ¼ teaspoon celery seed
½ teaspoon dry mustard   2 teaspoons salt
⅓ cup pickle relish   Dash pepper

Mix top 4 ingredients together and set aside. Mix the dressing ingredients. Toss together and let stand to blend. Chill before serving.

Hope Parks

Pretzel Salad

Must prepare ahead   Serves 8

2 cups crushed pretzels   1-8 ounce carton frozen
¾ cup margarine, melted   whipped topping, thawed
3 tablespoons sugar   1-6 ounce package strawberry
1-8 ounce package cream   gelatin
   cheese, softened   2 cups boiling water
1 cup sugar   2-10 ounce packages frozen
                                        strawberries

Mix crushed pretzels, margarine, and 3 tablespoons sugar together and press into a 9 x 13-inch pan. Bake at 400 degrees for 8 minutes. Cool thoroughly.

Mix softened cream cheese and 1 cup sugar. Fold the 2 cups thawed whipped topping into cream cheese mixture and spread over cooled pretzel crust. Dissolve strawberry gelatin in boiling water and add frozen strawberries. Chill until syrupy, then pour over the cream cheese layer and refrigerate. Cut into squares and garnish with whipped topping and a whole strawberry.

Mrs. Susan J. Jumper

German Potato Salad

May prepare ahead   Serves 8-10

4 cups sliced, boiled potatoes
4 slices bacon, cut into small
    slices
1 onion, diced
1 tablespoon flour

1 tablespoon sugar
1 teaspoon salt
1 teaspoon paprika
½ cup vinegar
½ cup water

Brown bacon and drain. Crumble bacon and sprinkle over the potatoes. Add onion to the hot bacon fat and cook only a few minutes to avoid burning. Add the flour to the bacon fat and onions; blend. Add sugar, salt, paprika, vinegar, and water. Cook until clear, stirring constantly. Pour the mixture over the potatoes and bacon. Mix well. Serve hot or cold.

Allison Decker Sonier

Cold Rice Salad

Must prepare ahead   Serves 8-10

1¾ cups uncooked rice
3 chicken bouillon cubes
¼ cup oil
2 tablespoons vinegar
1½ teaspoons salt
⅛ teaspoon pepper
2 hard-boiled eggs, chopped

1½ cups celery, diced
¼ cup dill pickle, chopped
¼ cup pimento, chopped
½ cup onion, chopped
½ cup mayonnaise
1 tablespoon mustard

Cook rice according to package directions adding bouillon cubes. Drain well in colandar. While still in colandar, pour mixture of salad oil, vinegar, salt, and pepper over rice. Let it drain. Then toss rice with egg, celery, pickle, pimento, and onion. Stir dressing of mayonnaise and mustard into salad. Chill until time to serve.

Mrs. Marilyn Johnson

Cold Rice and Artichoke Salad

Looks great in a big glass bowl with sprigs of parsley on top.

Must prepare ahead   Serves 12-16

4 cups chicken stock
2 cups uncooked long-grain
  white rice
3-6 ounce jars marinated
  artichoke hearts, drained
5 green onions, chopped
1-4 ounce jar pimento-stuffed
  olives

1 large green pepper, diced
3 large clery stalks, diced
¼ cup fresh parsley,
  chopped
Reserved artichoke marinade
1 teaspoon curry powder
2 cups mayonnaise
Salt and pepper to taste

Bring stock to boil and stir in rice. Return to boil. Lower heat, cover and simmer for 20 minutes or until liquid is absorbed; cool. Chop artichokes; add to rice with onions, olives, green pepper, celery, and parsley. Combine reserved marinade with curry, mayonnaise, salt, and pepper. Toss with rice and mix thoroughly; refrigerate.

Mrs. Kim Darnell

Hint: Put a tablespoon of butter in the water when cooking rice, dried beans, macaroni, to keep it from boiling over. Always run cold water over it when done to get the starch out. To reheat, put in colander over boiling water.

Maggie's Rice Salad

Must prepare ahead   Serves 8-10

1 package chicken
  Rice-A-Roni
1 teaspoon curry
Reserved artichoke marinade
1 cup mayonnaise

3 green onions, chopped
½ green pepper, chopped
1-8 ounce jar marinated
  artichokes, drained

Cook Rice-A-Roni as directed on package; adding curry. Mix artichoke juice with mayonnaise, onions, and peppers. In a mixing bowl, stir together Rice-A-Roni, mayonnaise mixture, and artichokes. Let chill and serve cold.

Mrs. Pam Warlick

California-Shrimp and Avocado Salad

May prepare ahead   Serves 4

3 tablespoons olive oil
2 tablespoons white wine
  vinegar
1 teaspoon Dijon mustard
1 pound fresh shrimp, cooked,
  shelled, deveined, and cubed
1 cup Hellman's mayonnaise
2 tablespoons chili sauce
1 large garlic clove, crushed

1 dash hot pepper sauce
1 dash salt
1 dash freshly ground pepper
1 large ripe avocado
Juice of ½ lemon
2 tablespoons fresh dill,
  minced
2 tablespoons chives, minced

Whisk together oil, vinegar, and mustard until well blended. Add this to shrimp; toss thoroughly. Cover and let marinate for 2 hours in refrigerator.

Whisk mayonnaise, chili sauce, garlic, hot pepper sauce, salt, and pepper until smooth; set aside.

Peel, seed, and cube avocado; sprinkle with lemon juice and set aside.

Drain cooked shrimp; add cubed avocado, dill, and chives; toss lightly. Fold in enough mayonnaise mixture to coat lightly. Taste and adjust seasoning, if needed. Cover and chill.

Serve on chilled plates and garnish with fresh herbs (dill or chives) and avocado.

Ms. Debbie Rhyne

Spinach-Beet Salad

Prepare same day   Serves 6-8

1-8¼ ounce can sliced beets,
  drained
¼ cup Italian dressing
1 stalk celery, chopped

2 green onions, chopped
3 spinach leaves, shredded
Fresh spinach leaves, whole
1 egg yolk, hard-boiled

Combine beets and dressing; marinate at least 2 hours, then drain. Add celery, onions, and shredded spinach leaves; toss gently. Arrange beet mixture on spinach leaves; sprinkle with sieved egg yolk.

Mrs. Holt Anthony Harris

131

Shrimp Hawaiian

May prepare ahead   Serves 8-10

1 pound cooked shrimp or
   2 pounds green shrimp
2 heads lettuce, chopped

2 slices bread, toasted on
   both sides and rubbed
   with garlic - then cubed
¾ of an 8-ounce can
   Parmesan cheese

Dressing:
¾ cup Wesson oil
Juice of ½ lemon

1 egg, beaten
Salt to taste

Mix dressing ingredients. Put shrimp, lettuce, and bread cubes in a bowl.
Pour dressing on top of salad and toss. Top with Parmesan cheese.

Mrs. Plato Pearson, Jr.

Barbeque Slaw

May prepare ahead   Serves 10-12

1 head cabbage, grated
1 tablespoon mayonnaise
1 tablespoon mustard
1 tablespoon Worcestershire
   sauce
1 tablespoon A-1 steak sauce
1 tablespoon sugar

1 tablespoon vinegar
½ bottle catsup
2 shakes Texas Pete
1 teaspoon chili powder
Salt and pepper to taste

Mix above ingredients and serve with barbeque.

Marjorie Kircus

Gingered Fruit Slaw

May prepare ahead   Serves 20

2-8 ounce cans pineapple
tidbits drained, reserve
⅓ cup juice
1-16 ounce package mixed
dried fruit bits (1½ cups)

2 large carrots, shredded
(1½ cups)
1 small head cabbage,
shredded (5 cups)
½ cup walnuts, chopped

Salad dressing:
Reserved pineapple juice
2 tablespoons honey
¼ to ½ teaspoon ground
ginger

2 tablespoons salad oil
1 tablespoon lemon juice

In a 3-quart container, layer pineapple, fruit bits, carrots, cabbage, and walnuts.

For dressing: In a screw top container, combine reserved pineapple juice, oil, honey, lemon juice, and ginger. Cover and shake well. Pour over cabbage mixture; cover and chill overnight. Toss first before serving.

Ann Roberts

Marinated Coleslaw

Must prepare ahead   Serves 8-10

1 head of cabbage
1 onion
1 green pepper
1 cup sugar
1 cup vinegar

1 tablespoon salt
1 teaspoon celery seed
1 teaspoon dry mustard
¾ cup vegetable oil

Shred cabbage and put into a 13 x 9-inch casserole. Add layer of sliced onion, separated into rings. Add layer of sliced pepper in rings. Pour sugar over this. DO NOT MIX. Combine vinegar, salt, celery seeds, mustard, and oil; bring to boil. Pour over cabbage while hot. DO NOT MIX. Put in refrigerator until cool or overnight. It is best when it has had time to marinate. Preparation time is 20 minutes.

Mrs. Phillip L. Hicks (Lou Anne)
Patti Hunter

Tortellini Salad

Must prepare ahead   Serves 4-6

1-8 ounce bag ravioletti
   tortellini (filled with
   Parmesan cheese)
¾ cup celery, sliced
¾ cup green onions, sliced
   diagonally
1 red or green pepper, diced
¾ cup canned artichoke
   hearts, chopped

Dressing:
½ cup mayonnaise
½ cup plain yogurt
2 tablespoons lemon juice
Salt and pepper to taste

Cook tortellini in salted, boiling water until tender. While pasta is cooking, whisk together the mayonnaise, yogurt, lemon juice, salt, and pepper; set aside. Drain tortellini; put into a large bowl with the vegetables. Add the salad dressing and toss to mix well. Chill for several hours.

Serve on a bed of lettuce leaves and garnish with cherry tomatoes and cucumber sticks, if desired.

Mrs. Barbara McCarthy

Vermicelli Salad

Great for cookouts.

Must prepare ahead   Serves 12

1-16 ounce package vermicelli
1 small can ripe, pitted olives
1 small jar sliced green olives
5 tablespoons olive oil
   (no substitutes)
2½ tablespoons vinegar

3 tablespoons crushed, dried
   oregano
Salt and pepper to taste
2 tablespoons Parmesan
   cheese

Cook pasta according to package directions. Blanch with cold water. Slice ripe olives. Drain green olives. Add to pasta and toss. Combine olive oil and vinegar; drizzle over pasta and toss again. Add oregano, salt, pepper, and Parmesan cheese; toss again. Refrigerate. This will keep for at least 3 days and can be made well ahead.

Pat McCloskey

Tabouli

*This is good to take on picnics or for backyard barbeques
as an accompaniment for grilled chicken.*

Must prepare ahead   Serves 6-8

1 cup bulgar wheat
1 cup boiling water
2 large carrots, diced
1 cup parsley, chopped
1 medium green pepper, diced

1 medium cucumber, diced
2 medium tomatoes, diced
1 cup green onions, sliced
½ cup mint leaves,
  chopped

Dressing:
½ cup lemon juice
1 teaspoon salt

½ cup olive oil
¼ teaspoon pepper

Place bulgar wheat in a large mixing bowl and pour boiling water over it. Let stand for 10 minutes, then stir gently. Combine lemon juice, salt, olive oil, and pepper in a screw-top jar; shake well to mix. Pour dressing over wheat. Add remaining ingredients and toss gently to mix. Cover and refrigerate for 3 hours.

Mrs. Barbara McCarthy

Herbed Tomatoes

May prepare ahead   Serves 6

6 tomatoes, sliced or cut into
  wedges
¼ cup spring onion, chopped
¼ teaspoon pepper
1 clove garlic, minced

⅔ cup salad oil
¼ cup vinegar
1 teaspoon salt
½ teaspoon thyme

Put tomatoes in a bowl. Shake together remaining ingredients in a jar; pour over tomatoes and let marinate for at least 1 hour.

Jane Petty

Tomato Aspic

This is a favorite family recipe of my mother-in-law's, Mrs. Mildred Horne. It is great in the summer and is also LOW CAL!

Must prepare ahead   Serves 12

1-46 ounce can V-8 juice
4 envelopes (1 box) Knox
  unflavored gelatin
1 tablespoon horseradish
2 or 3 dashes black pepper

1 cup celery, chopped
1 cup onion, chopped
½ cup olives, sliced
1 tablespoon lemon juice
1½ cups small shrimp or
  crabmeat, optional

Soften gelatin in 2 cups V-8 juice and heat until gelatin is dissolved. Mix rest of ingredients including remaining V-8 juice together and add to gelatin/V-8 mixture. Mix well and pour into a 9 x 13-inch Pyrex dish or mold and refrigerate until set. Serve on lettuce and top with a dot of mayonnaise. *Variation:* Add shrimp or crabmeat to mixture before it is set.

Loretta Horne

Tomato Aspic With Capers

Must prepare ahead   Serves 12-15

2½ envelopes unflavored gelatin
2 cups V-8 juice
1 bay leaf
Celery tops
1½ cups tomato juice
½ cup tarragon vinegar
1 teaspoon lemon juice

Salt, red pepper, and
  Tabasco sauce to taste
1-3 ounce bottle capers
Juice of 1 onion
1 cup celery, diced
½ cup olives, chopped

Soak gelatin in ½ cup V-8 juice. Heat 1½ cups V-8 juice with 1 bay leaf and celery tops. Strain and add gelatin. When gelatin is dissolved, add cold tomato juice, vinegar, lemon juice, salt, pepper, and Tabasco sauce. When cooled, add capers, onion juice, celery, and olives. Pour into ring-mold and chill thoroughly. Garnish with avocado and slices of egg.

Mrs. Ginny Ratchford

Tart Tomato Aspic Salad

Must prepare ahead   Serves 8

1 package lemon Jello
1 pint stewed tomatoes,
   strained
1½ teaspoons lemon juice
¼ teaspoon salt

1 teaspoon Worcestershire
   sauce
½ cup sweet pickle
½ cup celery, diced

Dissolve Jello in boiling tomato juice and add salt, lemon juice and
Worcestershire sauce. CHILL. When slightly thickened, fold in celery
and pickles. Turn into molds and chill to congeal. Unmold to serve.

Mrs. W. J. Pharr (Catherine)

James Forney's Tomato Aspic

Must prepare ahead   Serves 10-12

1 envelope unflavored gelatin
2-3 ounce packages lemon
   gelatin
4 cups V-8 juice
2 cups celery, chopped

1 medium onion, chopped
2 tablespoons Worcestershire
   sauce

Dissolve unflavored gelatin in 2 cups of cold V-8 juice. Heat the remaining 2 cups of V-8 juice and add lemon Jello. Combine the two mixtures.
Add chopped onion, celery, and Worcestershire sauce. Pour into a greased
8-cup mold or oblong pan. Chill until set. Unmold or cut into serving
portions.

*Variation: You can add ½ can each of chopped, globe artichokes and heart of palm
to mixture before it sets. Use remainder as garnish.*

Mrs. J. M. Carstarphen (Catherine Ann)

Virginia Lee Salad

Must prepare ahead   Serves 6-8

1 head lettuce, cut or torn
  into bite-size pieces
1 head cauliflower, cut into
  bite-size pieces
1 small onion, chopped

1-16 ounce package bacon,
  fried and crumbled
½ cup Parmesan cheese
¼ cup sugar
1-16 ounce jar Miracle Whip
  salad dressing

Layer each ingredient in large bowl starting with lettuce. Add remainder
of ingredients in order listed except salad dressing. Cover top completely
with the salad dressing, cover with plastic wrap and refrigerate overnight. Mix well before serving.

Mrs. Penny White

Bleu Cheese Salad Dressing

May prepare ahead   Yields: 3 cups

1 small carton Dannon yogurt
1 cup Hellman's mayonnaise
4 ounces bleu cheese

1 teaspoon fresh lemon juice
1 small clove garlic,
  pressed

Mix yogurt and mayonnaise. Crumble bleu cheese into mixture. Add
lemon juice and garlic; mix well.

Norman Hull-Ryde

Sour Cream Roquefort Dressing

May prepare ahead   Yields: 4 cups

2 cups mayonnaise
½ cup wine vinegar
6 ounces Roquefort or bleu
  cheese

1 cup sour cream
2 tablespoons lemon juice

Use blender to combine all ingredients. Let blender run until dressing
is creamy.

Janice Stowe

Honey-Creme Dressing

May prepare ahead   Yields: 1 cup

1-3 ounce package cream   Dash of salt
  cheese   2 tablespoons honey
1 tablespoon toasted sesame   2 tablespoons milk, to thin
  seeds
¼ cup sour cream

Whip all ingredients, except milk, with an electric mixer. Add milk to reach desired consistancy. Chill before serving.

Becca Mitchell

Lemon Dressing

May prepare ahead   Yields: 5 cups

3 cups oil   1 cup lemon juice
2 teaspoons Worcestershire   ½ cup Dijon mustard
  sauce   1 teaspoon garlic, minced
½ cup red wine vinegar   Salt and pepper to taste
1 tablespoon sugar

Blend ingredients together with a wire whisk. Serve with a green or spinach salad.

Joye Rankin

Poppy Seed Dressing

May prepare ahead   Yields: 2 cups

¾ cup sugar   1½ tablespoons grated
1 teaspoon salt   onion
1 tablespoon dry mustard   1 cup salad oil
⅓ cup vinegar   1½ tablespoons poppy seed

Mix sugar, salt, mustard, and vinegar. Add grated onion and stir well. Add oil slowly, beating until thick. Add poppy seed and beat longer. If you do not have dry mustard, use prepared mustard.

Cookbook Committee

139

Super Salad Seasoning Mix

This makes a great last minute Christmas gift.
Seal in a decorative container and include recipe.

May prepare ahead   Yields: 2½ cups

2 cups Parmesan cheese,   ½ teaspoon dried dill seed
  grated   2 tablespoons poppy seeds
2 teaspoons salt   3 tablespoons celery seed
½ cup sesame seed   2 teaspoons paprika
½ teaspoon garlic salt   ½ teaspoon pepper
1 tablespoon minced onion
  flakes
2 tablespoons parsley flakes

Mix together all ingredients. Store in a sealed container in a cool, dry place. Use within 2 to 3 months.

Uses: Sprinkle over tossed salads, baked potatoes, or buttered French bread before toasting. Garnish potato salads, macaroni salads, or egg salad. Mix 2 tablespoons of this mix with 1 cup sour cream to make a dip for chips or raw vegetables.

Joye S. Rankin

Tarragon Salad Dressing

May prepare ahead   Yields: 1⅓ cups

¼ cup sugar   ¼ cup white corn syrup
¼ cup tarragon vinegar   1½ teaspoons celery seed
1 teaspoon dry mustard   1 teaspoon salt
¼ teaspoon onion juice   Few grains white pepper
                                     ¾ cup oil

Put all ingredients EXCEPT THE OIL in a bowl and beat well with rotary beater until thoroughly mixed. Add the oil gradually (about ½ teaspoon at a time) while beating constantly to avoid separation. Continue beating until mixture is of desired consistency. Chill thoroughly. Shake well before serving. This should keep indefinitely.

Patti Hunter

Boiled Salad Dressing

This is great on chicken salad.

May prepare ahead   Yields: 2 cups

2 eggs, well beaten   2 tablespoons butter, melted
1 teaspoon dry mustard   1 teaspoon salt
Celery seed   Pepper to taste
⅓ cup sugar   ½ cup vinegar

Combine all ingredients and cook in a double boiler until thickened.

Cookbook Committee

Bud's Favorite Salad Dressing

May prepare ahead   Yields: 3 cups

1 cup salad oil   ¾ cup sugar
⅓ cup catsup   ¼ cup vinegar
1 tablespoon Worcestershire   1 medium onion, grated
  sauce   Dash of salt

Prepare by shaking ingredients in a jar. Pour over salad just before
serving.

Mrs. Bud Anthony

Cooked French Dressing

May prepare ahead   Yields: 5 cups

1 cup Wesson oil   1 cup vinegar
1 cup Del Monte catsup   1 cup sugar
1 teaspoon salt   1 teaspoon black pepper
1 teaspoon dry mustard   1 cup sharp Cheddar
1 medium onion, grated   cheese, grated

Put all ingredients except cheese in a heavy pan and bring to a boil.
Reduce heat and simmer for 5 minutes. As it cools, add cheese and stir.

Ann Cain

Ranch Dressing (Homemade)

*This is divine on baked potatoes and broccoli. Substitute sour cream
for the buttermilk to make dip for raw vegetables.*

May prepare ahead   Yields: 2 cups

1 cup mayonnaise
1½ teaspoons dried onion flakes
1 teaspoon Accent
¼ teaspoon garlic

1 cup buttermilk
1 tablespoon dried parsley
1 scant teaspoon onion salt
¼ teaspoon salt

Mix all ingredients together and store in refrigerator until ready to use.

Hope Parks

Salad Dressing

May prepare ahead   Yields: 1 cup

1 small clove garlic, pressed
1 tablespoon apple cider
   vinegar
1 teaspoon Coleman's dry
   mustard

⅔ cup safflower oil
1 teaspoon sugar
⅓ cup fresh lemon juice

Put all ingredients in a jar and shake well.

Anne Hull-Ryde

Brick's Roquefort Dressing

May prepare ahead   Yields: 1 quart

1½ cups buttermilk
2 tablespoons Worcestershire
   sauce
1 teaspoon garlic powder

2 cups mayonnaise
½ pound Roquefort or bleu
   cheese, crumbled

Blend thoroughly, but gently, so that there will be tasty bites of cheese.
Keep in a tightly covered jar in refrigerator.

Lin Lineberger

Main Courses

London Broil For 12

Serve immediately   Serves 12

2 thick-cut London broil

Marinade:

⅔ cup olive oil

3 tablespoons Worcestershire sauce

⅓ cup lemon juice

1 onion, sliced

½ teaspoon powdered ginger

2 teaspoons dry mustard

½ teaspoon salt

¼ cup soy sauce

⅓ cup wine vinegar

2 small bay leaves

1 teaspoon parsley flakes or 1 tablespoon fresh parsley, chopped

½ teaspoon freshly ground pepper

Mix all ingredients and pour over steaks and let stand in refrigerator at least 24 hours. Turn once or twice. Allow meat to stand at room temperature for one hour before putting steaks on hot grill. Grill about 8 minutes on each side for medium rare and about 10 minutes for medium. Baste with the marinade. When steaks are cooked, remove to large platter and allow the meat to rest for 5 to 10 minutes before slicing diagonally across the grain in very thin slices. Arrange slices on warm platter and drizzle with juices obtained when slicing; garnish with fresh parsley.

Mrs. John D. Bridgeman (Nan)

Beef Tenderloin

Must prepare 24 hours ahead   Servings depend on size of tenderloin

1 heaping teaspoon thyme

1 teaspoon seasoning salt

1 teaspoon garlic salt

1 tablespoon black pepper

¼ teaspoon oregano

1 whole beef tenderloin

Mix together the above spices and rub into the tenderloin. Then wrap in foil and refrigerate for 24 hours. (At this point you may freeze.) Remove from refrigerator two hours ahead of cooking. Put in pan with 1 ½ cups water. Cook 25 minutes in a 400-degree preheated oven.

Carolyn Sumner

Marinated Filet Mignon

Must prepare ahead   Serves 6-8

1 cup catsup
1 teaspoon Worcestershire
  sauce
2 envelopes Italian salad
  dressing mix

2 teaspoons prepared mustard
1½ cups water
6 to 8 filet mignons,
  1½ to 2-inches thick

Combine first 5 ingredients. Spear steaks with fork and place in zip-loc bag. Pour marinade over meat, seal bag, and place in shallow pan. Refrigerate 8 hours, turning once or twice. Drain off and reserve marinade for basting. For medium rare steaks (1½-inches thick), grill 6 minutes on first side. Turn and grill for 7 minutes on second side. (For 2-inch steaks, grill 8 minutes first side and 9 minutes second side.) Baste when turning. Serve with remaining marinade. Marinade is also excellent with beef tenderloin. Marinate 8 hours. Grill or bake in oven at 425 degrees until meat thermometer reaches 140 degrees (rare) or 150 degrees (medium-rare) or 160 degrees (medium).

Mrs. David W. Smith, III (Tracey)

Marinated Tenderloin

Glazed Filet of Beef

Must prepare ahead   Serves 8-10

1 cup soy sauce
4 garlic cloves, finely chopped
1 beef tenderloin, whole and
  trimmed

⅓ cup olive oil
½ cup sherry

Mix soy sauce, garlic, olive oil, and sherry together and marinate tenderloin for several hours or overnight turning several times. When ready to cook, roast on rack in 425-degree oven for 28 to 30 minutes. Baste with marinade from time to time.

Cookbook Committee

English Boiled Beef With Horseradish Sauce

May prepare ahead

Serves 8

1-4½ pound rump roast
1 medium onion, sliced
1 small carrot, sliced
2 tablespoons salt

1 bay leaf
Pepper to taste
2 tablespoons butter
2 tablespoons flour

Cook beef in just enough water to cover, with onion, carrot, and seasonings. Cover pot and simmer slowly for 3 to 4 hours or until meat is tender. Let stand in broth for 24 hours.

Melt butter, stir in flour, and add 2 cups of broth. Cook until thickened. Heat meat in remaining broth. Serve with gravy and horseradish sauce.

Horseradish sauce:
1 cup sour cream
1 teaspoon vinegar
Dash of Tabasco sauce
Grated onion to taste
Worcestershire sauce to taste

1 teaspoon horseradish
Pinch of sugar
Salt to taste
Mustard to taste

Mix all ingredients and refrigerate until chilled. Serve with beef for a delicious taste.

Mrs. Robert C. Clements ('Tuga' Wilson)

Eye of Round

May prepare ahead

Serves 10

1-4 to 5 pound eye of round
Accent
Salt and pepper to taste

Meat tenderizer
Garlic powder
Worcestershire sauce

Stab roast well all over. Sprinkle with meat tenderizer, Accent, garlic powder, salt, and pepper. Rub in Worcestershire sauce. Stab again all over and sprinkle with more tenderizer, Accent, and garlic powder. Bake at 225 degrees for 2 to 3 hours for rare.

Mrs. John B. Garrett, Jr. (Nancy)

Cold Steak With Mustard Sauce

Must prepare ahead   Serves 6

1½ to 2 pounds sirloin steak
  or London broil

Mustard sauce:
2 tablespoons red wine vinegar   2 green onions, minced
2 tablespoons coarse-grain   ¼ cup watercress, minced
  mustard   ½ cup mayonnaise
Salt and pepper to taste
⅓ cup olive oil

Grill steak medium-rare. Cool and slice thinly. In a small bowl whisk together the vinegar, mustard, salt, and pepper; whisk in the oil until the dressing thickens. Whisk in green onions, watercress, and mayonnaise. Arrange steak on a platter and serve with mustard sauce.

Connie Gibbons

Country Pot Roast

This recipe is great on cold winter days and is even good enough for company!

Serve immediately   Serves 6-8

1-3 to 4 pound lean   8 to 10 small carrots, peeled
  chuck roast or round steak   4 to 6 potatoes, peeled and
2 teaspoons salt   quartered
½ teaspoon pepper   2-8 ounce cans tomato sauce
1 tablespoon paprika   2 tablespoons parsley,
2 tablespoons corn oil   chopped
½ cup water   1 cup sour cream
1 bay leaf
8 to 10 small white onions,
  peeled

Trim fat from meat; sprinkle with salt, pepper, and paprika. Brown in hot oil in a Dutch oven. Add water and bay leaf. Cover and simmer for 1½ hours. Add onions, carrots, potatoes, and tomato sauce. Cover and simmer for 1 additional hour or until tender. Remove roast to a serving platter. Add parsley and sour cream to vegetables to make a sauce. Serve roast, topped with hot vegetables and sauce.

Mrs. Anne Neal

Oven Barbeque Brisket

Must prepare ahead   Serves 8-10

1-5 to 6 pound brisket, fresh   **Salt and pepper to taste**
Celery salt   **Worcestershire sauce**
Onion salt   **6 ounces barbeque sauce**
Garlic salt   **2 tablespoons flour**
3 ounces Liquid Smoke   **½ cup water**

Sprinkle each side with celery salt, onion salt, and garlic salt. Pour Liquid Smoke over brisket and place in refrigerator overnight. Turn once or twice. When ready to bake, sprinkle salt, pepper, and Worcestershire sauce in same pan with all ingredients. Cover and bake for 5 hours at 275 degrees. Add 6 ounces of barbeque sauce and bake one more hour uncovered.

Remove meat to a platter and let cool one hour at least. Slice thin (you may take this back to the butcher to slice if you wish).

Skim fat off the sauce in pan and add 2 tablespoons flour, ½ cup water and more barbeque sauce, if desired. Serve brisket at room temperature and with hot sauce.

Mrs. Alex Hall (Ginny)

Easy Brisket Barbeque

Prepare same day   Serves 8-10

1 beef brisket   **1-12 ounce can beer**
1-12 ounce bottle chili sauce

Place brisket in a heavy Dutch oven. Add chili sauce and beer. Cover and cook for 3 to 4 hours or until done in a 325-degree oven. Cool, slice thinly, and reheat in the sauce. Delicious served in buns.

Mrs. Clay Williamson (B. K.)

Beef Stroganoff

May prepare ahead   Serves 4-6

2 pounds round steak or
  sirloin
3 tablespoons Crisco
1½ cups onion, chopped
1 clove garlic, minced
2 tablespoons flour
1-8 ounce can or 1 cup tomato
  soup
½ cup celery, chopped

1 tablespoon Worcestershire
  sauce
1-3 ounce can sliced
  mushrooms and juice
1 teaspoon salt
Dash of pepper
1 cup sour cream

Brown meat in Crisco, add onions, celery, and garlic. Cook until tender but not brown. Stir in flour and remaining ingredients and mix well. Put in a 2-quart greased casserole (do not grease with butter). Bake uncovered for 2 hours at 300 degrees until meat is very tender. (If using sirloin less time is needed.) Add water as stroganoff dries during cooking time and stir occasionally (top only). Serve over rice.

Mrs. Charles Reeves

Beef Teriyaki

Serve immediately   Serves 8

½ cup soy sauce
¼ cup water
2 tablespoons sugar
2 medium onions, sliced
  lengthwise
1 tablespoon vinegar
2 garlic cloves, pressed
¾ teaspoon ground ginger
2 pounds round or flank
  steak, cut into thin diagonal
  strips

¼ cup oil
2 cups cabbage, thinly
  sliced
1 pound fresh mushrooms,
  sliced
1-1 pound can bean sprouts,
  drained
1-8 ounce can sliced water
  chestnuts, drained

Combine first 7 ingredients. Add beef, cover and refrigerate two hours. In a large wok or skillet, heat ½ of oil (in wok at 350 degrees). Add cabbage and stir fry for 3 minutes. Add mushrooms, fry 3 minutes. Remove to dish. Add remaining oil, heat. Add beef mixture; stir-fry for 5 minutes. Add bean sprouts and chestnuts; return cabbage and mushrooms to wok; stir fry for 5 minutes longer. Serve over rice.

Mrs. Charles Gray, III

Beef Kabob

Must prepare ahead   Sauce makes 2 cups

Sirloin tip roast or any beef suitable for kabob, cut in cubes - use ½ pound of beef per person.

Marinate the beef with Good Seasons Italian dressing for 30 minutes or longer before cooking.

Sauce:

2 sticks butter   **Juice of ½ lemon**
20 drops Worcestershire   **10 drops Tabasco**
  sauce   **¼ cup vinegar**
1 cup plus 2 tablespoons
  catsup

Mix ingredients for sauce and pour over meat and any vegetables that you choose to use: onions, mushrooms, tomatoes, peppers, etc. After soaking, put on skewers, alternating meat and vegetables. Cook on charcoal grill.

Mrs. David Allen Smith

Steak Casserole

Serve immediately   Serves 6-8

2 pounds round steak, cubed   **6 to 8 medium potatoes,**
  and cut in medium pieces   **peeled and quartered**
2 onions, sliced   **1 can mushroom soup**
                                                    Water

Flour steak, season to taste, and brown in pan. Transfer meat to baking pan lined with sliced onions. Add quartered potatoes and pour mushroom soup and 1 can water over ingredients. Season to taste with salt and pepper. Cover and bake at 350 degrees for one hour or until potatoes are done.

Jennie Stultz

Beef Casserole

This recipe was in the Gastonia Gazette a few years ago.

Serve immediately   Serves 4-6

1½ pounds stew beef	2 tablespoons sugar
1 medium onion, sliced	2 tablespoons cornstarch
4 carrots, sliced	1-12 ounce can V-8 juice
5 potatoes, sliced	Salt and pepper to taste

Cut meat into small pieces, cutting off fat. Put meat into greased casserole. Add a layer of onion, a layer of carrots, and a layer of sliced potatoes. Add salt and pepper to taste. Sprinkle with sugar and cornstarch. Pour V-8 juice over top and cover casserole tightly with aluminum foil. Bake at 250 degrees for 4 hours.

Mrs. William A. Current

Burgundy Beef

May prepare ahead   Serves 8

4 pounds round steak, 1-inch thick	2 teaspoons salt
¼ cup shortening or bacon drippings	¼ teaspoon marjoram
	¼ teaspoon thyme
5 large onions, sliced	¼ teaspoon pepper
1 pound fresh mushrooms, sliced	1 cup beef bouillon
3 tablespoons flour	2 cups Burgundy

Cut meat into 1-inch cubes, melt shortening in Dutch oven; brown meat. Remove meat and set aside. Cook and stir onions and mushrooms in Dutch oven until onion is tender, adding shortening if necessary. Remove vegetables; cover and refrigerate.

In Dutch oven sprinkle meat with flour and seasonings. Stir in bouillon and wine. Cover and simmer until meat is tender, about 1¼ hours. Liquid should just cover the meat. If necessary, add more bouillon and wine (1 part bouillon to 2 parts wine). Remove from heat. Cover and refrigerate. About 15 minutes before serving, add mushrooms and onions to meat in Dutch oven. Heat thoroughly, stirring occasionally.

Mrs. Holt Harris

Veal and Mushrooms

This veal dish is excellent with wild rice and a broccoli casserole.

Prepare same day   Serves 4

1 pound veal, sliced very thin   **Salt and pepper to taste**
Garlic powder to taste   **2 cups mushrooms, sliced**
½ cup oil   **½ cup sherry**
Flour to coat veal

Cut veal in small pieces and pound thin. Sprinkle with salt, pepper, and a dash of garlic powder. Flour lightly. Cook mushrooms in skillet approximately 5 minutes using ½ cup oil. Take mushrooms out and add meat. Brown over medium heat. When meat is brown, add mushrooms and sherry. Cook at high heat for 2 or 3 minutes. Scrape pan and pour scrapings over meat before serving.

Mrs. Stuart M. Jones (Peggy)

Roast Leg of Lamb

Serve immediately   Serves 8-10

1-6 pound leg of lamb   **1 soup can of water**
Salt and pepper to taste   **2 tablespoons vinegar**
2 to 4 cloves garlic, crushed   **1 onion, sliced**
1 can beef consomme

Rub leg of lamb with salt, pepper, and crushed garlic. (You may substitute powdered garlic if you wish.) Add consomme, water, vinegar, and onion slices to roasting pan. Insert meat thermometer to thickest part of lamb.

Put lamb in preheated 450-degree oven and bake for 15 minutes. Reduce heat to 350 degrees and continue roasting until thermometer registers 145 to 150 degrees for medium-rare, 160 to 170 degrees for well-done. Serve on warmed platter and garnish with watercress or fresh parsley. Drippings may be reduced if needed and passed in gravy boat.

Mrs. John Bridgeman (Nan)

Sukiyaki

(For an Oriental New Year)

Serve immediately   Serves 4-6

1 bunch scallions	½ cup sugar
1-3½ ounce can bamboo shoots	¾ cup soy sauce
1 pound fresh mushrooms	½ cup white wine
1 bunch fresh spinach	½ cup beef soup stock
1 block tofu (soybean curd)	Beef suet, for greasing the
1 pound thinly-sliced beef	pan
roast (as thin as bacon)	

Cut scallions diagonally; thinly slice bamboo shoots. Use just the mushroom caps. Remove heavy stems of spinach leaves. Cut tofu in half lengthwise, then in one-inch pieces. Place all the vegetables on a large platter decoratively....scallions bunched, then bamboo shoots, spinach leaves, mushrooms, then tofu. Place meat on a platter arranged decoratively with the suet on the side.

Mix together ½ cup white wine and ½ cup beef soup stock. Have the sugar, soy sauce, and the cup of wine and soup stock in small pitchers. Heat skillet on high. Grease the skillet with the suet and remove. Brown the meat in the skillet. As each ingredient is added to the skillet, add sugar/soy sauce/wine mixture to it. Each ingredient remains in its own area; however, the juices mingle. Sukiyaki is best served from an electric skillet placed at a table so that the cook begins to prepare the meal and the guests begin serving themselves as the ingredients are cooked to each person's satisfaction. Each guest has two bowls. A bowl of rice and bowl to place the sukiyaki from the skillet. Often a raw egg is provided. This egg is beaten in the bowl and each guest dips his food in his egg bowl.

Oriental pickles may be served with this and fresh fruit (tangarines) for dessert.

Cathy Harvey

Stir-Fried Beef with Broccoli

The oyster sauce is the key to the flavor of this dish.

May prepare ahead   Serves 7

1 pound beef flank or   1 tablespoon vegetable oil
  tenderloin steak   l teaspoon cornstarch
1 teaspoon salt   1 teaspoon sugar
1 teaspoon soy sauce   ⅛ teaspoon white pepper

Trim fat from beef and cut beef into strips. Toss beef, vegetable oil, cornstarch, salt, sugar, soy sauce, and pepper into a glass bowl. Cover and
refrigerate 20 minutes.

1½ pounds broccoli   ¼ cup oyster sauce (found
2 green onions   in grocery deli)
¼ cup chicken broth   2 tablespoons cornstarch

Cut broccoli into pieces. Cover with water, place in microwave, and cook
on high for 1 minute. Drain; rinse under cold water. Cut green onions
into 2-inch pieces. Mix ¼ cup chicken broth, the oyster sauce, and
2 tablespoons cornstarch.

3 tablespoons vegetable oil   1 teaspoon gingeroot,
1 teaspoon garlic, finely   finely chopped
  chopped

Heat wok or pan until one drop of water bubbles. Add vegetable oil; rotate
wok or pan to coat side. Add beef, gingeroot, and garlic; stir-fry until
beef is brown, about 3 minutes. Remove beef.

2 tablespoons vegetable oil   ½ teaspoon salt
½ cup chicken broth

Add 2 tablespoons vegetable oil to wok/pan; rotate. Add broccoli and salt;
stir-fry for 1 minute. Stir in ½ cup chicken broth; heat to boiling. Stir
in beef; heat to boiling. Stir in cornstarch mixture; cook and stir until
thickened, about 15 seconds. Garnish with green onions.

Microwave reheat directions: Prepare beef with broccoli as directed EXCEPT
omit green onions; cover and refrigerate no longer than 48 hours. Just
before serving, prepare green onions. Cover beef mixture tightly and
microwave on platter or bowl on high for 4 minutes. Stir. Cover and
microwave on high for 6 minutes or more. Garnish with green onions.

Mrs. Holt Harris

Sauerbraten With Gingersnap Gravy

Must prepare ahead   Serves 6-8

**4 pound roast (eye of round
roast or sirloin tip roast)**

Marinade:

2 onions, thinly sliced	8 peppercorns
4 cloves	1 bay leaf
1½ cups red wine vinegar	½ teaspoon salt
1 cup water	

Gravy:

¼ cup vegetable oil	2 cups boiling water
½ cup sour cream	1½ cups dry red wine
10 to 12 gingersnap cookies, crushed	

Place meat in large container. Add all of the ingredients for the marinade together and pour over raw meat. Turn meat 2 times each day for 3 days. Remove meat from marinade, dry well by patting with a paper towel and strain marinade in a bowl. Reserve onions and 1 cup of marinade.

In Dutch oven brown meat on all sides in ¼ cup hot vegetable oil. Sprinkle meat with a little salt. Pour 2 cups boiling water around meat. Pour in crushed gingersnaps and simmer with meat for 1½ hours. Cover while simmering, turning often. Next, add 1 cup of reserved marinade and cook for 2 hours more until tender. Remove meat; strain cooking juices into a 1-quart saucepan. In a small bowl mix sour cream with flour. Stir into cooking juice and cook stirring until sauce thickens and is smooth. Serve with egg noodles.

Mrs. Karen L. Staker

Sauerbraten

Must start 1 day ahead   Serves 6

2 cups wine vinegar
1 cup water
1 clove garlic
¾ cup onion, sliced
1 bay leaf
10 peppercorns
¼ cup sugar

3 whole cloves
4 pounds boneless chuck or
    rump roast
Salt and pepper to taste
Flour
2 tablespoons bacon
    drippings
1½ cups sour cream

Mix vinegar, water, garlic, onion, bay leaf, peppercorns, sugar, and cloves. Boil mixture. Salt and pepper the meat. Pour boiling mixture over meat. Refrigerate for 1 day.

Next day: Put liquid marinade mixture aside. Pat meat dry and flour lightly. In large Dutch oven, add bacon drippings and brown meat on all sides. Add 2 cups of marinade mixture. Cook meat slowly on top of stove on low for 2 to 3 hours. Take meat out. Thicken sauce with flour and add sour cream. Stir and pour back on meat. Cut meat and serve.

Mrs. Anne Carriel

Sicilian Meat Loaf

Serve immediately   Serves 4

1 cup bread crumbs (1 slice)
¾ cup tomato juice
2 tablespoons chopped parsley
1 egg, beaten
1 teaspoon oregano
1 onion, chopped

1 clove garlic, chopped
1½ pounds ground beef
1 package wafer-thin sliced
    ham
1 cup mozzarella cheese,
    shredded

Combine bread crumbs, tomato juice, parsley, egg, and spices. Add hamburger and mix thoroughly. Spread on wax paper (about 11 inches long) into rectangular shape. Place ham on top, then sprinkle cheese over ham. Roll up loaf. Place in loaf pan and bake at 350 degrees for 1 hour.

Jan P. Gray

McCosh's Texas Chili

*This is a favorite of ours. My husband makes this on very cold
winter days and believe me, it will keep you warm!!*

May prepare ahead   Serves 12-15
Freezes well

3 pounds lean stew beef	3 tablespoons paprika
¼ cup olive oil	6 tablespoons chili powder
1 quart water	5 cloves garlic, finely chopped
1 or 2 cans Mexican chili	1½ teaspoons salt
beans	1 teaspoon ground cumin
1 teaspoon ground oregano	½ teaspoon red pepper
½ teaspoon black pepper	1 tablespoon sugar

Chop beef into small cubes by hand (a food processor does it too fine).
Heat oil; add meat over high heat until it turns gray. Add water and
simmer this for 2 hours. Add chili beans and the remainder of the ingredients; simmer another 30 minutes. Thicken with the following
ingredients:

1 cup cold water	3 tablespoons flour
6 tablespoons cracker crumbs	

Mix the thickening ingredients together until smooth and stir into chili.
Let simmer for 10 minutes and serve with cornbread or crackers.

Cathy McCosh

Mexican Cornbread Pie

*My husband brought this recipe to me from a hunting trip with
a fraternity brother whose grandmother, Helen Taylor, made it for them.*

May prepare ahead   Yields: 8 slices

1 cup corn meal   2 tablespoons flour
1 cup milk   2 tablespoons bacon grease
¾ teaspoon salt   1 medium onion, diced
1-15 ounce can cream style corn   ½ pound ground beef
2 eggs, beaten   ½ pound Cheddar cheese,
½ teaspoon soda   grated
                                   3 pods hot pepper

Mix corn meal, milk, salt, corn, eggs, soda, flour, and bacon grease
together to form a batter. Saute onion and ground beef together and
drain. Grease large iron skillet. Pour ½ batter into pan. Sprinkle cheese,
peppers, and meat and onion mix evenly on top of batter. Pour
remaining batter on top. Bake at 350 degrees for 45 to 60 minutes.

Mrs. John M. Templeton (Beth)

Moussaka-Stuffed Eggplant

Freezes well   Serves 8-10

2 eggplant, washed and salted   ½ cup butter or margarine,
                                    melted

Meat Sauce:
1 cup onion, finely chopped   ½ teaspoon oregano
1½ pounds ground chuck   ½ teaspoon cinnamon
2 tablespoons butter or   1 teaspoon salt
   margarine   Dash of pepper
1 clove garlic, crushed   2-8 ounce cans tomato sauce
1 teaspoon dried basil leaves

Cream Sauce:
2 tablespoons butter or   Dash of pepper
   margarine   2 cups milk
2 tablespoons flour   2 eggs
½ teaspoon salt

Other ingredients:
½ cup Parmesan cheese, grated   2 tablespoons dry bread
½ cup Cheddar cheese, grated   crumbs

To prepare eggplant:
Half whole eggplant lengthwise. Slice crosswise ½-inch thick and place in bottom of broiler pan. Brush with melted butter, broil 4 inches from heat for 4 minutes per side, or until golden.

To prepare meat sauce:
Sauté onion and ground beef in butter in a 3½-quart Dutch oven. Add garlic and stir until lightly browned. Add herbs, spices, and tomato sauce. Bring to boil, stirring. Reduce heat and simmer uncovered for 30 minutes.

To prepare cream sauce:
In a medium saucepan melt butter. Remove from heat, stir in flour, salt, and pepper. Add milk gradually. Bring to boil, stirring until mixture is thickened. Remove from heat. In small bowl beat eggs with wire whisk. Beat in some hot cream sauce mixture. Return mixture to sauce pan and mix well. Set aside. Preheat oven to 350 degrees.

To assemble casserole:
In bottom of shallow 2-quart baking dish (12 x 7½ x 2-inch) layer half of the eggplant, overlapping slightly. Sprinkle with 2 tablespoons each of the Parmesan and Cheddar cheese. Stir bread crumbs into the meat sauce. Spoon evenly over eggplant. Sprinkle 2 tablespoons each of the cheeses. Layer rest of eggplant slices overlapping as before. Pour the cream sauce over all. Sprinkle with remaining cheese and bake for 35 to 40 minutes or until golden and cream sauce is cooked and set. Cool slightly to serve. Cut into squares.

To freeze:
Bake casserole for 20 minutes, seal well and freeze. On day you wish to serve, defrost and finish baking.

Tami Pearson

Stuffed Cabbage Rolls

May prepare ahead   Serves 4-6

1 head of cabbage
1 pound ground beef
2 green peppers, chopped fine
2 medium onions, chopped
  fine
1 cup bread crumbs
⅓ to ½ cup chili sauce
2 teaspoons Worcestershire
  sauce

½ teaspoon marjoram
½ teaspoon salt
¼ teaspoon pepper
1-8 ounce can tomato sauce
2 tablespoons margarine
½ to ¾ cup sour cream

Cook cabbage for 7 to 9 minutes in boiling salt water, covered. Drain, cool and remove 12 large outer leaves. Meanwhile cook ground beef, green peppers, and onion until meat is browned and drain off all grease. Add bread crumbs, chili sauce, seasonings, and Worcestershire sauce, mix well. Place equal amounts of meat mixture on each cabbage leaf, roll up, secure with toothpicks, and place in large skillet. It may take 2 cabbage leaves (1 for top and 1 for bottom, be sure to secure with toothpicks so they don't fall apart). Pour tomato sauce over the rolls, dot with margarine, cover, and simmer about 1 hour. Remove cabbage rolls to a platter. Stir sour cream into tomato sauce in skillet. Pour this mixture over cabbage rolls.

Mrs. Susan B. Garrett

Spaghetti Sauce

Freezes well   Serves 8

1 pound ground chuck
1 onion, diced
1 green pepper, diced
1 can Hunt's tomato sauce
1 package herb-spice mix
  (from Kraft tangy Italian
  style spaghetti dinner)

2-15 ounce cans Hunt's
  Special tomato sauce
¼ cup Heinz tomato catsup
1-8 ounce can mushrooms
2 tablespoons Worcestershire
  sauce
1 teaspoon sugar

Brown ground chuck, onion, and green pepper together until done. Drain grease. Then add all other ingredients. You may cook this in a crockpot on low heat all day (8 to 10 hours) or on stove top on low for 2 hours. Serve over spaghetti noodles and sprinkle Parmesan cheese on top. Serve with tossed salad and garlic bread for a complete meal.

Mrs. Kristi Hickson Medlin

Spaghetti

May prepare ahead   Serves 8

2 pounds ground beef
Olive oil
Large V-8 juice
Large tomato juice
3 onions, chopped
2 bell peppers, chopped
Celery to taste, chopped

Fresh mushrooms to
  taste, chopped
1 clove garlic, chopped
1-8 ounce can tomato paste
Italian dressing
1 box vermicelli

Brown beef in olive oil and drain. Bring to simmer V-8 and tomato juice. Add chopped onion, pepper, celery, mushrooms, and garlic. Add browned beef and tomato paste. Sprinkle beef with fresh olive oil before adding to vegetable mixture. Season lastly with Italian seasoning to taste. Cook vermicelli with a little cooking oil. Serve sauce over noodles.

Mrs. Cookie McLean Jackson

Meats

Spaghetti and Meatballs

Serve immediately   Serves 8

½ pound ground pork, halved   1 teaspoon onion, chopped
½ cup oil   ½ clove garlic
1 medium onion, chopped   Salt and pepper to taste
3 cloves garlic   Bread crumbs
3-14 ounce cans tomatoes   1 small can tomato paste
1½ pounds ground chuck   1 teaspoon sugar
1 egg   ½ teaspoon cayenne pepper
½ teaspoon Parmesan cheese   More salt to taste

Fry together ¼-pound ground pork, oil, onion, and garlic until cooked, not brown. Add 3 cans tomatoes (if whole, cut up). Cook in 5-quart saucepan slowly for 2 hours. Meanwhile, make meat balls from ground chuck, ¼-pound ground pork, egg, Parmesan cheese, onion, garlic, and salt and pepper to taste. Add enough bread crumbs to stiffen for balls. Brown meat balls and drop into sauce after 2 hours. Then add tomato paste, sugar, cayenne pepper, and more salt to taste. Cook an additional 20 minutes. Spoon over hot spaghetti noodles.

Mrs. Sam Howe (Cherry)

Spaghetti Alla Carbonara

Serve immediately   Serves 6-8

1-1 pound package spaghetti   ¼ cup fresh parsley
3 large eggs, beaten   ¼ teaspoon dried basil
1 cup Parmesan cheese, grated ⅛ teaspoon garlic powder
½ cup whipping cream   ¼ cup butter
8 slices bacon, cooked
  and crumbled

Cook spaghetti according to package directions. While it is cooking, combine eggs and ½ cup cheese in small bowl. Mix well. Heat cream in heavy saucepan or double boiler until scalded. Stir in bacon, parsley, basil, and garlic. Reduce to low heat. When spaghetti is cooked, drain thoroughly and put in serving bowl. Immediately add egg mixture, cream mixture, and butter; toss gently until butter is melted. (It is important that the spaghetti be hot when the other ingredients are added to it because it is the heat of the spaghetti that cooks the eggs.) Sprinkle with remaining ¼ cup cheese, garnish with parsley and serve immediately.

Mrs. Elizabeth Neisler Sumner

162

Blondie's Carbonara

This is a favorite of the entire Davis family.
It was created by my husband and me so Rob got to name it.
Note that this looks a lot harder than it really is.
From start to finish, it takes only about 45 minutes.

Serve immediately   Serves 4-6

1½ pounds bacon, diced
½ cup, plus 3 tablespoons
  olive oil
1 large onion, diced
1 large pepper, diced
½ cup chopped mushrooms
Dry white wine
1-12 ounce box fettucini
  (green or yellow)

1 stick butter, melted
2 eggs
¾ cup Parmesan and Romano
  cheeses, grated and mixed
⅓ cup parsley, chopped
Lots of fresh ground pepper

Fry bacon until lightly browned, pour off ALMOST all grease and set aside. In same pan add 3 tablespoons olive oil and sauté onion, pepper, and mushrooms until soft. Return bacon to pan and deglaze with ¾ cup of wine; let simmer for 5 to 10 minutes, always keeping enough wine in the pan to keep moist.

In a very large pot boil water. Add a small amount of olive oil and salt to water. When rapidly boiling, add pasta and cook only until barely tender. While pasta is boiling, melt butter. In another bowl beat eggs. Have cheese, pepper, parsley, and olive oil on hand and ready.

When pasta is nearly ready, prepare for a flurry of activity. Drain pasta quickly but thoroughly in a colander, and return to warm pot. Immediately add beaten eggs, melted butter, cheese, parsley, olive oil, and bacon/vegetable/wine mixture. Stir all together. Sprinkle with pepper (fresh-ground is best).

This recipe is best served with a light salad, hot garlic bread, and lots of red wine.

Sharron Davis

Italian Spinach Shells

Serve immediately   Serves 6-8

1 pound ground beef
1 quart Ragu sauce
1 box of jumbo shells for
  stuffing
2-9 ounce packages frozen
  creamed spinach

15 ounces ricotta cheese
  (or small curd cottage
  cheese)
8 ounces mozzarella cheese,
  shredded

Brown ground beef and drain. Add Ragu sauce. Boil jumbo shells for 5 to 10 minutes just until soft but still firm. Drain shells and let cool.

Mix thawed spinach with ricotta and mozzarella cheese. Stuff cooled shells with mixture. Arrange side by side in a 3-quart rectangular Pyrex dish. Pour sauce with ground beef over the top of stuffed shells. Sprinkle a little of shredded mozzarella cheese over the top. Bake at 400 degrees until bubbly.

Mrs. William L. Beam (Anne)

Stuffed Manicotti Shells

Freezes well   Serves 4

1-8 ounce package manicotti
  shells
1 pound ground beef
1-10 ounce can spinach
  (frozen can be used)
1 small onion, chopped (¼ cup)
2 beef bouillon cubes, crushed
½ teaspoon garlic powder
⅛ teaspoon dried thyme leaves

1½ cups cottage cheese
2 eggs
½ cup Parmesan cheese,
  grated
2-8 ounce cans tomato sauce
1 cup mozzarella cheese,
  grated
1 can herbed tomato sauce

Cook manicotti shells according to directions on package. Brown, then drain ground beef and onions. Drain canned or frozen (cooked) spinach. In large bowl mix ground beef, spinach, onion, bouillon cubes, garlic powder, thyme, cottage cheese, eggs, and Parmesan cheese. Fill manicotti shells with mixture. Arrange in greased 13 x 9-inch pan. Pour tomato sauce over shells and sprinkle with mozzarella cheese. Bake at 350 degrees for 25 minutes.

Susan Stover

Kathryn Stowe's Lasagna

Everybody loves this recipe and it is great for company.
It is excellent served with a spinach or Greek salad and a light dessert.

May prepare ahead   Serves 12-15
Freezes well

1 pound ground chuck	2-12 ounce cartons (3 cups) large curd cottage cheese
1 tablespoon olive oil	
1 clove garlic	
1 tablespoon parsley flakes	2 eggs, beaten
1 tablespoon basil	2 teaspoons salt
2 teaspoons salt	½ teaspoon pepper
1-No. 2 can (2½ cups) tomatoes	2 tablespoons parsley flakes
1-6 ounce can (⅔ cup) tomato paste	½ cup Parmesan cheese, grated
1-10 ounce package lasagna noodles	1 pound provolone cheese
	1 pound mozzarella cheese

Brown the meat in hot olive oil. Add the next 6 ingredients. Simmer uncovered until thick, about one hour, stirring occasionally. Cook noodles in boiling salted water according to package directions. (Adding a little oil to the water keeps the noodles from sticking together.) Meanwhile combine cottage cheese with the next 5 ingredients. Cover the bottom of a 13 x 9-inch baking dish with noodles. Spread some of the cottage cheese mixture, then the meat mixture and a layer each of provolone and mozzarella cheeses. Repeat layers. (This usually makes 2 dishes.) Bake at 375 degrees for 30 minutes until bubbly.

Patti Hunter

Crafty Crescent Lasagna

Serve immediately   Serves 8

½ pound bulk sausage
½ pound ground beef
¾ cup onion, chopped
1 clove garlic, minced
1 tablespoon parsley
½ teaspoon basil
½ teaspoon oregano
½ teaspoon salt

1-6 ounce can tomato paste
1 cup cottage cheese
1 egg
¼ cup Parmesan cheese
1½ cups mozzarella
  cheese, grated
1 can Pillsbury French loaf
Poppy seed or sesame seeds

Meat filling:
Brown sausage, ground beef, and onion. Add garlic, parsley, basil, oregano, salt, and tomato paste and simmer for 25 minutes.

Cheese filling:
Mix together cottage cheese, egg, and Parmesan cheese. Unroll dough on cookie sheet. Place half of meat mixture down the center. Put half mozzarella cheese on top, then put cottage cheese mixture on top of that. Next top with last half of meat mixture and mozzarella cheese. Fold dough edges around to cover. Pinch edges so that it is well sealed. Sprinkle with poppy seed or sesame seeds. Bake at 375 degrees for 25 minutes or until browned.

Mrs. Laura Lineberger

Sausage-Apple Pie

May prepare ahead   Serves 6-8
Freezes well

1 stick butter
¼ cup sugar
¼ cup orange juice
1 package Neese's hot
  sausage, fried and drained

4 to 6 green apples, peeled,
  cored, and chopped
½ pound Cheddar cheese,
  grated
1 deep-dish pie shell

Boil butter, sugar, and juice. Pour over other ingredients in pie shell. Bake at 350 degrees for 50 to 60 minutes.

Mrs. Joanna Woods Owen

Fool Proof Country Ham

*This is the way country hams were cooked for years in Tennessee
and it is really moist and good!*

Must prepare 1 day ahead   Servings depend on size

Country ham, any size   Whole cloves
1 cup brown sugar   2 tablespoons hot mustard
Enough Coca Cola to make
  a paste

Soak ham in water overnight. Scrub WELL with stiff brush. Place ham in roaster and add 5 cups boiling water. Cover. Place in cold oven, turn oven on to 500 degrees for 15 minutes and turn oven off. Leave ham in oven for 3 hours; do not open oven door. Then turn oven to 500 degrees again for 15 minutes and turn off. Leave ham in oven overnight and do not disturb.

Next day, cut off fat except for 1 inch. Score ham and cover with brown sugar paste. Make paste with brown sugar, hot mustard, and Coca Cola. Place whole cloves in each diamond. Bake at 350 degrees until brown which should be about 25 to 30 minutes.

Sandy Rankin

Smoked Sausage-Pasta Jambalya

Serve immediately   Serves 6-8

1 cup rotini, sea shells, or   ½ cup green pepper,
  large noodles, cooked   chopped
1 pound Hillshire Farms   ½ cup celery, chopped
  smoked sausage or Polish   1 can tomatoes
  Kielbasa, cut into 2-inch   ½ teaspoon garlic
  pieces   ½ teaspoon thyme
½ cup onion, chopped   ⅛ teaspoon cayenne pepper

Cook noodles in salted water and drain. Cook sausage and drain. In skillet brown vegetables in small amount of margarine until tender. Add tomatoes, spices, and sausage. Cook for 10 to 15 minutes. Fold in noodles.

Cookbook Committee

Polynesian Ribs

This is especially good served with a spinach salad and sourdough bread.

Serve immediately   Serves 4

2 packages ribs   1 cup soy sauce
½ cup sugar   1 teaspoon ginger
1 teaspoon Hickory smoked salt   2 tablespoons brown sugar
1 cup catsup   1 teaspoon monosodium
                                           glutamate (optional)

Rub ribs with sugar and Hickory smoked salt; let stand for 1 hour. Combine the catsup, soy sauce, ginger, brown sugar, and monosodium glutamate (if desired) and rub on ribs. Let them stand for 2 hours. Place in a preheated 400-degree oven. Reduce heat to 325 degrees and cook until tender, about 40 minutes.

Patti Hunter

Cream Cheese and Ham Loaf

This is pretty sliced on a tray with parsley or great to take on a picnic.

Must prepare ahead   Yields 10-12 slices

1 loaf unsliced French bread   ½ cup Cheddar cheese,
¼ cup mayonnaise   grated
1-8 ounce cream cheese   1 tablespoon lemon juice
¾ cup celery, chopped   1 tablespoon Worcestershire
2 tablespoons onion, minced   sauce
⅓ cup parsley, chopped   Dill pickle strips
                                    8 slices cooked ham

Split bread and hollow out each half. Blend cream cheese with mayonnaise; add celery, onion, parsley, cheese, lemon juice, and Worcestershire sauce. Spread on bread halves; roll pickle strips in ham slices and place in middle of bottom half. Cover with top and wrap in foil; chill for 24 hours. Slice and serve.

Mrs. Clay Williamson (B.K.)

Smoked Barbecue Picnic

May prepare ahead
Freezes well

Serves 10-12

2-4 or 5 pound pork loin
  roasts or Boston butts
½ cup lemon juice

½ cup clear Italian
  dressing
½ cup oil

On a charcoal grill over indirect heat, place the roasts in the center over a drip pan. Using hickory chips according to the directions on the bag or fresh green hickory branches, smoke the roasts all day at as low a temperature as possible, basting about every hour with the Italian dressing, lemon juice, and oil mixture. If the fire goes out (it is sometimes difficult to keep burning at a low temperature), simply restart it and continue smoking. Continue adding hickory and charcoal all day. When ready to serve, remove from the grill and chop the meat. The outside will look charred. Serve with sauce below.

Sauce:
3 tablespoons brown sugar
½ cup Worcestershire sauce
3 tablespoons prepared
  mustard
1½ cups catsup

1 cup vinegar
1 onion, minced
¼ teaspoon pepper

Mix all sauce ingredients together thoroughly and serve with your delicious smoked barbecue picnic.

Patti Hunter

Marinated Pork Chops

This is great for summer cookouts and a change from beef.

Must prepare ahead

Serves 6

½ cup lemon juice
½ teaspoon garlic powder
6 pork chops, ¾ to 1-inch
  thick

½ cup soy sauce
2 tablespoons fresh ground
  ginger, chopped

Combine ingredients and pour over pork chops. Refrigerate for 6 hours or overnight turning once. Cook on an outdoor grill.

Hope Parks

Stromboli

Freezes well   Yields: 8 small loaves

4 loaves frozen bread dough   1 pound fresh bulk sausage,
Poupon mustard   browned and crumbled
1 pound Genoa salami, sliced   1 stick butter, melted
   very thin   Parmesan cheese
1 pound provolone cheese,   Pepper to taste
   sliced thin   Oregano
1 pound ham, shaved   Garlic powder
1 pound mozzarella cheese,
   grated

Thaw dough and let rise. Roll dough into a rectangle. Spread Poupon mustard down the middle of dough. Layer the following ingredients in a row down the center: salami, provolone cheese, ham, and mozzarella cheese ;add the crumbled sausage along the sides.

Bring both ends of dough to center and pinch shut. Place on cookie sheet, seam side down. Brush the top with melted butter and sprinkle with Parmesan cheese, pepper, oregano, and garlic powder (as much or as little as you like). Bake at 350 degrees for 30 minutes. You may make 4 large loaves or for easier handling, cut each loaf in half prior to filling for 8 smaller loaves.

Lynda Nelson

Make Your Own Open-Faced Sandwich

This is great for a Sunday evening with soup.

Serve immediately   Makes as many as you need

Ingredients per serving:
1 slice toast   1 slice cheese, any kind
Mayonnaise or Dijon mustard   Cooked vegetable, asparagus,
1 slice meat, ham, turkey,   broccoli, cauliflower
   Canadian bacon, or bologna   Another slice cheese,
                                                       any kind

Spread toast with mayonnaise or mustard. Top with meat, cheese, vegetable, and additional slice cheese. Broil on cookie sheet until cheese melts and enjoy!

Candy Grooms

Popover Pizza

Serve immediately   Serves 4-6

½ pound pork sausage
½ pound lean ground beef
1-15 ounce can tomato sauce
1 cup plus 2 tablespoons flour
1 teaspoon oregano
½ teaspoon salt, divided

2 eggs
1 cup milk
1 tablespoon corn oil
½ cup fresh Parmesan
  cheese, grated
¾ pound mozzarella cheese,
  sliced

Preheat oven to 425 degrees.

Sauté meat until brown and crumbly. Drain excess fat. Add tomato sauce, 2 tablespoons flour, oregano, and ¼ teaspoon salt. Heat to boiling and cook, stirring for 1 minute. Pour into 13 x 9-inch baking pan; cover with mozzarella cheese slices. To make crust: Beat eggs with milk, oil, remaining ¼ teaspoon salt, and 1 cup flour. Pour over cheese and meat. Sprinkle with Parmesan cheese. Bake until pizza is puffy and cheese has melted, about 25 to 30 minutes.

Loosen edges when the pizza comes out of the oven, then turn onto a platter and cut. Serve with a salad or cut into squares as an appetizer.

Ms. Mary Loughridge Hendricks

Wyche's Stuffed Rolls

May prepare ahead   Makes 12 rolls
Freezes well

12 French or sour dough rolls
⅔ cup water
½ cup parsley, minced
¼ cup Dijon mustard
2 eggs, beaten
½ teaspoon oregano

½ teaspoon pepper
1 pound sausage
1 pound ground beef
1 medium onion, chopped
6 tablespoons margarine
1 minced garlic clove

Scoop out insides of rolls, leaving ¼-inch shell with lid. After drying, put inside bread in blender to make crumbs. Put in bowl and add water, parsley, mustard, eggs, oregano, and pepper. Brown meat and onion together until meat is done; drain well and add to above mixture. Pack rolls lightly. Melt butter/garlic and brush top to cover. Bake for 10 to 15 minutes at 400 degrees.

Mrs. Clay Williamson (B. K.)

Charcoal Dove

Serve immediately   Serves 8-10

1 bottle Wishbone Dressing   **1 pound bacon**
12 to 18 doves

Use dressing to marinate birds for 24 hours. Wrap each bird with bacon
and cook on charcoal grill until done.

Hope Parks

Doves in Foil

*Men love this! Add a tossed salad and
"Voila", you've got a banquet.*

Serve immediately   Serves 6

12 doves, split   **2¼ slices green pepper, diced**
6 strips of bacon   **Salt and pepper**
4 medium potatoes, peeled   **Seasoning salt**
  and quartered   **2 to 3 tablespoons**
1 small onion, quartered   **Worcestershire sauce**
1 carrot, cut into ½-inch
  pieces

Place 2 doves on a 12-inch square piece of foil and repeat with remaining doves. Place ½ strip bacon over breast of each dove. Place vegetables
around doves. Salt and pepper and add seasoning salt to taste. Sprinkle
Worcestershire sauce over doves. Fold foil to seal. Bake at 325 degrees
for 90 minutes.

Hope Parks

Marinated Doves

A delight! This is our family's favorite dove recipe.

Must prepare ahead   Serves 4

Salt and pepper to taste   12 dove breasts
1½ cups salad oil   ½ cup butter
½ cup vinegar   3 tablespoons flour
½ cup red wine   1 onion, chopped
2 to 3 bay leaves   2 bouillon cubes or
1 onion, sliced   1-10¾-ounce can bouillon
1 clove garlic, minced   or consomme
1 teaspoon Worcestershire   2 cups boiling water
  sauce   Salt and pepper to taste

Combine first 8 ingredients and marinate dove breasts in it for 7 to 8 hours or overnight.

Brown doves in butter over high heat until browned on all sides. Add flour and onion to drippings and stir until flour is brown. Dissolve bouillon cubes in boiling water and slowly add to roux or add the can of bouillon or consomme and water to equal 2 cups. Put doves in roaster and cover with gravy. Bake at 225 degrees for 2 to 3 hours or until tender.

Hope Parks

Sauteed Doves

May prepare ahead   Serves 6

6 doves, split   2 tablespoons celery leaves,
½ cup butter   minced
1 cup Vermouth or white dry   Salt
  wine   ½ teaspoon tarragon
¼ cup onion, minced

Sauté doves in butter for 5 minutes or until browned. Add wine, onion, celery leaves, and salt. Cover and simmer over low heat for 20 minutes. Add tarragon and simmer, uncovered, for 15 minutes.

Hope Parks

Easy Wild Duck

Must prepare ahead   Serves 6

3 wild ducks
3 apples, quartered
3 onions, quartered
Salt and pepper

12 slices bacon
1-12 ounce can orange juice
   concentrate

Put apples and onions in duck cavities. Salt and pepper outside of duck.
Cover each breast with 2 slices bacon and secure with toothpicks. Line
bottom of roaster with heavy aluminum foil. Pour orange juice over ducks.
Cover and bake with vent open at 350 degrees for 3 hours.

Hope Parks

Faisan Saute Aux Herbes

Sauteéd Pheasant With Herbs

Serve immediately   Serves 4

1 cleaned, ready-to-cook
   pheasant (about 2 pounds),
   cut in serving pieces (must
   check weight)
2 tablespoons butter
Salt to taste, if desired
Freshly ground pepper to taste
2 whole cloves garlic, peeled

1 bay leaf
2 sprigs fresh thyme or
   ½ teaspoon dried
¾ cup dry white wine
3 tablespoons cold butter
2 tablespoons parsley,
   finely chopped

Sprinkle the pheasant pieces with salt and pepper. Heat the butter in
a skillet and add the pieces skin side down. Cook about 2 or 3 minutes
until skin is golden brown. Turn the pieces and continue cooking about
3 minutes more. Add the garlic, bay leaf, thyme, and wine. Cover and
cook 20 minutes or until the pheasant is tender. Transfer the pheasant
pieces to a serving dish. Swirl the 3 tablespoons of cold butter into the
pan sauce. Pour and scrape the sauce (including garlic and thyme sprig)
over the pheasant and serve sprinkled with chopped parsley.

Lin Lineberger

Roast Pheasant
(Or Cornish Hen Or Quail)

Our favorite dish for candlelit dinners as newlyweds and it is still a simple, but special, entree now that our children are grown and we are enjoying candlelit dinners for two again.

Serve immediately   Serves any number.

Pheasant (or Cornish hen   **Seedless grapes**
  or quail)   **Bacon**
Butter   **Sherry**
Salt

Rub bird with butter; sprinkle with salt. Stuff bird with seedless grapes. Lay bacon across breast of bird. Roast, uncovered, in a very hot 500-degree oven for 15 minutes. Baste often. When browned, reduce heat to 350 degrees. Cook for 1 hour, basting every 15 minutes. Pour a wineglass full of sherry over birds. Add an additional handful of grapes to pan. Cook an additional 15 minutes.

Reduce cooking times for smaller birds. This recipe can easily be varied in quantity as needed.

Arrange on serving dish with grapes. Garnish with grape leaves or parsley.

Mrs. Kay Kincaid Moss

Marinated Quail

Must prepare ahead   Serves 3-4

4 quail   **1 cup (6 ounces) frozen**
2 tablespoons Kitchen Bouquet   **orange juice concentrate**
Oil for browning   **2 tablespoons flour**

Brush quail with Kitchen Bouquet. Let stand ½ hour. Brown on all sides in oil. Add orange juice concentrate and 1 can water. Cover and cook over low heat for 1 hour. Mix flour with a little water and use to thicken sauce for gravy.

Hope Parks

Smothered Quail

This recipe may be cooked in a crockpot for
5 to 6 hours instead of in the oven.

May prepare ahead   Serves 4-6

6 quail, cleaned
6 tablespoons butter or
  margarine
3 tablespoons flour
½ cup sherry

2 cups chicken broth, canned
  or homemade
Salt and pepper to taste
Cooked wild rice

Brown quail in heavy saucepan or Dutch oven in butter or margarine. Remove quail to an 8 x 11-inch oblong dish. Add flour to butter in saucepan and brown, stirring well. Slowly add sherry, chicken broth, salt, and pepper. Blend well and pour over quail. Cover baking dish and bake at 350 degrees for 1 hour. Serve over wild rice.

Mrs. Anne Neal

Georgia Quail

Serve immediately   Serves 6

12 birds
Flour
½ cup water

Salt and pepper to taste
¾ cup white wine

Roll quail in flour; place in flat pan and brown in 450-degree oven. When brown, add water, salt, and pepper. Cover with foil. Reduce heat to 350 degrees and bake for 45 minutes. Add wine and cook for another 45 minutes, tightly covered. Thicken pan gravy before serving if desired.

Janice Stowe

Cornish Hens With Parsley Sauce

This recipe is great with wild rice on the side.

May prepare ahead   Serves 4-6

3 rock Cornish hens   ¼ teaspoon thyme
4 tablespoons flour   ¼ teaspoon sage
4 teaspoons salt   ¾ teaspoon chili powder
1 teaspoon pepper   ¾ teaspoon paprika
6 tablespoons butter   2 tablespoons sherry
¼ teaspoon dried marjoram   1 cup parsley, chopped

Cut the hens in half. Combine the flour, salt, and pepper in a paper bag. Add the hens and shake to coat evenly. Melt the butter in a Dutch oven and stir in marjoram, thyme, sage, chili powder, and paprika. Add the hens, several halves at a time, and brown. Place all halves in the Dutch oven and cover tightly. Cook over low heat until fork tender. Place on a heated platter and keep warm.

Pour the sherry into the Dutch oven and stir to loosen browned particles. Add the parsley and cook for 2 minutes. Pour sherry over hens (¼ cup white wine may be substituted for sherry).

Debbie Brake

Venison Chili

May prepare ahead   Serves 6-8

1 pound of ground venison   1-15 ounce can tomato sauce
1 tablespoon oil   1-16 ounce can pureed
1 teaspoon chopped onion or   tomatoes
  flakes   1-16 ounce can kidney beans
2 stalks celery, chopped   1 package Chili-O-Mix

Brown ground venison meat until done; drain. Saute onion and celery in oil until tender; add cooked and drained meat. Combine meat, onion, celery, tomato sauce, tomatoes, and Chili-O-Mix. Add drained kidney beans and simmer for 10 minutes more. Serve over cooked rice and top with grated Cheddar cheese.

Hope Parks

Chicken Cordon Bleu

People will think you cooked all day.

Serve immediately   Serves 6-8

8 chicken breasts, skinned
   and boned
8-1 ounce slices cooked ham
8-1 ounce slices Swiss cheese
3 tablespoons parsley, chopped
¼ teaspoon pepper
1 egg, beaten

½ cup milk
½ cup Italian bread crumbs
½ cup butter
1-10¾ ounce can mushroom
   soup
1-8 ounce carton sour cream
1-4 ounce can sliced
   mushrooms

Place each piece of chicken between 2 sheets of waxed paper. Flatten
to ¼-inch thickness using meat mallet or rolling pin. Place 1 slice of
ham and 1 slice of cheese in center of each piece. Sprinkle with parsley
and pepper. Roll up lengthwise and secure with a toothpick. Dip each
piece of chicken in egg mixed with milk, then cover with breadcrumbs.
Melt butter in heavy skillet, brown chicken on all sides. Remove chicken
to baking dish, reserving drippings in skillet. Add remaining ingredients
to drippings and stir well. Pour sauce over chicken. Bake uncovered at
350 degrees for 40 to 45 minutes.

Melissa Morris

Sherried Chicken Breasts

Serve immediately   Serves 8

8 large boned chicken breasts
8 slices Swiss cheese
2-10¾ ounce cans cream of
   chicken soup

1 cup dry sherry
1½ cups dry herb stuffing
   mix
½ cup margarine, melted

Arrange chicken breasts in a greased 9 x 13-inch baking dish. Arrange
cheese slices over chicken breasts. Mix together chicken soup and sherry.
Pour over chicken. Sprinkle top thoroughly with herb stuffing mix. Drizzle with melted margarine. Bake uncovered for 1½ hours at 300 degrees
or until chicken is tender and done.

Mrs. J. Caswell Taylor, Jr.
Julie Solomon

Bacon-Wrapped Chicken Breasts

Serve immediately   Serves 6

6 boneless chicken breasts   **12 strips of bacon**
6 slices thin ham   **Tarragon**
6 slices Swiss cheese   **Parsley**

Pound chicken breasts until ¼-inch thick. Top each piece with 1 slice
of ham and 1 slice of cheese. Fold chicken over ham and cheese. Wrap
each bundle with 2 strips of bacon. Place in shallow baking dish and
sprinkle with tarragon. Bake in preheated oven at 350 degrees for 40
to 45 minutes or until chicken is cooked and bacon is browned. Garnish
with parsley.

Mrs. William Cain (Monica)

Chicken Parmesan

Serve immediately   Serves 4

¼ cup fine dry bread crumbs   **2 pounds chicken parts or**
4 tablespoons Parmesan   **4 breasts**
  cheese, grated, and divided   **1-10¾ ounce can cream of**
¼ teaspoon oregano   **mushroom soup**
Dash garlic powder   **½ cup milk**
Dash pepper   **Paprika**

Combine crumbs, 2 tablespoons Parmesan, oregano, garlic, and pepper;
roll chicken in mixture. Arrange in 2-quart baking dish. Bake at 400
degrees for 20 minutes, turn chicken, and bake for another 20 minutes.
Blend soup and milk, pour over chicken. Sprinkle with paprika and
remaining Parmesan cheese. Cook for an additional 20 minutes.

Microwave Directions: Cook in microwave oven on HIGH for 7 minutes. Turn
dish and cook for another 7 minutes. Blend soup and milk, pour over
chicken. Sprinkle with paprika and remaining Parmesan. Cook for
another 7 minutes. All microwave cooking is on HIGH. May need to adjust cooking time, based on the size of the chicken.

Kerry Jarman

Chicken Eden Isle

Serve immediately   Serves 4-6

1-3 ounce jar dried beef
4 to 6 boneless chicken breasts
1-10¾ ounce can chicken
  mushroom soup

1-8 ounce carton sour cream
6 slices bacon, fried and
  crumbled
Noodles, cooked

Line a 2½-quart Pyrex casserole (one with a cover) with dried beef. Place chicken breasts on dried beef. Mix mushroom soup and sour cream and pour over chicken. Bake covered at 325 degrees for 2 hours. Brown 6 slices bacon and crumble over chicken when done. Serve over noodles. Add extra cream of mushroom soup if needed for extra sauce. Serve with hot rolls and assorted vegetables.

VARIATION: Wrap each chicken breast with uncooked bacon strip and lay on top of chipped beef. Bake at 275 degrees for 3 hours total (cover the first hour and uncover the last two).

Mrs. R. Spencer Eaves
Mary Lou Norcross

Chicken Marsala

My family enjoys fettucini with this dish.

Serve immediately   Serves 4

4 boned chicken breast halves
4 tablespoons butter or
  margarine
12 mushrooms, sliced
¼ teaspoon salt
Dash of pepper

2 teaspoons lemon juice
1 cup Marsala wine
2 teaspoons fresh parsley,
  chopped

Place each piece of chicken between two sheets of waxed paper, and flatten to ¼-inch thickness using a meat mallet. Melt butter in a skillet; add chicken and cook over low heat 5 to 6 minutes on each side or until golden brown. Remove chicken breast to serving platter. Add next 5 ingredients to skillet; cook until mushrooms are tender. Pour wine mixture over chicken; sprinkle with parsley.

Mrs. Joe B. Maynard

Chicken Supreme

Must prepare 12 hours ahead   Serves 4-6

4-6 chicken breasts, boned
2 cups sour cream
¼ cup lemon juice
4 teaspoons Worcestershire
  sauce
4 teaspoons celery salt
4 teaspoons paprika

4 teaspoons salt
Dash of pepper
Garlic salt to taste
Pepperidge Farm stuffing
  mix, crushed
½ cup margarine
½ cup oil

Marinate chicken breasts in marinade made from sour cream, lemon juice, Worcestershire, celery salt, paprika, salt, pepper, and garlic salt. Marinate in refrigerator for 12 hours or more. Roll chicken breasts in crushed stuffing mix, and arrange in baking dish. Melt together margarine and oil. Slowly pour ½ mixture over chicken. Bake at 350 degrees for 1 hour. After 30 minutes pour remainder of melted mixture over chicken.

Mrs. Nancy H. Wallace

Chicken With Almonds

*Serve over rice and add a tossed salad,
green vegetable, and bread for a complete meal.*

Freezes well   Serves 6

6 to 8 chicken breasts, boned
¼ cup shortening
¼ cup onions, chopped
3 tablespoons flour
2 cups chicken broth
¼ cup sherry

1 teaspoon dried tarragon
1 teaspoon salt
1 teaspoon pepper
1½ cups sour cream
4 tablespoons slivered
  almonds

Brown chicken in shortening and remove. Sauté onions. Stir in flour. Slowly add chicken broth and sherry. When liquid begins to simmer, return chicken to skillet. Add tarragon, salt, and pepper. Cook covered on low for about 45 minutes. Stir in the sour cream and heat; do not boil. Garnish with slivered almonds.

Mrs. Susan B. Garrett

181

Sesame Chicken In Acorn Squash

*This is a Martha Stewart recipe that can be used
for a family dinner or an elaborate candlelit meal.*

Prepare ahead   Serves 4

Marinade:

1 piece fresh ginger (1-inch),
peeled and thinly sliced
Pinch of dried chili pepper
or 1 fresh chili, minced
½ cup white wine

2 tablespoons sesame oil
3 cloves garlic, peeled and
split
1 teaspoon chili powder
½ cup soy sauce

Other ingredients:

2 whole chicken breasts, boned,
skinned and cut into ¾-inch
strips
2 acorn squash, halved
lengthwise
½ cup flour
2 tablespoons black sesame
seeds
2 tablespoons white sesame
seeds

3 tablespoons unsalted
butter
3 carrots, cut and blanched
20 snow peas, blanched
1 small head broccoli, cut into
small flowerets, blanched

Mix all marinade ingredients together in a bowl. Put chicken in
marinade and let set overnight preferably, or at least 30 minutes. Preheat
oven to 350 degrees. Put squash halves, cut side down, in baking pan.
Add ½-inch water and bake until squash is tender, 30 to 40 minutes.
About 15 minutes before squash is done, combine flour and sesame seeds.
Roll chicken in mixture. Melt butter in a skillet and saute chicken for
4 to 5 minutes, until golden. Remove chicken and set aside. Pour off excess butter and crumbs. Deglaze skillet with ¼ cup of strained marinade.
Add carrots, snow peas, and broccoli and cook just enough to heat
vegetables. Add chicken strips and toss well. Serve chicken and
vegetables spilling over squash halves.

Mrs. H. Garrett Rhyne

Poppy Seed Chicken Casserole

Prepare same day   Serves 4

2½ cups diced chicken
1-8 ounce carton sour cream
1 can cream of chicken soup
Salt and pepper to taste

2 tablespoons poppy seeds
1½ rolls of Ritz crackers
1 stick butter, melted
Poppy seeds for topping

Combine chicken, sour cream, soup, salt, pepper, and 2 tablespoons of poppy seeds. Crumble Ritz crackers on top of casserole and pour melted butter over cracker crumbs. Sprinkle top with poppy seeds. Bake at 325 degrees for 1 hour.

Ginny Ratchford

Poulet Chasseur

I learned this recipe when I took gourmet cooking lessons from Mme. Phillipe Bret in Montpellier, France.

May be prepared ahead   Serves 4

½ pound very small white
  onions or 1 large white
  onion, sliced
1 tablespoon butter
1 tablespoon oil
4 chicken breasts
1 cup beef bouillon

½ pound fresh mushrooms,
  sliced
Salt and pepper to taste
2 tablespoons heavy cream
Fresh parsley, chopped

Sauté the onions in the butter and oil in a large pot on high heat for 2 or 3 minutes. If using sliced onions, remove the onions from the pot. If using small onions, leave them in the pot. Brown the chicken. Add the bouillon, mushrooms, salt, pepper, and onions, if they were removed. When the bouillon comes to a boil, cover and reduce heat to low. Cook for approximately 30 minutes per pound of chicken. When done, remove chicken from pot. Add the cream to the gravy in the pot and stir thoroughly.

You may serve the gravy over the chicken or on the side. Garnish with chopped parsley.

Mrs. Elizabeth Neisler Sumner

Chicken Breasts Lombardy

Serve immediately   Serves 8

6 whole chicken breasts; boned,   **¾ cup dry white wine**
  skinned, and quartered   **½ cup chicken stock**
½ cup flour   **½ cup mozzarella cheese,**
1 cup butter, divided   **shredded**
Salt and pepper   **½ cup Parmesan cheese,**
1½ cups mushrooms, sliced   **grated**

Place each piece of chicken between 2 sheets of waxed paper and flatten to ⅛-inch thickness using a meat mallet or rolling pin. Dredge chicken lightly with flour. Place 4 pieces at a time in 2 tablespoons melted butter in a large skillet. Cook over low heat for 3 to 4 minutes on each side or until golden brown. Place chicken in a greased 13 x 9 x 2-inch baking dish, overlapping edges. Sprinkle with salt and pepper to taste. Repeat procedure with remaining chicken, adding 2 tablespoons butter to skillet each time. Reserve drippings in skillet.

Sauté mushrooms in ¼ cup melted butter until tender; drain and sprinkle evenly over chicken. Stir wine and chicken stock into drippings in skillet. Simmer for 10 minutes, stirring occasionally. Stir in ½ teaspoon salt and ⅛ teaspoon pepper. Spoon about ⅓ of sauce evenly over chicken, reserving remainder. Combine cheeses and sprinkle over chicken. Bake at 450 degrees for 10 to 12 minutes. Place under broiler 1 to 2 minutes or until lightly browned. Serve with reserved sauce.

Mrs. Mona L. Fulton

Romertopf Chicken

Prepare same day   Serves 4-6
Freezes well

1-3½ pound chicken   **⅔ cup dry white wine or**
1 clove garlic, pressed   **red wine**
1 tablespoon dried herbs

Soak romertopf (clay pot) for ten mintues. Truss the chicken. Rub chicken with garlic and put in pot. Add ⅔ cup wine. Sprinkle dried herbs over chicken. Cover pot and place in a cold oven. Bake at 450 degrees for 1½ hours.

Mrs. Norman Hull-Ryde

Chicken Stuffed With Crab

Serve immediately   Serves 6

1 pound fresh crab
1-8 ounce package cream cheese
3 egg yolks
2 teaspoons Worcestershire
  sauce

8 chicken breasts, boned
Eggs, 2 or more
1 to 2 cloves garlic, crushed
Ritz crackers
Real butter

Sauce:
1 cup sour cream

4 tablespoons Dijon mustard

Combine crab, cream cheese, egg yolks, and Worcestershire sauce. Pound chicken breasts to ¼-inch thickness. Pat hefty tablespoon of mixture in center of chicken breast and roll up. (May need to secure with toothpicks.) Chill! Dip chilled chicken breast in eggs, beaten with garlic. Roll in Ritz cracker crumbs. Sauté in butter. Serve with warmed sour cream and Dijon mustard.

Mrs. William P. Adams (Becky)

Quick And Easy Chicken Squares

*Quick for the family but nice enough
to serve at a ladies' luncheon.*

Serve immediately   Serves 4

2-5 ounce cans boned chicken
1-3 ounce package cream
  cheese with chives

Dash of pepper
1-8 ounce package crescent
  rolls

Stir chicken into softened cream cheese. Add pepper. Separate crescent dough into 4 rectangles; firmly press perforations to seal. Spoon ¼ of chicken mixture onto each rectangle. Pull 4 corners of dough around the chicken mixture and seal together on top and sides. Bake at 350 degrees for 25 minutes.

Mrs. Gail Hardin

Chicken Spectacular

May be frozen before baking   Serves 12

3 cups cooked chicken
1 box Uncle Ben's wild rice,
  cooked
1 can cream of celery soup
2 cups frozen French-style
  green beans

1 cup mayonnaise
1 small can sliced
  mushrooms
1 can sliced water chestnuts
1 medium jar chopped
  pimento
1 medium onion, chopped

Mix all ingredients together. Place in a large flat casserole dish. Bake at 350 degrees for 30 minutes. The last few minutes of baking, add crushed potato chips to the top if you choose.

Ms. Carol G. Matthews

Spanish Chicken And Rice

Serve immediately   Serves 6

1 teaspoon garlic powder
1 teaspoon celery salt
1 teaspoon paprika
1-3 pound chicken broiler,
  cut up
1 cup uncooked rice
¾ cup onion, chopped
¾ cup green pepper, chopped

¼ cup parsley, chopped
1½ cups chicken broth
1 cup canned tomatoes,
  drained and chopped
1½ teaspoons salt
1½ teaspoons chili powder

Blend garlic powder, celery salt, and paprika and sprinkle on chicken. Place skin side up in a greased, shallow, 2½-quart casserole or a 9 x 13-inch pan. Bake at 425 degrees for 20 minutes. Push chicken to one side. Add rice, onion, green pepper, and parsley. In a saucepan combine remaining ingredients and heat to boiling. Pour over rice mixture and stir well. Arrange chicken on rice, cover and continue baking for 30 minutes longer or until rice is tender and all liquid is absorbed.

Mrs. John M. Templeton (Beth)

Wyman Chicken and Wild Rice

This recipe was given to me by Mrs. Frank Wyman (Margaret),
one of our Camp Seafarer doctors' wives. Mrs. Wyman lives in Columbia
and is a member of the Junior League. She has used
this recipe many times for large dinner parties.

May prepare ahead   Serves 20

5 to 6 pounds chicken
3-6½ ounce boxes Uncle Ben's
  quick-cooking wild rice
1 large onion
1 stick margarine
6 tablespoons flour
2½ cups milk

3-10¾ ounce cans
  mushroom soup
2-3 ounce cans sliced
  mushrooms
1½ teaspoons salt
½ teaspoon pepper
1 pound Cheddar cheese,
  grated

Cook chicken breasts or fryers; bone and cut into bite-size pieces. Set aside. Cook rice according to directions on box and set aside. To prepare sauce, sauté onion in butter until transparent. Add flour. Mix 2½ cups of milk and 3 cans of soup. Add to onion and flour. Add drained mushrooms, salt, and pepper. Set aside. Spray two 13 x 9-inch Pyrex dishes with Pam. Layer sauce on bottom of each dish. Next layer the rice; then the chicken; then the remainder of sauce; and finally the cheese. Bake at 350 degrees for 30 to 45 minutes.

Mrs. Carl Ellis Fisher

Country Captain

This is an original recipe from the late Mrs. W. L. Bullard
of Columbus, Georgia. We have enjoyed this many times
especially when we go to Columbus for a great Sunday family
dinner. It feeds as many as you need if you just add more chicken.

Prepare same day   Serves 8-10

Choice pieces from 2 chickens
Flour to coat chicken
Salt and pepper to coat chicken
Shortening or oil to fry chicken
2 onions, finely chopped
2 green peppers, chopped
1 small garlic clove
1 teaspoon salt
½ teaspoon white pepper

2 teaspoons curry powder
2 cans of tomatoes
1 teaspoon parsley, chopped
1 teaspoon thyme
3 tablespoons currants
½ pound blanched, roasted
    almonds, divided
2 to 3 cups uncooked rice
Parsley

Remove skin from chicken and dredge in flour, salt, and pepper. Fry until golden in hot shortening. Remove chicken from the skillet, but keep it hot. This is a secret of the dish.

Add to 1 cup of the same oil onions, green peppers, and garlic. Cook very slowly, stirring constantly. Season with a "good" teaspoon of salt, white pepper, and two "good" teaspoons of curry powder. Add 2 cans of tomatoes, chopped parsley, and thyme. Pour mixture over chicken in a roaster. If mixture does not cover the chicken, add water. Cover and cook in a 350-degree oven about 45 minutes. Add ¼ pound of the almonds and the currants. Cook the rice and pile in center of large platter. Place chicken around rice and pour the sauce over the rice. Sprinkle remaining ¼ pound of almonds over the sauce. Garnish with parsley.

Cathy McCosh

Chicken Divan I

This recipe came from a caterer in Gainesville, Florida.
Every time I serve this, I am asked to share this recipe. It is excellent!

May prepare ahead   Serves 12

2-10 ounce boxes frozen
  broccoli, cooked or steamed
1 cup Parmesan cheese, grated
1 cup cooked rice

4 chicken breasts, cooked in
  1½ cups water with
  carrots and celery

Sauce:
1 stick butter
½ cup flour
2 cups chicken broth or
  chicken bouillon

1 can evaporated milk
1 cup sour cream
1 teaspoon lemon juice
½ cup Hellman's mayonnaise

To prepare sauce: Melt butter, blend flour, and stir in broth or bouillon
and milk until thickened and smooth. Add sour cream, lemon juice, and
mayonnaise; remove from heat.

To prepare recipe: Line 3-quart casserole dish with broccoli and sprinkle
with one half of the cheese. Drizzle a little sauce, layer boned chicken,
layer all of rice, sprinkle remaining cheese, then pour sauce over all.

Topping:
½ stick butter, melted
½ cup bread crumbs

½ cup Parmesan cheese, grated
1 teaspoon paprika

Mix together all topping ingredients and spread on top of recipe. Bake
for 30 minutes at 400 degrees.

Trinie Terry

Chicken Divan II

We have used this recipe since 1960 and always get raves!

May prepare ahead   Serves 6
Freezes well after cooking

2-10 ounce packages frozen
  broccoli or 2 bunches
  fresh broccoli
2 cups sliced cooked chicken
  or 3 chicken breasts, cooked
  and boned
2-10¾ ounce cans condensed
  cream of chicken soup
1 cup mayonnaise or salad
  dressing

1 tablespoon lemon juice
½ teaspoon curry powder
½ cup sharp process
  cheese, shredded
½ cup soft bread crumbs
1 tablespoon butter or
  margarine, melted
Pimento strips
Parsley

Cook broccoli in boiling salted water until tender; drain. Arrange broccoli in greased 11½ x 7½ x 1½-inch baking dish. Place chicken on top. Combine soup, mayonnaise, lemon juice, and curry powder; pour over chicken. Sprinkle with cheese. Combine bread crumbs and butter, and sprinkle over top. Bake in a moderate 350-degree oven for 25 to 30 minutes or until thoroughly heated and bubbly. Trim with pimento strips and parsley.

Mrs. Paul Quinn

Chicken And Dumplings

Must prepare ahead   Serves 6

Early in the day put a large chicken or hen in a stew pot and cover with water. Add salt and pepper to taste. Bring to a boil and reduce heat and simmer until meat is falling off bone. Remove chicken and let cool. Bone chicken and put back in pot.

Dumplings:
6 tablespoons margarine or
  butter
2 tablespoons Crisco
1 cup milk

1½ teaspoons salt
1 egg, beaten
3 cups flour

Melt butter and Crisco. Add milk, then salt and egg. Stir in flour and mix well. Chill at least one hour. Roll out thin and cut in strips. Bring chicken and broth to a boil and drop dumplings in and cook for 10 to 15 minutes.

Ginny Hall (Mrs. Alex)

Chicken Tetrazzini

*This recipe was given to me by Jim's aunt, Mrs. Samuel A. McCosh,
from Forsyth, Georgia. We have enjoyed this when visiting them at the family
home which was a Confederate hospital during the Civil War.*

Serve immediately   Serves 6-8

1-5 to 6 pound hen
1 small box thin spaghetti
1 cup chicken broth
1 tablespoon celery salt
3 cups Cheddar cheese, grated

½ cup chopped pimento
2-10¾ ounce cans cream of
  mushroom soup
1 large onion, chopped
1 can mushrooms

Boil chicken until tender and remove meat from bones; cut into bite-
size pieces. Cook spaghetti until tender and drain. Mix rest of ingredients
and pour into a buttered casserole. Bake at 350 degrees for 1 hour.

Cathy McCosh

Martha Love's Chicken Jubilee

Must prepare ahead   Serves 8

4 fryers, halved
2 teaspoons salt
¼ teaspoon pepper
½ cup butter, melted
1 cup water
½ cup raisins
1 tablespoon Worcestershire
  sauce
½ cup brown sugar

1-12 ounce bottle chili
  sauce
1 teaspoon garlic salt
  (optional)
2 medium onions, sliced
  (optional)
1-16 ounce can Bing cherries
1 cup sherry

Place chicken in shallow roasting pan, skin side up. Season and dribble
with butter. Brown under medium flame. Combine remaining ingredients, except canned cherries and wine. Mix thoroughly. Pour over
chicken and cover pan with aluminum foil. Bake an hour (or longer)
in a 325-degree oven. Add wine and cherries. Remove foil the last 15
minutes of roasting time. To serve, place on a platter and pour sauce
over all.

Mrs. W. J. Pharr (Catherine)

Chicken and Asparagus Casserole

Freezes well   Serves 6-8

2 cans asparagus, drained
2 to 4 chicken breasts, cooked
  and chopped
2-10¾ ounce cans cream of
  chicken soup

1 cup mayonnaise
1 tablespoon lemon juice
1 cup sharp Cheddar cheese,
  grated
1 cup bread crumbs

Layer asparagus in buttered 9 x 13-inch pan. Layer chicken. Mix soup, mayonnaise, and lemon juice; pour over chicken. Top with cheese and bread crumbs. Bake 350 degrees for 30 to 40 minutes.

Mrs. Cathy Foster

Fried Chicken

Serve immediately   Serves 6-8

½ quart buttermilk
1 tablespoon poultry seasoning
2-3 pound chickens, cut in
  pieces or chicken parts
  already cut

1 tablespoon salt, divided
4½ cups flour, divided
Vegetable oil for frying

In a large bowl combine the buttermilk, poultry seasoning, ½ tablespoon of salt, and ½ cup flour. Mix well. Place 4 cups flour and ½ tablespoon of salt in another large bowl or baking pan. Dip chicken pieces in batter and then roll them in the flour. In a heavy skillet (preferably cast iron) add about 1 inch of oil. Heat oil over high heat to about 375 degrees. Add chicken pieces and reduce heat to medium. Cook 10 to 12 minutes on each side, or until dark golden-brown. Do not allow oil to smoke (if it looks too hot adjust as you go along). Turn up the heat just before flipping the chicken pieces (this seals the batter when you flip), then return to medium.

Mrs. James S. Stewart

Hot Chicken Salad I

Freezes well   Serves 4-6

1-10¾ ounce can cream of
   chicken soup
½ cup Hellman's mayonnaise
2 tablespoons soy sauce
2 tablespoons lemon juice
2 cups cooked chicken, cubed
1½ cups celery, chopped

1 small can sliced water
   chestnuts
½ cup green onion, sliced
8 ounces twist macaroni,
   cooked 5 minutes and
   drained
1 cup chow mein noodles

In bowl stir together soup, mayonnaise, soy sauce, and lemon juice until blended. Stir in chicken, celery, water chestnuts, and green onion. Add macaroni and toss to coat well. Spoon into a 2-quart casserole. Top with chow mein noodles. Bake at 375 degrees for 20 to 25 minutes or until heated.

Mrs. Andrew H. Rutledge, Jr.

Hot Chicken Salad II

May prepare ahead   Serves 4-6

2 cups chicken, chopped
1 can water chestnuts
Celery salt to taste
1 cup cheese, grated
1 cup mayonnaise

½ cup sliced almonds
2 ounces chopped pimento
Salt and pepper to taste
1 can French fried onion
   rings

Mix all ingredients except onion rings and put in shallow baking pan. Cover with onion rings and bake at 350 degrees for 20 minutes.

Cacky Moser

Hot Chicken Salad Casserole
This is my most requested recipe and is one that men like.

Must prepare ahead   Serves 8

8 chicken breasts
1 bottle of clear French
  dressing (Girard's is good)
1 cup celery, chopped
1 cup mayonnaise

1 cup pecans or almonds
  (optional)
1 pound jar Cheese Whiz
1 can French fried onion
  rings

Day before boil chicken, cool, remove from bones, and cut into bite-size pieces. Toss in French dressing and marinate overnight. Next day add celery and mayonnaise to taste to make a chicken salad. Add nuts if desired. Place in baking dish and cover with jar of cheese spread. Cook at 350 degrees for ½ hour or a little longer if not starting from room temperature. Put can of onions on top and bake 5 minutes longer.

Janice Stowe

Lemon Chicken

Must start 1 day ahead   Serves 6

1 medium onion, sliced
3 pounds chicken pieces
¼ cup olive oil
¼ cup lemon juice
1 clove garlic, crushed
  (optional)

1 teaspoon crushed oregano
4 teaspoons butter, melted
3 teaspoons water
Salt and pepper to taste
3 large potatoes, peeled
  and sliced

Slice onion and spread on bottom of baking pan. Place chicken pieces on top of onion. Mix together the rest of the ingredients except potatoes. Pour over chicken, cover with foil, and marinate all night in refrigerator. Bake uncovered at 425 degrees until lightly browned. Turn chicken pieces and baste. Add peeled and sliced potatoes and cover with aluminum foil. Reduce temperature to 325 degrees and bake for 1 to 1½ hours. Uncover, baste, and turn chicken pieces; baste and bake at 400 degrees until potatoes and chicken are lightly browned.

Tami Pearson

Sesame Chicken

Must prepare 12 hours ahead   Serves 8
Freezes well

½ cup soy sauce
¼ cup water
½ cup vegetable oil
2 tablespoons onion, minced
⅛ teaspoon red pepper
2 tablespoons sesame seeds

1 tablespoon sugar
¾ teaspoon salt
½ teaspoon instant minced
  garlic
2 chickens

Combine above ingredients except chicken. Cut chickens into quarters or pieces and pour mixture over chicken and marinate for 12 hours. Cook chicken on grill until done.

Mrs. Davis Patton

George's Barbequed Chicken on the Grill

Must prepare ahead   Serves any number

Boil chicken parts in salt water for 20 minutes and refrigerate overnight, covered in your favorite barbeque sauce. Grill the next day on low heat, basting with sauce until crispy and done. Variation: You may use thick center cut pork chops as an alternative.

Margie Kircus

Reid's Favorite Charcoaled Chicken

Must prepare ahead   Serves 2-4

½ cup Wesson oil (or ¼ cup
  Wesson and ¼ cup olive oil)
1 envelope Good Seasons
  Italian dressing mix

¼ cup lemon juice (fresh)
1 whole fryer, halved or
  quartered

Mix together oil, dressing, and lemon juice. Pour over chicken (bone side up) and marinate overnight or for several hours. Charcoal over large bed of coals which have begun to turn gray for 1 hour to 1 hour and 20 minutes turning and basting with sauce every 10 minutes or so.

Mrs. Nancy McLeod Reid

195

Roasted Hen or Turkey Breast

May prepare ahead

Serves 6-8

3 to 6 pound hen or turkey
breast
2 tablespoons peanut, corn,
or vegetable oil
Salt and pepper to taste
1 teaspoon thyme, crushed
1 teaspoon rosemary, crushed

1 clove garlic, peeled
1 bay leaf
2 onions, peeled and cut
in half
1 carrot, cut in pieces
1-10¾ ounce can chicken
broth

Preheat oven to 450 degrees. Rub hen inside and out with oil. Sprinkle with salt and pepper. Rub with thyme and rosemary. Put garlic clove and bay leaf inside, and place hen in a roasting pan (I do not use a rack). Put onion and carrot around the hen. Bake at 450 degrees for 45 minutes. Cover loosely with foil and bake for 30 minutes. Pour broth over hen and cover loosely with foil. Bake at 350 degrees for 30 minutes more or until done. May thicken gravy with arrowroot or flour.

Mary Jane Stewart

Turkey Breast

Must prepare ahead

Serves 4-6

1½ sticks of butter
1-5 to 7 pound turkey breast
Juice of ½ lemon
(approximately ⅛ cup)
2 teaspoons salt

½ teaspoon pepper
2 celery stalks
2 medium-small onions
1 cup hot water

Clarify the butter. Wash the turkey breast and wipe dry. Rub the lemon juice on the entire turkey breast, inside and outside. Then rub on the mixture of salt and pepper.

Coat inside and outside with the melted clarified butter. Be generous particularly in the cavities. Then "stuff" with pieces of celery and large pieces of onion. Secure with skewers and place in a shallow pan, meat side up. Pour 1 cup very hot water in the pan and bake at 350 degrees approximately 2½ hours or until meat thermometer registers 180 degrees. You must baste the turkey every 30 minutes. Serve hot, or if you plan to serve it cold, cool at room temperature or remove skewers and cover with plastic wrap and refrigerate.

Tami Pearson

Turkey In A Bag

*I've been doing my turkey this way for about 10 years,
and I've never been disappointed. The turkey is always moist
and beautifully browned.*

Must start a few hours ahead   Serves 8-12

Prepare the turkey precisely the same way you would any turkey, complete with stuffing* or not. (Salt and pepper the turkey and grease with margarine.)

Next slide the turkey into a brown grocery paper bag. Be sure there are no holes in it. Twist the end shut and tie with a string or twist tie. If your turkey is big, just slip another bag on the open end. Place your bagged bird on the rack of your broiler pan. Place in a preheated 325-degree oven. The bag will not scorch at this temperature.

Turkey which is 12 pounds or under is roasted at 25 minutes per pound; over 12 pounds, allow 20 minutes per pound. I usually cook it 30 minutes longer.

When cooking time is up, lift rack and all to the top of stove. Some of the juices may have seeped through to the drip pan,but a lot will still be in the bag. Carefully tear sack away, allowing juices to run into drip pan. Slide turkey to platter. Remove the rack and make gravy right in pan.

GRAVY: Put browned flour in drippings using a whisk to stir lumps out. Then add liquid broth to desired consistency. Salt to taste.

BROTH: Cook giblets and neck in large amount of water. You may add giblets, if you like, to gravy.

*Dressing For Stuffed Turkey:

Cornbread (I use bags of cornbread mix)
1 onion, chopped
2 or 3 slices raw bacon, chopped
Salt and pepper to taste

Toasted bread (Use equal amounts of cornbread and toasted bread)
1 or 2 ribs of celery, chopped

Mix and stuff neck cavity first. Sew up skin with a needle and thread. Then stuff body before cooking.

Ginny Hall (Mrs. Alex)

Crab and Artichoke Casserole

This is great served with tossed salad, bread and a green vegetable.

Serve immediately   Serves 10-12

1 stick margarine
3 tablespoons onions,
  chopped
½ cup flour
1 quart half-n-half, heated
  to boiling
½ cup Madeira
Salt and pepper to taste
2 tablespoons lemon juice

4 cups canned crab meat
3-9 ounce packages frozen
  artichoke hearts, cooked
  according to directions
2½ cups shell macaroni,
  cooked and drained
2 cups Swiss cheese, grated
Paprika

Preheat oven to 350 degrees. Melt margarine in a large heavy pan. Sauté onion. Stir in flour, cooking over low heat until flour is pale yellow. Remove from heat. Add cream and stir. Return to moderate heat and stir until sauce comes to boil. Reduce heat and add Madeira. Season with salt and pepper. Pour lemon juice over crab meat, toss lightly. Combine crab meat, cooked hearts, cooked macaroni, and sauce in a 6-quart buttered casserole. Sprinkle with cheese and then with paprika. Bake for 25 to 30 minutes until heated thoroughly.

Mrs. Susan B. Garrett

Crab Meat Puget

Serve immediately   Serves 10-12

1 can cream of shrimp soup
⅔ cup milk
¼ cup New York sharp Cheddar
  cheese, grated
½ cup mayonnaise
1 pound crab meat

2 cups raw thin noodles
1 cup water chestnuts,
  sliced
1 can fried onion rings or
  Chinese noodles or
  Pepperidge Farm crumbs

Heat soup, milk, cheese, mayonnaise, crab meat, and noodles. Mix until smooth. Add water chestnuts. Put in greased casserole. Cover and bake at 350 degrees for 30 minutes. Uncover and top with crumbs or other topping. Bake 10 minutes longer.

Mrs. Marilyn Johnson

Crab Supreme

Serve immediately   Serves 8-10

1 cup celery, chopped
2-13 ounce cans crab meat or
  1 pound fresh crab meat
1 medium onion, chopped
¼ cup green pepper, chopped
½ cup mayonnaise

8 slices bread, chopped
4 eggs, beaten
3 cups milk
1 can cream of mushroom soup
1 cup sharp Cheddar cheese,
  grated
Salt and pepper to taste

Cook celery in small amount of water for 5 minutes. Mix crab, onion, celery, green pepper, and mayonnaise. Put 4 slices of chopped bread in casserole. Spoon crab mixture over top. Add remaining 4 slices of chopped bread. Beat eggs and milk and add salt and pepper to taste. Pour over bread crumbs. Spoon soup on top. Cook at 325 degrees for 1 hour, adding grated cheese last 10 to 15 minutes.

Clarissa Craig

Pawley's Baked Crab

This is great with fresh asparagus or fresh broccoli with cheese sauce.

Serve immediately   Serves 4

1 pound fresh lump crab meat
½ cup celery, finely chopped
1½ teaspoons fresh lemon juice
¼ teaspoon salt (or less)
¾ to 1 cup Hellman's
  mayonnaise
2 tablespoons butter, melted
1½ teaspoons Worcestershire
  sauce

½ cup Progresso seasoned
  bread crumbs
2 hard-boiled eggs, chopped
  or grated
1½ teaspoons Dijon
  mustard
Dash cayenne pepper

Preheat oven to 400 degrees. Combine all ingredients, leaving crab meat in as big lumps as possible. Place in a 2-quart casserole that has been sprayed with Pam. Bake 15 to 20 minutes (may take longer if casserole has been refrigerated).

Mrs. Charlton Torrence (Sis)

Blackened Redfish

Serve immediately   Serves 6

¾ pound (3 sticks) unsalted
   butter, melted in a skillet

6-8 to 10 ounce fish fillets
   (preferably redfish,
   pompano or tilefish) cut
   about ½-inch thick

Seasoning mix:
1 tablespoon sweet paprika
1 teaspoon onion powder
1 teaspoon ground red
   pepper (preferably cayenne)
½ teaspoon dried thyme
   leaves

2½ teaspoons salt
1 teaspoon garlic powder
¾ teaspoon white pepper
¾ teaspoon black pepper
½ teaspoon dried oregano
   leaves

Melt the butter in a small skillet. Heat a second (large cast-iron) skillet over very high heat until it is beyond the smoking stage and you see white ash in the skillet bottom (the skillet cannot be too hot for this dish), at least 10 minutes. Meanwhile, pour 2 tablespoons melted butter in each of 6 small ramekins; set aside and keep warm. Reserve the remaining butter. Heat the serving plates in a 250-degree oven.

Thoroughly combine the seasoning mix ingredients in a small bowl. Dip each fillet in the reserved melted butter so that both sides are well coated; then sprinkle seasoning mix generously and evenly on both sides of the fillets, patting it in by hand. Place in the hot skillet and pour 1 teaspoon melted butter on top of each fillet (be careful, as the butter may flame up). Cook, uncovered, over the same high heat until the underside looks charred, about 2 minutes (the time will vary according to the fillet's thickness and the heat of the skillet). Turn the fish over and again pour 1 teaspoon butter on top; cook until fish is done, about 2 minutes more. Repeat with remaining fillets. Serve each fillet while piping hot.

To serve, place one fillet and a ramekin of butter on each heated serving plate.

Lin Lineberger

Escoveitch Fish

Escoveitch fish and variations of this dish can be found in many Latin American countries. This particular recipe comes from our housekeeper who cooked for us in Jamaica. The dish originated in southern France and Spain where it appears as "escabeche".

May prepare ahead   Serves 4

**2 pounds fresh fish (red
   snapper is best)
Freshly ground black pepper**

**Juice of 2 fresh limes
Salt
Cooking oil**

**Sauce:
1 green pepper, cut into strips
2 medium onions, sliced
2 hot peppers, sliced**

**2 tablespoons whole
   allspice
1 cup vinegar
Salt to taste**

Clean and wash fish; rub them with lime juice, and dry them with a kitchen cloth. Sprinkle fish on both sides and inside with salt and pepper. Heat oil in a frying pan until very hot and begins to smoke slightly. Place the fish one at a time into the pan. Reduce heat slightly and fry on both sides. When the fish flakes, remove and drain. Arrange on a large platter.

Sauce: In a saucepan combine green pepper, onions, hot peppers, whole allspice, vinegar, and salt to taste. Bring the mixture to a boil, simmer for 2 minutes, and remove from the heat. Pour this hot "pickling" sauce over the fish and arrange on the platter. The fish can be left to marinate in the pickling sauce for up to 2 days. I prefer to serve the dish immediately, particularly while the ingredients are still crisp.

Mrs. Kenneth W. Harvey (Cathy)

Grilled Monkfish
(Poor man's lobster)

*This is a most unique fish. It really does taste like
lobster and because it is a thick fish, it grills beautifully.*

Can be prepared ahead   Serves 4

4 pieces of Monkfish   **1 stick butter, melted**
1 bottle Viva Italian dressing **¼ cup lemon juice, fresh**
Salt and pepper to taste   **squeezed**

Wash and dry pieces of fish. Place in a large glass baking dish and pour
dressing evenly over each fish. Sprinkle with salt and freshly ground
pepper. Let marinate for at least 1 hour.

When coals are very hot, place fish on grill and cover. Cook on each side
6 to 10 minutes, turning only once. Just before fish are done, mix melted
butter and lemon juice and drizzle over fish.

Sharron Davis

Oriental-Style Flounder

Serve immediately   Serves 4

Freshly ground pepper to taste   **½ teaspoon fresh lemon**
2 cloves of garlic, minced   **juice**
½ teaspoon powdered ginger   **1 teaspoon soy sauce**
2 tablespoons peanut oil   **1½ pounds flounder fillets**

Make marinade with pepper, garlic, ginger, peanut oil, lemon juice, and
soy sauce. Grease pan or line with foil. Marinate fillets in pan 20 to 30
minutes, reserving some marinade for basting later. Broil about
6 minutes or until they lose translucency and flake when touched with
a fork. Baste fillets 2 or 3 times while cooking.

Alternate method of cooking using wok and bamboo steamer: Bring
water to boil in wok. Line bamboo steamer with cabbage leaves. Place
fillets on top of cabbage leaves. Pour all of marinade over fillets. Cover
with top of bamboo steamer. Cook 10 minutes per inch of thickness or
until fillets flake when touched with fork.

Mrs. David Allen Smith (Ada Ellen)

Flounder Fillets in Shrimp Sauce

Serve immediately   Serves 2

2-16 ounce flounder fillets
1 teaspoon lemon juice
1 tablespoon dry white wine

1½ cups water
½ pound unpeeled small
   shrimp

Sauce:
2 tablespoons butter
2 tablespoons flour
¾ cup milk
½ teaspoon salt
¼ teaspoon dried whole
   tarragon
1-3 ounce can sliced
   mushrooms, drained

2 tablespoons dry white
   wine
1½ teaspoons parsley,
   chopped
¼ teaspoon Worcestershire
   sauce

Fillets: Place fillets in a shallow dish. Combine lemon juice and 1 table-spoon wine; pour over fillets. Cover and chill for at least 1 hour.

Shrimp: Bring water to boil; add shrimp, and return to a boil. Reduce heat and simmer, uncovered, 3 to 5 minutes or until shrimp are pink. (Precooked shrimp may be substituted.) Drain well, and rinse with cold water. Peel and devein. Set aside.

Sauce: Melt butter in a heavy saucepan over low heat; add flour, stir-ring until smooth. Cook 1 minute, stirring constantly. Gradually add milk; cook over medium heat, stirring constantly until thickened and bubbly. Stir in the remaining sauce ingredients and the shrimp. Drain fillets, roll up, and place seamside down in a lightly greased baking dish. Pour sauce over top and bake uncovered at 375 degrees for 25 minutes, basting occasionally with sauce.

Mrs. Holt Anthony Harris

Sybil Arant's Catfish Baked With Cheese

Serve immediately   Serves 6-8

6 to 8 catfish fillets, about
  3 pounds
Milk to soak fish
½ cup Parmesan cheese,
  freshly grated (you can use
  canned cheese)
½ cup flour

Salt and pepper to taste
1 teaspoon paprika
1 egg, lightly beaten
1 tablespoon milk
1 stick margarine, melted
¼ cup slivered almonds

Salt and pepper fish and soak them in milk for at least 30 minutes (the longer you soak them, the more moist they will be). Blend together the cheese, flour, salt, pepper, and paprika. Combine the egg and 1 tablespoon milk in a flat dish. Dip the fillets in the egg mixture and then coat with the cheese mixture. Arrange the fillets in one layer in a baking dish and pour the melted butter over each fillet. Use enough butter to keep the fish from sticking to the pan. Sprinkle the almonds on top and bake at 350 degrees for 20 minutes. Broil fish for 3 to 5 minutes to brown almonds and cheese.

Note: if you need more cheese mixture, just be sure to use equal amounts of cheese and flour when increasing the amounts.

Cathy McCosh

Marinated Salmon Steaks

Must prepare ahead   Serves 4

4 salmon steaks
¾ cup brandy or vermouth
¼ teaspoon marjoram
⅛ teaspoon rosemary
⅛ teaspoon sage
½ teaspoon thyme

¾ cup salad oil
2 tablespoons lemon juice
¾ teaspoon salt
¼ teaspoon pepper
1½ teaspoons parsley

Mix all ingredients except salmon. Let stand for 5 minutes. Mix ingredients again and pour over salmon steaks. Let covered salmon steaks marinate in refrigerator at least 4 hours or overnight, turning once. Grill over very hot coals, or broil in oven, for 7 to 8 minutes on each side. Garnish with parsley.

Mrs. Elizabeth Neisler Sumner

Scalloped Oysters

Serve immediately   Serves 6

1 stick unsalted butter, melted   **1 quart oysters**
1 bag Pepperidge Farm   **2 tablespoons milk or cream**
stuffing mix

Melt butter. Mix together all ingredients. Put in greased baking dish.
Bake for 30 minutes at 350 degrees.

Anne Hull-Ryde

Spa Pasta With Scallops

Serve immediately   Serves 4-6

1½ cups vegetable stock   **1 tablespoon Dijon mustard**
or water   **2 tablespoons Neufchatel**
2 tablespoons shallots, sliced   **cream cheese**
½ tablespoon tarragon,   **1 teaspoon lime juice**
chopped   **1 pound fresh fettuccini or**
Dash white pepper   **linguine**
Dash nutmeg   **12 large sea scallops, sliced**
1 bunch asparagus, stems   **into thirds**
separated from tops   **2 tablespoons chives, chopped**
¼ cup dry white wine

Combine vegetable stock, shallots, tarragon, pepper, and nutmeg in
saucepan. Bring to boil over medium heat. Add asparagus stems. Cook
2 minutes. Add asparagus tops and wine, cooking until tender. Remove
asparagus tops, slice into small rounds and reserve. In blender combine
contents of saucepan with mustard, cream cheese, and lime juice. Blend
30 to 60 seconds or until smooth. Strain through cheesecloth or metal
strainer. (Sauce can be prepared in advance to this point.)

Cook pasta until al dente. Drain well. Return sauce to pan. Add scallops
and simmer over medium heat 30 to 45 seconds. Be careful not to overcook. Add pasta and asparagus tips to sauce. Toss lightly. Garnish with
chives.

Lin Lineberger

Seafood Linguine

This dish is well worth the effort.

Serve immediately   Serves 6

2 cups fresh mushrooms, sliced
(about 6 ounces)
4 shallots or green onions,
finely chopped
½ cup butter or margarine
1½ cups Madeira wine
1 tablespoon tomato paste
1 tablespoon fresh snipped
tarragon or 1 teaspoon
dried tarragon, crushed
¼ teaspoon salt
Fresh tarragon sprigs (optional)

Dash freshly ground black
pepper
10 ounces linguine,
spaghetti, or other
pasta
1½ pounds fresh or frozen
shelled shrimp
4 cups boiling water
1½ cups whipping cream
4 egg yolks, beaten
Salt to taste
Freshly ground black pepper

In a 10-inch skillet cook mushrooms and shallots in the butter or margarine over medium-high heat for 4-5 minutes or until vegetables are tender but not brown. Remove with slotted spoon and set aside. Stir wine, tomato paste, tarragon, salt, and pepper into skillet. Bring to a boil. Boil vigorously for 10 minutes or until mixture is reduced to ½ cup. Meanwhile cook pasta according to package directions. Drain; keep warm. Drop fresh or frozen shrimp into boiling water, return to boiling. Reduce heat and simmer for 1 to 3 minutes or until shrimp turn pink. Drain; keep warm. In a small bowl stir together whipping cream and egg yolks; add the wine mixture. Return to skillet. Cook and stir until thickened. Stir in the shrimp and mushroom mixture; heat thoroughly. Season to taste with salt and pepper. Toss with the cooked pasta. Transfer to a serving platter. Garnish with fresh tarragon sprigs.

Mrs. Alex Hall (Ginny)

Jambalya

Serve immediately   Serves 6

1 stick butter	1 teaspoon salt
3 tablespoons onion	1 teaspoon pepper
3 tablespoons flour	1 bay leaf
2 cups clam juice	1 green pepper, chopped
1 can tomatoes	1 cup clams
1 teaspoon parsley	1 cup oysters
1 cup uncooked long grain rice	2 cups shrimp

Melt butter; add onions, sauté until translucent. Stir in flour; add 1 cup clam juice to make paste. Add tomatoes, parsley, rice, salt, bay leaf, and green pepper. Cook covered over low heat until rice is tender and liquid is absorbed. Add shrimp, clams, oysters, and remaining 1 cup clam juice; heat for 5 minutes until oysters begin to curl.

Carolyn Sumner

Oyster Casserole

A must at Christmas dinner.

May prepare ahead   Serves 4-6

1½ cups coarse cracker crumbs	Dash of nutmeg
8 tablespoons butter, melted	2 tablespoons parsley, chopped (optional)
1 pint oysters	¼ cup oyster liquor
½ teaspoon salt	2 tablespoons milk
⅛ teaspoon pepper	

Combine cracker crumbs and butter. Put thin layer in bottom of a 1-quart casserole dish; alternate layers of oysters and crumb mixture, sprinkling each layer with seasonings. Never use more than 2 layers of oysters. Pour oyster liquor and milk over layers; top with crumbs. Bake at 450 degrees for 30 minutes.

For a different flavor substitute canned cream of mushroom soup for all the liquids.

Mrs. T. Dale Ward (Ann)

Mixed Seafood Casserole

Serve immediately   Serves 12

6 tablespoons butter
6 tablespoons flour
1 teaspoon dry mustard
Salt to taste
3 cups milk
1 cup sharp Cheddar cheese,
  grated
Dash of paprika

4 small or 2 large frozen
  lobster tails, cooked
2 pounds cooked shrimp
8 ounces crab meat
1-4 ounce can sliced
  mushrooms, drained
Buttered bread crumbs
12 teaspoons sherry

To make sauce: Melt butter in heavy saucepan; add flour, mustard, and salt; blend well. Gradually add milk, stirring and cooking over medium heat until smooth and thickened. Add cheese and remove from heat; stir until cheese is melted; add paprika and blend.

Remove cooked lobster from shells and cut in chunks. If shrimp are extra large, cut in pieces. Combine seafoods, mushrooms, and sauce. Taste and adjust seasonings. Put in large casserole or individual baking shells and cover with buttered bread crumbs. Bake for 15 minutes in a 400-degree oven. After baking, sprinkle 1 teaspoon of sherry over each shell and broil for a few seconds. Serve while piping hot over rice.

Mrs. Morris W. Keeter

Shrimp-Crab Medley in Patty Shells

Serve immediately   Serves 12-15

2 cans cream of shrimp soup
1 can cream of mushroom soup
1 pound crab meat, lump if
  possible

2 pounds medium shrimp,
  cooked, shelled, and
  deveined
Fresh mushrooms, cooked
  and drained

Heat soups; add seafood and mushrooms and serve hot in patty shells. Patty shells may be frozen or homemade. Sherry may be added when hot if desired.

Cookbook Committee

Seafood Coquille

Serve immediately   Serves 6

⅓ cup onion, minced
1 clove garlic, crushed
⅓ cup butter or margarine
¼ cup flour
½ teaspoon salt
¼ teaspoon pepper
1 cup cleaned, cooked shrimp
  (¾ pound in shells)

1⅓ cups milk
⅔ cup sauterne or, if desired,
  apple juice
1-7½ ounce can crab meat,
  drained
6 tablespoons Swiss cheese,
  grated or 6 teaspoons
  Parmesan cheese, grated

Sauté onion and garlic in butter until onions are tender. Remove from heat. Blend in flour, salt, and pepper. Cook over low heat stirring until bubbly. Remove from heat. Stir in milk and wine and heat to boiling, stirring constantly. Boil and stir for 1 minute. Stir in crab and shrimp. Divide into 6 baking shells and top each with 1 tablespoon Swiss or 1 teaspoon Parmesan cheese. Broil for 3 to 4 minutes.

Mrs. J. Philip Coyle

Jim's Shrimp Etoufee

When we lived in New Orleans, Shrimp Etoufee with a green salad, followed by bread pudding with whiskey sauce for dessert was our favorite meal at a local cafe.

Serve immediately   Serves 6-8

2 sticks butter
2 cups yellow onions, chopped
1 cup green onions, chopped
1 cup celery, chopped
4 large cloves garlic, minced

2 teaspoons basil
2 tablespoons parsley flakes
1 teaspoon oregano
2 pounds raw medium
  shrimp, peeled
3 cups cooked rice

Over medium heat sauté onions, celery, and garlic in 1 stick of butter until celery is soft and onions are translucent. Add second stick of butter and spices. Increase heat to high. When butter is melted and hot add shrimp and cook until pink and opaque (about 3 mintues). Don't overcook the shrimp! Serve over fluffy rice.

Mrs. Barbara McCarthy

Artichoke and Shrimp Casserole in Patty Shells

May prepare ahead

Serves 6-8

1 package Pepperidge Farm
 patty shells
1 No. 2 can artichoke hearts
 (or 1 package frozen
 artichoke hearts, cooked
 by directions)
¾ pound medium-sized
 cooked shrimp (if fresh
 shrimp, use one pound,
 allowing for shrinkage)
2 tablespoons butter

¼ pound fresh or canned
 mushrooms
1 tablespoon Worcestershire
 sauce
¼ cup good dry sherry
Salt and pepper to taste
Cream sauce (recipe below)
¼ cup Parmesan cheese,
 grated
Paprika

Cook patty shells according to package directions. While this is cooking, drain can of whole artichokes and arrange in buttered baking dish.
Spread the cooked shrimp over them. Saute sliced mushrooms in butter
for 6 minutes and add them to baking dish. Add Worcestershire sauce,
salt, pepper, and sherry to cream sauce and pour over contents of baking dish. Sprinkle the top with Parmesan cheese and paprika. Bake at
375 degrees for 20 minutes. Cover dish with chopped parsley just before
serving. Spoon into patty shells to serve.

Cream Sauce:
2 tablespoons butter or
 margarine
1½ to 2 tablespoons flour

1 cup milk
¼ teaspoon salt

Melt butter over low heat. Stir in flour until the mixture is smooth.
Slowly stir in milk until smooth. Cook, stirring constantly, until thick;
remove from heat. Add salt.

Cookbook Committee

Louisiana Barbequed Shrimp

This was a favorite dinner when we lived in New Orleans. We spread the dining table with newspapers (barbequed shrimp are VERY messy) and served the shrimp in the baking pan. We peeled and ate the shrimp with our fingers, sopping up the sauce with lots of French bread. Serve with cold beer and maybe some vegetable crudites with ranch-style dip. It makes a great party.

Serve immediately   Serves 4

**2 to 3 pounds large shrimp,
  heads removed**

Sauce:

1 pound butter or margarine　　**2 teaspoons salt**
4 lemons, sliced　　**1 tablespoon black pepper**
1 tablespoon rosemary　　**¾ cup Worcestershire**
1 teaspoon Tabasco sauce　　** sauce**
2 to 4 cloves garlic, crushed

In a saucepan melt butter or margarine. Add lemon slices, rosemary, Tabasco, garlic, salt, and pepper. Mix thoroughly. Add Worcestershire sauce and stir over medium-low heat until heated thoroughly. Arrange shrimp in a large shallow baking pan and pour heated sauce over them. Cook at 400 degrees about 15-20 minutes, turning once. Shrimp are ready when their shells are pink, and the meat is white, not translucent.

Mrs. Barbara McCarthy

Dan's Boiled Shrimp

May prepare ahead   Serves 4

1 pound of shrimp　　**1 cup of cold water**
1 tablespoon vinegar　　**Black pepper to taste**
Dash of red pepper　　**1 tablespoon salt**

Put all ingredients except salt in a saucepan. Bring to a boil. Add salt and stir shrimp continuously. Boil for 5 minutes. Drain and eat hot or cold. Does not require sauce.

Claire Kincaid

Shrimp Chinoise

May prepare ahead   Serves 6

2 pounds jumbo shrimp, unpeeled

½ pound snow peas, strings removed

½ pound carrots, peeled and cut diagonally into 2-inch pieces

½ head cauliflower, cut into florets

½ bunch fresh broccoli, cut into florets

¼ pound shitake mushrooms, cleaned and sliced

1 cup bok choy cabbage, cut into 1½-inch pieces

3 red peppers, seeded and cut into thin strips

Dressing:

2 tablespoons Japanese rice vinegar

1 tablespoon cider vinegar

2 tablespoons soy sauce

1 tablespoon chili oil

1 cup vegetable oil

½ cup sesame oil

Juice of 1 lemon or orange

2 cloves garlic, finely minced

1 teaspoon Dijon mustard

1 tablespoon honey

¼ cup toasted sesame seeds (toast in hot pan)

Cook shrimp in rapidly boiling salted water for 3 to 4 minutes, or until shrimp turn pink. Drain and cool under cold water. Peel shrimp, leaving tails attached if possible. Refrigerate. In separate pots of boiling water blanch snow peas for 30 seconds, the carrots for 3 minutes, the cauliflower for 4 minutes, and the broccoli for 4 minutes. Remove vegetables with slotted spoon or Chinese strainer and put them in ice water to stop cooking. Drain and set aside. The vegetables should still be crunchy. Combine all ingredients for dressing in small mixing bowl. In large bowl combine cooked shrimp, cooked vegetables, mushrooms, cabbage, and red peppers. Pour on dressing, toss well, and refrigerate for at least 1 hour. Serve cold.

Mrs. H. Garrett Rhyne

Low Country Boil

This is great for a patio, river, or beach party, or a winter supper.

May prepare ahead   Serves 4

Small new potatoes, 4 per   Hillshire Polish sausage,
person   ¼ pound per person
Corn on Cob, 1 ear per   Unpeeled headless green
person, cut in half   shrimp, ⅓ pound per person
Seafood seasoning bag, either
1 bag or loose seasoning
tied in cheese cloth

Boil potatoes in water for 15 minutes. Add sausage cut into 3-inch sections and cook for 20 minutes. Remove potatoes and sausage from water and reserve. Add corn to water, cook for 7 minutes, and remove. Add seafood seasoning bag and simmer for 5 minutes. Remove and add shrimp to boiling water. Cook 1 minute or until pink. Drain well. Spread on large platter and top with potatoes, sausage, and corn on the cob. (Hot shrimp will reheat the rest.) Note: For easy way to serve, cover tables with newspaper and peel your own. Supply butter, cocktail sauce, and plates for shrimp shells. Add green salad or layered cole slaw and French bread for a complete meal. Cooking time: approximately 50 minutes.

Mrs. Phillip L. Hicks (Lou Anne)

Emily's New Orleans Shrimp

I drain the sauce and serve the shrimp with hot cocktail sauce.
This is a "peel 'em and eat 'em" recipe.

Serve immediately   Serves 2-4

1 pound shrimp in shells   1 stick margarine
½ cup bottled Italian dressing   Pepper to taste
Juice of 1 lemon

Put shrimp in roasting pan. In a saucepan melt margarine and add pepper, salad dressing, and lemon juice. Pour over shrimp. Cover and bake for 20 minutes at 350 degrees. Serve the shrimp with the cooking sauce (along with napkins and bibs.)

Mrs. David Simpson (Emily)

Shrimp Pilau

Serve immediately   Serves 12

1 stick butter
1 green pepper, chopped
1 onion, chopped
½ cup celery, chopped
1-4 ounce can pimento
Dash of sugar, salt, and pepper
  to taste

1 pound cooked shrimp,
  shelled and chopped
  small
1-10 ounce can consomme
1 soup can of water
1½ cups raw rice

Melt butter. Add green pepper, onion, and celery and sauté until tender.
Add pimento, sugar, salt, pepper, and cooked shrimp. Mix consomme and
water together. Measure. This should equal 3 cups of liquid. If it does
not, add enough water to make 3 cups total. Combine shrimp mixture
with consomme mixture and rice. Cover and cook about 25 minutes or
until rice is tender.

Mrs. Alex Hall (Ginny)

Shrimp Spaghetti

May prepare ahead   Serves 4

1-8 ounce box thin spaghetti
½ cup margarine
2 dozen medium shrimp, diced
4 to 6 cloves garlic, minced
1-4 ounce can sliced mushrooms

6 tablespoons Romano cheese,
  grated
½ teaspoon salt
½ teaspoon pepper
Parmesan cheese to top
Parsley sprigs to garnish

Cook spaghetti in rapidly boiling salted water for 10 minutes. Drain,
rinse with cold water and set aside. Melt margarine in a 1- inch skillet.
Add shrimp, garlic, and mushrooms. Cook slowly for 5 minutes. Add
spaghetti to the skillet. Sprinkle with cheese, salt, and pepper. Toss in
skillet until spaghetti is hot but do not let margarine brown. Turn onto
warm serving dish and sprinkle with Parmesan cheese. Garnish with
sprigs of parsley for color.

Mrs. Joye S. Rankin

Wild Rice and Shrimp

May prepare ahead   Serves 10-12

1½ pounds (or more) cooked   6 drops of Tabasco sauce
  shrimp   1 can cream of chicken soup
½ cup margarine   2 tablespoons cream
½ large onion, chopped   Buttered bread crumbs
½ cup bell pepper, chopped   1 small box wild rice,
1 large can sliced mushrooms   cooked as directed
1 tablespoon Worcestershire
  sauce

Sauté onion, pepper, and mushrooms in margarine. Add cooked shrimp, Worcestershire, and Tabasco. Heat soup with cream. Fold all together with cooked rice. Pour into a greased 3-quart casserole. Cover with bread crumbs. Bake at 325 degrees for 30 minutes.

Mrs. David Simpson (Emily)

Cajun Shrimp Creole

Must prepare 1 to 2 days ahead   Serves 6-8

2 pounds medium shrimp   ½ teaspoon cayenne pepper
2 cups shrimp stock   ½ teaspoon black pepper
3 tablespoons bacon drippings   1 tablespoon thyme
3 cups onion, finely chopped   1 teaspoon basil
2 cups celery, finely chopped   2 teaspoons parsley flakes
2 cups green pepper, finely   3 cups canned tomatoes
  chopped   with liquid, chopped
4 large cloves garlic, minced   1 cup canned tomato sauce
1 bay leaf   3 cups cooked rice
1 teaspoon white pepper

Peel shrimp and cook shells in 2½ cups water for stock. In bacon drippings saute ½ of the onions, celery, peppers, and garlic over medium-high heat until onions are browned, about 20 minutes. Add remaining onions, celery, and peppers and continue cooking until onions are translucent. Add garlic and spices; saute briefly. Add tomatoes, shrimp stock, tomato sauce and heat to boiling. Cool and refrigerate 1 to 2 days to allow flavors to mix. Reheat to boiling, add shrimp and cook until pink, about 3 minutes. Serve immediately over fluffy rice.

Mrs. Barbara McCarthy

Seafood Casserole

May prepare ahead   Serves 8-10

2 cans cream of chicken soup
½ cup Miracle Whip salad
  dressing
1 small onion, grated
¾ cup milk
¼ teaspoon nutmeg
¼ teaspoon cayenne pepper
2 tablespoons Worcestershire
  sauce
Salt and pepper to taste

Sherry to taste
3 pounds cooked shrimp
1-7½ ounce can crab meat or
  1 pound scallops
1-5 ounce can sliced water
  chestnuts, drained
1½ cups celery, diced
3 tablespoons parsley, minced
Paprika (optional)
Slivered almonds (optional)

Preheat oven to 350 degrees. Butter large casserole dish. Combine soup
and salad dressing. Add onion and milk. Mix thoroughly. Season with
nutmeg, cayenne pepper, Worcestershire sauce, salt, pepper, and sherry
to taste. Add remaining ingredients and combine thoroughly. Pour into
casserole dish. Top with paprika and slivered almonds, if desired. Bake
at 350 degrees for 30 minutes or until bubbly.

Gayle Kersh
Elizabeth Neisler Sumner

Shrimp Pie

This recipe originated in Georgetown, South Carolina.

May prepare ahead   Serves 6

1 onion, diced
1 green pepper, diced
1 stick margarine
1 can mushroom soup
1 can celery soup
1 tablespoon Worcestershire
  sauce

Salt and pepper to taste
1 teaspoon Tabasco sauce
3 hard-boiled eggs
2 pounds shrimp
Pastry for a 2-crust pie

Sauté onion and pepper in margarine. Add soups and seasonings. Add
diced eggs and shrimp. Line a 2-quart casserole dish with half of pastry.
Pour in mix and cover with pastry. Dot with butter, and bake at 350
degrees until brown, about 45 minutes.

Mrs. George F. Henry, III

Sherried Shrimp Rockefeller (For Microwave)

Serve immediately   Serves 4

2 packages frozen, chopped
  spinach
1 pound medium to large raw
  shrimp, peeled and deveined
2 cans cream of shrimp soup
2 cups sharp Cheddar cheese,
  shredded

3 tablespoons cooking sherry
4 slices bread
6 tablespoons margarine
Paprika

In a 10-inch square casserole place frozen spinach and defrost 10 minutes. Break into blocks and microwave on high 3 to 4 minutes until thawed. With hands squeeze out all juice and spread over bottom of casserole. Place shrimp over spinach. In a 1-quart glass bowl combine shrimp soup, cheese, and sherry. Microwave on high for 2 minutes, stir, and microwave 2 minutes more. Crumble bread in glass bowl and add margarine. Microwave on high for 1 minute and stir after 30 seconds. Pour sauce over shrimp and sprinkle crumbs over top. Sprinkle paprika over top. Microwave on high for 12 to 14 minutes, uncovered. Let stand covered for 5 minutes before serving.

Mrs. Susan B. Garrett

Pickled Shrimp

This also makes an elegant salad in an avocodo half.

Must prepare ahead   Serves 15-20

3 pounds medium shrimp
2 pounds crabmeat
3 medium onions (Vidalia,
  when available)
4 lemons

Bay leaves
1-8 ounce bottle Catalina
  dressing
1-8 ounce bottle Russian
  dressing

Boil and clean shrimp (do not overcook). Slice onions and lemons as thinly as possible. In a large 5-quart plastic covered container layer shrimp, crabmeat, onions, and lemons placing 2 to 3 bay leaves per layer. Pour bottled dressings over and close tightly. Marinate 2 to 3 days in refrigerator, inverting container or stirring gently daily. Serve with crackers.

Mrs. Eva Ann McLean

Marinated Shrimp

This will keep for a week or longer.

May prepare ahead   Serves 10

2 cups vinegar   **½ cup Wesson oil**
¼ cup whole allspice

Bring vinegar and allspice to a boil. Add Wesson oil and set aside.

Make a paste out of the following ingredients:
1 tablespoon salt   **1 tablespoon sugar**
1 tablespoon powdered mustard   **1 teaspoon black pepper**
1 teaspoon paprika   **Enough water to make paste**

When vinegar, allspice, and Wesson oil mixture is cool, mix in paste.

5 pounds shrimp, cleaned and   **3 or 4 lemons, sliced thin**
** deveined**   **3 or 4 onions, sliced thin**
Bay leaves

Cook shrimp and layer the above ingredients in the following manner: shrimp, lemon slices, onion, and bay leaves. Repeat until all ingredients are used. Pour the vinegar mixture over the layers and refrigerate. Serve with crackers.

Mrs. David Allen Smith

Side Dishes

Apples In A Dish

May prepare ahead   Serves 6-8

8 Golden Delicious apples   **10 to 12 pieces day-old**
½ cup sugar   **white bread**
Juice of 1 fresh lemon   **1 stick butter or margarine,**
Grated lemon rind   **melted**

Peel, core, and slice apples. Place in greased 9 x 11-inch glass dish.
Sprinkle with ¼ cup sugar. Pour lemon juice over apples; then sprinkle
with rind. Bake covered at 350 degrees until tender. Remove crust from
bread and cube. Mix with melted butter and ¼ cup sugar until well
coated. Place bread over apples and bake until bread is golden and crispy.

Mrs. Joanna Woods Owen

A Friend's Scalloped Apples

May prepare ahead   Serves 6

1-20 ounce can sliced apples   **¼ to ½ cup Ritz**
¾ cup Cheddar cheese, grated   **crackers, crushed**
3 tablespoons flour   **½ stick butter, melted**
¾ cup sugar

Mix apples and Cheddar cheese. Add flour and sugar mixed together.
Top with crushed Ritz crackers and melted butter. Bake uncovered at
400 degrees for 20 minutes.

Mrs. Carole Fuller

Pineapple Casserole

Great with ham!

Serve immediately   Serves 8

8 slices bread (king-size)   **3 eggs**
2 cups sugar   **2 cups pineapple chunks**
1 cup butter, melted   **¾ cup milk**

Cube the slices of bread and mix with 2 cups of sugar and 1 cup of butter.
Set aside. Mix eggs, drained pineapple, and milk together; combine with
bread mixture. Pour into casserole dish and bake at 325 degrees for
approximately 45 minutes.

Mrs. J. Wylie Goble

Baked Pineapple With Cheese

May prepare ahead   Serves 8

½ cup sugar
3 tablespoons flour
2-15¼ ounce cans pineapple
   tidbits (packed in own
   juice), drained

2 cups mild Cheddar cheese,
   grated or 1 cup each
   Cheddar and Velvetta
   cheese
1 stick butter
1 stack Ritz crackers, crushed

Mix sugar and flour together. Add drained pineapple and grated cheese. Toss thoroughly. Place in a 1½-quart casserole dish. Melt butter. Add crushed crackers and toss to coat. Spread on pineapple mixture. Bake at 350 degrees for 30 minutes.

Connie Gibbons
Mrs. William P. Adams (Becky)

Cranberry-Apple Casserole

This is great at Christmas with turkey, ham, or as a dessert with ice cream.

May prepare ahead   Serves 8-10
Freezes well

2 cups uncooked, washed
   cranberries

3 cups apples, diced
1 cup sugar

Place cranberries, raw apples, and sugar that have been mixed together in bottom of pan.

Topping:
½ cup brown sugar
⅓ cup plain flour
1 cup oatmeal

¾ cup nuts, chopped
1½ sticks margarine,
   melted

Mix together topping ingredients and heat. Cover fruit evenly and cook uncovered for 1½ hours at 275 degrees. This recipe fits in a 9-inch square pan. Double this for a 9 x 13-inch pan.

Mrs. Nan Anthony

Apple-Cranberry Compote

Serve warm, plain or with vanilla ice cream as a dessert.
Can also serve plain as a meat accompaniment or served chilled.

May prepare ahead   Serves 4

3 medium (1 pound) cooking   ⅓ cup honey
  apples   Dash of salt
1-16 ounce can whole-berry   1-2 inch cinnamon stick
  cranberry sauce

Peel apples, cut in quarters and put in SLOW COOKER. Mix remaining ingredients and pour over apples. Cover and cook on high (stirring after the first hour) for 2½ hours or until apples are tender.
Conventional stove directions: Follow above recipe. Put quartered apples in saucepan with ¼ cup water. Bring to boil, cover and simmer for 10 to 15 minutes or until apples are nearly tender, adding more water if necessary. Add remaining ingredients, cover and cook gently for 10 minutes longer.

Mrs. Paulette H. Elmore

Anne Byrd's Brandied Fruits

Must prepare ahead   Serves 10-12

1 stick butter   9 to 10 cups of assorted
2 tablespoons flour   canned fruits (4 ½ to
½ cup sugar   5 pounds) - such as
1½ cups brandy   peach halves, pineapple,
                                      pears, apricots, plums,
                                      or maraschino cherries

Melt butter and stir in flour, whisking to avoid lumps. Add sugar and brandy. Cook over moderate heat until thickened. Pour syrup over drained fruits and marinate in refrigerator overnight. Remove from refrigerator and allow to come to room temperature. Bake fruits and syrup in ovenproof dish in a 325-degree oven for 30 minutes. Serve hot.

Roseanne Nichols

Baked Beans

May prepare ahead   Serves 4

3 slices very thin ham,   1-16 ounce can pork 'n beans
  chopped very small   1 tablespoon brown sugar
1 small onion, chopped   1 tablespoon catsup
1 tablespoon Grandma molasses   ½ teaspoon salt

Sauté onion and ham together. After onion has turned yellow, add
molasses and cook for 1 minute. Turn off heat. Mix together beans
(remove any fat back), brown sugar, catsup, and salt. Then pour in
onion/ham mixture and mix well in a 1½-quart casserole dish. Cover
and bake at 350 degrees for 25 to 30 minutes.

Mrs. Robin Bean

Macaroni Deluxe

Serve immediately   Serves 8

1 package macaroni, cooked   1 cup Cheddar cheese, grated
  and drained   Mushrooms, sliced and
2 cans cream of mushroom   cooked (optional)
  soup
1½ pounds sharp Cheddar
  cheese (optional)

Heat soup and cheese until cheese is melted. Layer macaroni and then
cheese sauce in a 11 x 13-inch oven proof glass server, using two layers.
Sliced mushrooms and a small bit of cheese may be added to macaroni
layer, if desired, before layer of sauce. Cook slowly at 350 degrees or less
until bubbly.

Mary Margaret S. Hunter

Special Macaroni and Cheese

May prepare ahead   Serves 6

1-8 ounce package macaroni   1 tablespoon butter
1 cup Longhorn cheese, cubed   1 tablespoon flour
1 cup Swiss cheese, cubed   1 cup milk
¼ cup Parmesan cheese, grated   Salt and pepper to taste

Prepare macaroni as instructed on package. Add cheeses and mix well.
Combine butter, flour, milk, salt, and pepper in a small saucepan; bring
to a boil; pour over casserole. Bake at 350 degrees for 30 minutes.

Mrs. Ann R. Cline

Twice-Baked Potatoes

Serve immediately   Serves 4

2 medium baking potatoes   1 tablespoon chives,
2 tablespoons butter   chopped
1 tablespoon mayonnaise   2 tablespoons Cheddar
¼ teaspoon salt   cheese, shredded
⅛ teaspoon pepper   Paprika
½ cup cream-style cottage
  cheese

Scrub potatoes, rub skins with oil; bake at 400 degrees for 1 hour. Allow potatoes to cool to touch. Cut potatoes in half lengthwise; scoop out pulp, leaving shells intact. Mash pulp. Combine potato pulp with butter, mayonnaise, salt, pepper, cottage cheese, and chives. Mix well. Stuff shells with potato mixture; sprinkle with cheese and paprika. Place in a shallow baking dish and bake at 375 degrees for 20 minutes.

Mrs. Holt Anthony Harris

Stuffed Baked Potatoes A-La-Microwave

May prepare ahead   Serves 8
Freezes well

4 medium potatoes, cleaned   ½ teaspoon salt
  and drained   ⅛ teaspoon pepper
¼ cup butter   ¾ cup milk
½ cup Cheddar cheese, grated   Paprika
1 tablespoon onion, grated

Prick potatoes once and bake potatoes for 8 minutes on high. Turn over and bake 8 minutes more. While hot slice lengthwise. Scoop out insides, saving shell. Whip together potatoes, butter, cheese, onion, salt, and pepper. Gradually blend milk. Spoon potato mixture back into shells. Return to oven for 5 more minutes. Sprinkle with paprika.

Hope Parks

Hash Brown Potato Casserole

May prepare ahead   Serves 8-10

1 box frozen Ore-Ida Hash
  Brown Patties, thawed and
  crumbled
1-10¾ ounce can cream of
  chicken soup, undiluted
1 cup Cheddar cheese, shredded

½ cup margarine, melted
½ cup onion, chopped
1-16 ounce carton sour cream
¼ cup butter, melted
2 cups corn flakes, crushed

Combine above ingredients except corn flakes and ¼ cup melted butter. Spread into greased baking dish. Crush cornflakes and combine with melted butter. Sprinkle over potatoes and bake at 350 degrees for 50 minutes.

Variation: Mix together hash browns, soup, ½ cup margarine, onion, and sour cream. Spread into greased baking dish. Top with shredded Cheddar cheese. Bake at 350 degrees for 50 minutes.

Mrs. Melissa Morris
Mrs. Holt Harris

Potato Souffle

May prepare ahead   Serves 6-8

1-8 ounce package cream
  cheese, softened
4 cups hot mashed potatoes,
  (instant are fine)
Dash pepper

1 egg, beaten
1 teaspoon salt
⅓ cup pimento, finely
  chopped (optional)
Grated cheese

Preheat oven to 350 degrees. Combine cream cheese and potatoes, mixing until well blended. Add remaining ingredients except cheese. Place in a 1-quart casserole. Bake for 45 minutes, adding cheese on top during the last few minutes of baking time.

Clarissa Craig

Grated Sweet Potato Pudding

This is an excellent dish to accompany Thanksgiving or Christmas holiday dinner. This is an old family recipe and may also be used as a dessert for other occasions.

May prepare ahead   Serves 6
Freezes well

1 egg, beaten   2 cups raw sweet potatoes,
1 cup sugar   grated
Pinch of salt   2 tablespoons butter, melted
1½ cups whole milk

Melt butter in 9 x 9-inch pan or Pyrex dish in oven. Mix together egg, sugar, salt, and milk. Add raw grated sweet potatoes. Pour melted butter from pan into sweet potato mixture and stir. Pour this into the 9 x 9-inch pan, which should already be warm. Cook at 350 degrees for 1 to 1¼ hours depending on oven.

Mrs. William Thrower, Jr. (Price)

Sweet Potato Casserole

May prepare ahead   Serves 6

Potato mixture:
2 cups cooked sweet potatoes   ⅓ stick margarine, melted
1 cup sugar   ½ teaspoon salt
2 eggs   1 teaspoon vanilla
2 teaspoons flour   1 teaspoon milk
1 teaspoon butternut flavoring   1 teaspoon to 1 tablespoon
  (optional)   sherry (optional)

Topping:
1 cup pecans, chopped   ⅓ cup flour
1 cup brown sugar   ⅓ stick margarine, melted

Mix together all the ingredients for the potato mixture and pour it into greased baking dish. Mix together topping ingredients and place on top of potato mixture and cook for 35 minutes at 350 degrees.

Beverly Poag
Jennie Stultz

Baked Rice

*This recipe was given to my mother by
a good friend in New Jersey about 26 years ago.*

Serve immediately   Serves 4-6

**2 cups chicken or beef
    bouillon
6 tablespoons butter or
    margarine
¼ cup onion, chopped**

**1 cup Uncle Ben's rice,
    uncooked
2 bay leaves
Dash of cayenne pepper**

Dissolve 2 cubes of bouillon in 2 cups of water. In a large skillet sauté
butter and onions until onions are tender. Then add to them (in pan)
the rice and bouillon. Pour this into a 2 or 2 ½-quart casserole dish. Place
bay leaves on top and sprinkle with cayenne pepper. Cover and bake in
a preheated 300-degree oven for 30 minutes.

Mrs. Charles Reeves

Mama Avery's Rice

Serve immediately   Serves 4

**3 tablespoons butter
1 onion, sliced
2 stalks celery, sliced
1 tablespoon Worcestershire
    sauce
A few shakes of garlic powder**

**A few shakes of Mrs. Dash
1 tablespoon instant chicken
    bouillon
1½ cups minute rice
Parmesan cheese (optional)**

Melt butter in skillet; sauté onion and celery until tender. Add all other
spices. Add rice and an equal amount of water. Bring to a boil; add
Parmesan cheese, if desired, cover; and remove from heat. Let stand for
5 minutes.

Mrs. Virginia Avery

227

Mushroom-Pecan Rice

Serve immediately   Serves 6-8

1 cup uncooked rice	¾ cup pecans, chopped
1 can cream of mushroom soup	½ cup butter, melted
1 cup fresh mushrooms, sliced	

Cook rice and rinse. Into a well-greased 1½-quart casserole layer half the rice, soup, mushrooms, and nuts. Repeat, ending with nuts on top. Pour melted butter over nuts. Bake at 350 degrees for 20 minutes.

Mrs. J. Caswell Taylor, Jr.

Rice Casserole

Men love it. Excellent with steak or London broil.

May prepare ahead.   Serves 6-8

¼ cup butter or margarine	½ teaspoon salt
1 cup onion, chopped	½ teaspoon pepper
4 cups cooked rice	Crushed red pepper to taste
2 cups sour cream	2 cups Cheddar cheese,
1 large bay leaf	grated
	Chopped parsley

Sauté onion in butter until translucent. Remove from heat. To the cooked rice add sour cream, bay leaf, salt, pepper, and the desired amount of crushed red pepper (1 teaspoon to 1 tablespoon). Mix well. Layer rice and cheese and repeat in the casserole. Top with cheese. Bake at 350 degrees for 25 minutes or until bubbly. Sprinkle with parsley.

Patti Hunter

Wild Rice

Serve immediately   Serves 6

1½ cups wild rice
4-10½ ounce cans undiluted
  bouillon or beef broth
1 cup onion, chopped
1 cup green pepper, chopped

1 cup mushrooms, sliced
¼ cup butter, softened
1 cup thick cream
Salt and pepper to taste

Wash wild rice and then cook in bouillon or beef broth until most of liquid has been absorbed. This takes 45 minutes to 1 hour. Saute onion, pepper, and mushrooms in butter. Add cream, salt, and pepper. Mix with rice and put in casserole dish and bake at 350 degrees for 20 minutes.

Ginny Hall

Fresh Asparagus Baked For A Crowd

May prepare ahead   Serves 12

4 pounds asparagus (or less)
1 tablespoon olive oil
2 tablespoons salad oil

4 tablespoons butter, melted
Salt and pepper to taste
5 tablespoons parsley, minced

Cover asparagus with warm water and let stand for 5 to 10 minutes. Rinse under warm running water and break off stalks as far down as they snap easily. Arrange on a flat cookie pan and drizzle oil and butter over it. Sprinkle with salt, pepper, and parsley and seal with foil. Bake at 400 degrees for 20 minutes.

Jane Petty

Broccoli Casserole I

May prepare ahead   Serves 8

1 medium onion, chopped
¼ stick margarine, melted
1 can cream of mushroom soup
1 cup Cheddar cheese, grated

1 cup mayonnaise
1 large package broccoli,
  thawed
Cheez-it crackers

Sauté onion in margarine in a saucepan. Add and warm to spreading consistency the mushroom soup, grated cheese, and mayonnaise. Spread over broccoli. Crumble Cheez-it crackers over top. Bake uncovered at 375 degrees for 25 to 30 minutes, until bubbly.

Patti Hunter

Broccoli Casserole II

May prepare ahead   Serves 10

¼ cup onion, chopped
½ cup celery, chopped
3 tablespoons margarine
½ cup milk
1-8 ounce jar Cheese Whiz
1 can cream of chicken soup

2 cups cooked rice (not
  Minute rice)
1-8 ounce can water
  chestnuts, chopped
1-10 ounce package chopped
  broccoli, thawed and
  drained

Sauté onion and celery in margarine. Add milk, ⅓ jar Cheese Whiz, soup, rice, water chestnuts, and uncooked broccoli. Place in a 13 x 9-inch casserole and top with remaining cheese. Brown at 350 degrees until bubbly.

Mrs. John B. Garrett, Jr. (Nancy)
Mrs. John S. Lowery (Kathy)

Cabbage Casserole

This is unusual and good!

May prepare ahead   Serves 6

1 medium to small cabbage
8 slices bacon, fried crisp and
  crumbled
1 medium onion, diced
1 medium green pepper, diced
1 can cream of mushroom or
  cream of chicken soup

½ cup milk
1½ cups Cheddar cheese,
  grated
Salt and pepper to taste
3 slices bread, cut in small
  cubes and soaked in
1 stick melted butter

Cook cabbage until tender in well salted water (do not overcook), drain. Use ½ of bacon grease to saute onion and pepper. Add mushroom soup, milk, cheese, salt, pepper, and crumbled bacon. Cook and stir until cheese is melted. Toss with drained cabbage. Pour into baking dish and add bread cubes. Bake at 350 degrees for 30 to 35 minutes.

Lin Lineberger

Skillet Cabbage

Serve immediately   Serves 6-8

4 cups cabbage, chopped   **2 teaspoons sugar**
2 large onions, sliced   **¼ cup vegetable oil**
1 green pepper, chopped   **Salt and pepper to taste**
2 tomatoes, chopped

Combine all of the above ingredients in a heavy skillet and cook over medium heat for 5 minutes or until tender.

Peggy Cooke

Red Cabbage With Apples

"Rotkohl mit Apfeln"

Serve immediately   Serves 8-10

2 to 2½ pounds purple cabbage   **½ cup onions, finely**
⅔ cup red wine vinegar   **chopped**
2 tablespoons sugar   **1 whole onion, peeled and**
2 teaspoons salt   **pierced with 2 whole**
2 tablespoons bacon grease   **cloves**
2 medium-size cooking apples,   **1 bay leaf**
** peeled, cored, and cut**   **1 cup boiling water**
** into ⅛-inch wedges**   **½ cup red wine, added to**
                                         cabbage after cooked

Wash cabbage and shred like coleslaw. Place cabbage in a bowl. Sprinkle with vinegar, sugar, and salt (evenly coated). In a 4 or 5-quart casserole melt bacon fat. Add apples and chopped onions; cook for 5 minutes, stirring frequently (until apples are lightly browned). Add cabbage, whole onion with cloves, and bay leaf. Stir thoroughly and pour in boiling water. Bring to a boil, cover, and simmer for 1½ to 2 hours (until cabbage is tender). If cabbage is dry add 1 tablespoon boiling water. When done, there should be almost no liquid left in casserole. Before serving remove onion and bay leaf and stir in wine. (The wine evaporates quickly.)

Karen Staker

Citrus Honey Carrots

May prepare ahead   Serves 6

1 bunch carrots
¼ cup butter, melted
¼ cup honey
1½ teaspoons grated orange
  peel

1½ teaspoons grated lemon
  peel
½ cup slivered almonds

Wash and slice carrots. Steam until crispy tender. In small saucepan melt butter and honey. Add citrus peels. When ready to serve, pour sauce over carrots and mix in nuts.

Miss Becca Mitchell

Microwaved Cauliflower and Sauce

May prepare ahead   Serve 6-8

1 head cauliflower
¼ cup water
½ cup mayonnaise
1 tablespoon onion, minced

½ teaspoon mustard
¼ teaspoon salt
Grated Cheddar cheese
Paprika

Wash and core cauliflower. Put in glass pie plate with ¼ cup water. Cover with plastic wrap. Microwave on high for 9 minutes. Mix mayonnaise, onion, mustard, and salt. Cover cooked cauliflower with sauce and cheese. Return to microwave and cooked uncovered on 70-percent power for 1½ minutes. Sprinkle with paprika.

Cookbook Committee

Grace's Creole Eggplant

May prepare ahead   Serves 8
Freezes well

1 large eggplant	2 teaspoons salt
3 tablespoons bacon grease or butter	Black pepper to taste
	1 cup Cheddar cheese, grated
1 medium onion, chopped	1 cup bread crumbs
1 cup tomatoes	½ teaspoon baking powder

Peel, slice, and boil eggplant in water until tender, about 15 to 20 minutes. Drain and mash. Put 2 tablespoons of bacon grease or butter into frying pan and add chopped onion. Saute onion, add tomatoes, salt, and pepper; simmer a few minutes. Combine with eggplant, cheese, and ¾ cup bread crumbs. Add baking powder. Put into greased casserole. Sprinkle with other tablespoon of bacon grease or butter and remaining crumbs. Bake at 325 degrees for 25 minutes.

Mrs. Joseph S. Stowe (Janice)

Eggplant Parmesan

Prepare same day   Serves 6-8

1-2 pound eggplant	¾ pound mozzarella cheese, sliced
Salt to taste	
3 eggs	3 cups tomato sauce
1½ to 2 cups dried bread crumbs	1 cup Parmesan cheese, grated
½ to ¾ cup oil	4 teaspoons fresh oregano, chopped

Peel eggplant and slice into ⅜-inch slices. Salt and let drain for 30 minutes; pat dry. Beat eggs with 2 tablespoons water. Dip the eggplant slices first into the eggs, then into the crumbs. Heat ¼ cup oil in a large frying pan and saute the eggplant slices until golden brown on both sides. Remove and drain on brown paper. Continue cooking the eggplant, using additional oil if needed. Place half the eggplant slices in a 9 x 13-inch pan. Sprinkle with ⅓ of the mozzarella cheese. Cover with half the tomato sauce and oregano. Repeat the layers. Top with the last of the Parmesan and mozzarella cheeses. Bake in a preheated oven at 350 degrees for 30 minutes.

Mary Jane Stewart

Ghivetch

Serve this recipe hot. This is SO pretty and is wonderful for a buffet dinner! Vegetables may be varied according to your tastes and/or what is available.

May prepare ahead   Serves 10-12

1 cup carrots, thinly sliced
1 cup potato, diced
2 medium tomatoes, quartered
1 small Bermuda onion, sliced
Red and green julienne sweet
  pepper (use 2-ounce jar
  sliced pimento if red pepper
  is not available)

1 cup fresh green beans
½ cup celery, diced
1 small yellow squash
½ to 1 cup cauliflower
  florets
½ to 1 cup broccoli
  florets
1 small zucchini

Sauce:
1 cup beef bouillon
3 cloves garlic, crushed
½ bay leaf, crumbled
¼ teaspoon Tarragon

⅓ cup olive oil
2 teaspoons salt
½ teaspoon savory

Preheat oven to 350 degrees. Arrange vegetables in ungreased 13 x 9 x 2-inch casserole. Mix ingredients to make sauce and heat to boiling. Pour over vegetables; cover tightly. Bake 1 to 1¼ hours; stir once or twice so that vegetables cook evenly.

Mrs. Eva Ann McLean

Different Marinated Beans

May prepare ahead   Serves 8

2-16 ounce cans French style
  beans
4 tablespoons bacon grease
4 tablespoons brown sugar
2 tablespoons prepared
  mustard

4 tablespoons vinegar
4 strips bacon, crisply-
  fried

Heat beans in own liquid. When warm, drain and put into a 1½-quart casserole. Heat grease, sugar, mustard, and vinegar. Pour over beans. Crumble bacon over top. Serve at room temperature.

Mrs. Frank P. Cooke, Jr.

Simple Spinach Casserole

May prepare ahead   Serves 6

1 package frozen chopped
  spinach, cooked and drained
  well
1 cup sharp Cheddar cheese,
  grated
1 can cream of mushroom soup

1 egg, beaten
Dash of nutmeg
1 cup Pepperidge Farm
  dressing

Prepare spinach and mix with remaining ingredients except dressing. Put in a 1½-quart casserole. Sprinkle dressing on top and bake for 30 to 40 minutes at 350 degrees.

Mrs. Paul Quinn

James Forney's Spinach Timbale

Serve immediately   Serves 8-10

4 tablespoons butter
4 tablespoons flour
1 cup milk
1 teaspoon salt
¼ teaspoon black pepper
½ teaspoon nutmeg
2-9 ounce packages frozen
  spinach, cooked and
  drained

5 eggs, beaten
1 medium onion, grated
1 cup sharp Cheddar cheese,
  grated
Bread
Mayonnaise
Tomato slices
Hollandaise sauce
Paprika

Grease 8 to 10 individual salad molds and set aside. Melt butter and add flour. Stir in milk, salt, pepper, and nutmeg. Cook until very thick. Cool for 10 minutes. Then add drained spinach, beaten eggs, onion, and sharp cheese. Mix well and pour into greased molds. Place molds in a pan and add enough water to come up ⅓ to ½ the height of the mold. Cover pan with foil and cook in a 350-degree oven for 35 to 40 minutes or until mixture is firm.

Cut large rounds from bread (or use packaged Holland rusk). Fry 10 fresh bread rounds in hot oil until lightly browned. Remove, drain, and cool. Spread some mayonnaise on bread slices. Add a slice of tomato, then turn out a spinach mold on top of the tomatoes. Top with Hollandaise sauce. Add a dash of paprika and serve.

Mrs. J.M. Carstarphen (Catherine Ann)

Spinach-Artichoke Casserole

May prepare ahead   Serves 10-12

1 can artichoke hearts, drained
3 packages frozen chopped
   spinach, cooked and
   drained well
1-8 ounce package cream
   cheese, cubed
2 cans cream of mushroom soup

Juice of one small lemon
Dash or two of nutmeg
3 eggs, well-beaten
1 cup Parmesan cheese,
   grated
Ritz cracker crumbs

Grease a 2-quart casserole and place artichoke hearts, cut side down in dish. Mix together spinach, cream cheese, soup, lemon, nutmeg, eggs, and Parmesan cheese; pour over artichokes. Top with cracker crumbs and bake at 350 degrees until bubbly, approximately 45 to 50 minutes.

Mrs. John Bridgeman (Nan)

Squash Pancakes

Serve immediately   Serves 4

2 cups raw yellow squash,
   grated
½ medium onion, grated
1 teaspoon sugar
2 eggs

6 tablespoons flour
1 teaspoon salt
Dash pepper

Mix all ingredients together and cook on hot greased griddle like pancakes. Barely salt after cooking and don't let griddle get too hot.

Hope Parks

Squash Casserole I

This is light and airy and is good served with London broil and rice pilaf.

May prepare ahead   Serves 4

2 cups yellow squash, sliced   Salt to taste
¼ small onion, chopped   Dash of black pepper
1 egg, beaten   1 tablespoon butter
½ cup evaporated milk   Bread crumbs
1 tablespoon sugar   ⅓ cup Cheddar cheese,
                                      grated

Cook squash and onion together in small amount of water. Cool and drain. Add beaten egg, milk, sugar, salt, and pepper. Butter bottom of casserole and add squash mixture. Top with crumbs and cheese. Bake at 350 degrees for 35 minutes.

Hope Parks
Mrs. Frank Mayes (Marion)

Squash Casserole II

May prepare ahead   Serves 12

3 cups cooked squash,   1-8 ounce carton sour cream
  drained (approximately   Ritz crackers
  2 pounds)   1 cup sharp Cheddar cheese,
1 can cream of chicken soup   grated
½ green pepper, finely chopped   4 ounces Pepperidge Farm
1 small onion, finely chopped   herb stuffing mix
1 carrot, finely grated   1 stick butter

Mix all ingredients except butter, one ounce stuffing and ¼ cup cheese. Grease a 9 x 13-inch casserole dish and place squash mixture in dish. Mix 1 cup crushed Ritz crackers, 1 ounce Pepperidge Farm stuffing, and ¼ cup cheese to top casserole. Dot with slices of butter. Bake at 350 degrees for 30 minutes or until bubbly.

Kathy Linker Jenkins

Broiled Tomatoes

Serve immediately   Serves 4-6

2 tablespoons sour cream
2 tablespoons mayonnaise
1 tablespoon Parmesan
  cheese, grated
¼ teaspoon garlic salt

1½ teaspoons lemon juice
¼ teaspoon parsley, chopped
1 green onion, chopped
2 or 3 tomatoes, halved

Mix together all ingredients except tomatoes. Top tomatoes with mixture. Broil until bubbly.

Mrs. David Simpson (Emily)

Broiled Herbed Tomatoes

Prepare mixture in a jar to be stored.

May prepare ahead   Serves 6-8

Large ripe tomatoes,
  sliced ¾-inch thick

Butter

Mixture:
½ cup Parmesan cheese, grated
½ cup fine bread crumbs
1 tablespoon parsley flakes
1 teaspoon dill weed

1 teaspoon onion powder
¼ teaspoon oregano
⅛ teaspoon garlic powder
Salt and pepper to taste

Place tomato slices on broiler pan. Mix all mixture ingredients and sprinkle over top of each tomato slice thickly. Dot with butter. Bake at 350 degrees for 15 minutes. Stick under broiler for a few minutes until bubbly.

Peggy Cooke

Anne Byrd's Crusty Tomato Casserole

May prepare ahead   Serves 6

5 slices toasted bread or biscuits	¼ cup light brown sugar
1 stick butter	1 tablespoon vinegar
1-16 ounce can tomatoes	½ teaspoon salt
¼ cup onion, chopped	¼ teaspoon pepper

Preheat oven to 350 degrees. Cube the bread or break it into large chunks. Melt the butter in a skillet over medium heat. Stir until the bread cubes become slightly brown. Set aside.

Mix tomatoes, onion, brown sugar, vinegar, salt, and pepper in a 1½-quart oven-proof casserole. Bake at 350 degrees for 30 minutes. Then add toasted bread cubes to the top of the tomatoes and cook for 10 more minutes. Serve hot.

Roseanne Nichols

Tomato Cheese Puffs

Serve immediately   Serves 6

6 large tomatoes	¼ cup sharp Cheddar cheese, grated
½ teaspoon salt	1 tablespoon butter
1 cup milk	3 eggs, separated
1 cup soft bread crumbs	

Remove stem and scoop out tomatoes. Drain and sprinkle with salt. Combine all the other ingredients except eggs and cook over low heat until smooth. Remove from heat and add three slightly-beaten egg yolks. Fold in three stiffly-beaten egg whites. Fill tomato shells with mixture. Bake in shallow pan at 350 degrees for 20 to 25 minutes until puffed and brown.

Mrs. J. Caswell Taylor, Jr.

Tomato Pie

May prepare ahead   Serves 6

1 deep dish pie crust
3 firm tomatoes, thick-sliced
1 teaspoon salt
1 teaspoon pepper

1 teaspoon basil
1 tablespoon chives
1 cup mayonnaise
1 cup sharp Cheddar cheese, grated

Cook pie shell according to directions. Put layer of tomatoes on bottom. Sprinkle with salt, pepper, basil, and chives. Layer again. Combine mayonnaise and cheese and spread on top, sealing all edges. Bake at 350 degrees for 30 minutes.

Mrs. Davis Patton

Scalloped Tomatoes

May prepare ahead   Serves 6

1 cup celery, chopped
½ cup onion, chopped
2 tablespoons butter
1 tablespoon flour
1-28 ounce can tomatoes, chopped

2 cups (4 slices) ½-inch crisp toast cubes
1 tablespoon sugar
1 teaspoon salt
2 teaspoons prepared mustard
Dash pepper

Cook celery and onion in butter just until tender. Remove from heat, sprinkle with flour and blend. In a 2-quart casserole, combine celery-onion mixture with tomatoes, half the toast cubes, sugar, and seasonings. Bake at 350 degrees for about 30 minutes. Top with remaining cubes and bake 10 minutes longer.

Sis Torrence (Mrs. Charlton)

Corn Patties

I remember this old Virginia recipe as a favorite one of mine made by my grandmother. It has been passed down through many generations. This recipe makes a very good breakfast, a delicious Sunday night supper, or a great accompaniment for a meal (similar to a fritter).

Serve immediately   Serves 6

1 cup flour
1 teaspoon baking powder
½ teaspoon salt
2 tablespoons cornmeal
1 egg, beaten

1½ cups buttermilk
½ teaspoon soda
1 tablespoon Mazola corn oil
4 small ears of white corn

Mix flour, baking powder, salt, and cornmeal. Add beaten egg and buttermilk to soda stirring until bubbly. Beat until smooth, add Mazola and stir again with corn cut from cob. Have griddle hot and pour small amounts of mixture to make small-sized patties.

Serve only with butter as it is not as good with syrup. You may accompany this with Canadian bacon or sausage and fried apples to make a complete meal.

Mrs. William Thrower, Jr. (Price)

Corn Pudding

May prepare ahead   Serves 4-6

3 cups fresh corn, cut off
   the cob
¼ teaspoon pepper
2 cups milk

1 teaspoon salt
2 eggs, beaten
2 tablespoons butter, melted

Combine ingredients and pour into greased round casserole dish. Bake in 350 to 400-degree oven until set.

Susie Henry

Vegetable Casserole

May prepare ahead   Serves 8

1 can French green beans,   1 can shoe peg corn,
   drained   drained
1 cup celery, chopped   1 cup green pepper, chopped
½ cup sour cream   ½ cup (or more) Cheddar
1 can cream of celery soup   cheese, grated

Mix well and put in greased casserole.

Top with a mixture of the following:
1 stack Ritz crackers, crushed   1 stick butter or margarine,
¼ cup almonds, chopped   melted

Bake at 350 degrees for 45 minutes.

Anne Decker

Zucchini Deluxe

Serve immediately   Serves 6

6 fresh zucchini   ½ pound Velvetta cheese
¼ cup onion, chopped   2 tablespoons margarine,
1 medium tomato, chopped   melted
1 cup bread crumbs   ¼ cup milk
½ teaspoon salt   6 slices cooked bacon,
¼ teaspoon pepper   crumbled

Cook whole zucchini covered in boiling salted water for 5 to 8 minutes
and drain. Trim off ends and cut in half lengthwise. Scoop out center
and chop. (Be careful not to cut into the shell.) Combine zucchini, onions,
and tomato, and let drain to get rid of excess water. Add bread crumbs,
seasonings, and butter; toss lightly. Fill each shell. Place in baking dish
and bake at 350 degrees for 25 to 30 minutes. Heat cheese and milk in
pan over low heat until smooth and pour over zucchini. Add bacon to top.

Mrs. Susan B. Garrett

Eggs and Cheese

Brunch Grits Casserole

May prepare ahead   Serves 6-8

1 cup grits, uncooked
2 cups Cheddar cheese, grated
2 eggs, beaten

¼ teaspoon cayenne pepper,
** or more to taste**
Paprika

Cook grits according to package directions. Add 1½ cups cheese. Add eggs and pepper and mix well. Pour into greased shallow 1 ½-quart casserole. Top with remaining cheese. Sprinkle with paprika and bake at 375 degrees for 20 minutes.

Patti Hunter

Microwave New Year's Day Casserole

Serve immediately   Serves 4-6

1-12 ounce package frozen
** hash brown potatoes**
6 pieces bacon, cut-up
1-8 ounce carton sour cream

6 hard-boiled eggs, sliced
Salt and pepper to taste
Paprika

Microwave hash brown potatoes on HIGH on plate (leave in box) for 7 minutes.

Microwave bacon, cut in pieces, on HIGH in loaf dish for 6 minutes. Drain bacon, combine bacon drippings with sour cream (or to taste).

In loaf dish make layers of hash browns, eggs, crumbled bacon, sour cream, and salt and pepper; then one more layer of same sprinkled with salt, pepper, and paprika. Microwave at MEDIUM for 8 minutes.

Marsha Jones

Breakfast Casserole

May prepare ahead   Serves 8

2 pounds sausage   **9 eggs**
12 slices bread, cubed   **2 cups milk**
2 cups Cheddar cheese, grated **1½ teaspoons dry mustard**

Grease a 13 x 9-inch pan. Brown sausage and drain well. Layer bread, sausage, and cheese twice. Beat together eggs, milk, and mustard. Pour over layers. Refrigerate overnight. Bake at 350 degrees for 45 minutes to 1 hour until knife comes out clean. Cut into squares and serve.

May freeze layers ahead of time. Remove from freezer day before and add egg mixture. Refrigerate until ready to cook and serve.

Mrs. Joye S. Rankin

Brunch Casserole

May prepare ahead   Serves 6
Freezes well

6 hard-boiled eggs, sliced   **1½ cups Cheddar cheese,**
1 pound hot bulk sausage   **grated**
1½ cups sour cream   ` **Salt and pepper to taste**
½ cup dry bread crumbs

Place eggs in buttered casserole and season to taste. Cook sausage, drain, and sprinkle over eggs. Pour sour cream over sausage. Combine crumbs and cheese. Sprinkle over casserole. Place in oven to heat thoroughly and then brown top under broiler.

Mrs. Richard Akers (Gretchen)

Eggs and Sausage Casserole

Prepare same day   Serves 6

½ pound sharp cheese, grated   ½ cup sour cream
½ teaspoon salt   1 pound sausage, cooked,
½ teaspoon paprika   drained, and cooled
½ teaspoon dry mustard   10 to 12 eggs, beaten

Spray a 7 x 11-inch casserole with Pam. Cover bottom of dish with ½ of the cheese. Mix salt, paprika, and mustard into the sour cream and pour ½ of this over cheese. Sprinkle with sausage and top with remaining sour cream. Pour eggs on top and sprinkle with remaining cheese. Bake at 325 degrees for 30 to 40 minutes until firm.

Leslie Seabrook

Cottage Cheese Cake

*This has been a breakfast dish at our house. It is especially good
in the summertime because it is cool, but has staying power.*

May prepare ahead   Serves 6-8

Mix well the following and pour into buttered 2-quart casserole (use a deep dish for creamy, and a shallow dish for chewy).

2 pounds creamed cottage   5 eggs, beaten
  cheese   Rind of 2 lemons
Juice of 1½ lemons   1 teaspoon vanilla
1½ cups sugar

Sprinkle top with cinnamon and bake at 350 degrees for 35 to 45 minutes. This may be tested with clean knife. It sets up like custard. Refrigerate.

Marilyn Price

Egg and Rice Brunch Casserole

Must prepare day before   Serves 8

8 eggs, beaten
1 cup milk
¼ teaspoon salt
⅛ teaspoon pepper

2 cups cooked rice
1-4½ ounce jar mushrooms,
 drained

Combine eggs, milk, salt, and pepper; mix well. Stir in rice and mushrooms. Pour into greased 12 x 8 x 2-inch casserole. Refrigerate overnight. Bake at 350 degrees for 30 to 35 minutes or until set. Cut into squares. Serve with cheese sauce.

Cookbook Committee

Open Face Cheese Dreams

Serve immediately   Serves 6

3 English muffins, split in half
 and buttered
6 slices bacon, cut in half

Tomato, sliced
6 slices processed cheese

Place muffins in oven and broil. Slightly microwave bacon and drain. Top muffin half with tomato slice, bacon and slice of cheese. Return to broiler and broil for 5 minutes or until cheese melts.

Mrs. Holt Harris

Irene's Swiss Eggs

A good idea for Christmas morning.

May prepare day ahead   Serves 12

3 to 4 tablespoons butter,   12 eggs
  softened   Milk, 1 tablespoon for each
1-8 ounce package fresh   egg
  mushrooms, sliced   2 cups Cheddar cheese,
1 to 1½ cups Swiss cheese,   grated
  grated

Grease a 9 x 13-inch glass dish with butter. Place layer of mushrooms in bottom of dish and top with Swiss cheese. Drop eggs into dish. Put 1 tablespoon milk on each egg. Sprinkle grated Cheddar cheese over entire pan. Bake at 325 degrees for 20 minutes. Cover and refrigerate if preparing night before.

Mary Lou Norcross

When recipe calls for adding raw eggs to hot mixture, always begin by adding a small amount of hot mixture to the beaten eggs slowly to avoid curdling.

Eggs For A Crowd

Serve immediately   Serves as many as you want

Frozen patty shells,   Canadian bacon, 1 slice per
  one per person   shell
Eggs, one per person   Knorrs Hollandaise sauce mix
                                       1 envelope per six eggs

Bake patty shells according to directions (can be done ahead). Undercook so they are not too brown (approximately 20 minutes). Remove tops, scoop out middle dough, being careful not to make holes in basket.

Place on a cookie sheet and crack a raw egg into each. Bake at 300 degrees until egg is set (about 30 minutes). Serve each egg on a slice of Canadian bacon. Top with Hollandaise sauce.

Pat McCloskey
Connie Gibbons

French Scrambled Eggs

These are soft and custardy without being runny.
The secret is to cook VERY slowly.

Serve immediately   Serves 8

12 eggs   **2 tablespoons soft butter**
¼ teaspoon salt   **2 tablespoons whipping cream**
Pinch of pepper

Beat eggs in bowl with salt and pepper until lemony in color. Smear cold frying pan with butter. Pour in eggs and set over low to moderate heat. Stir constantly until eggs thicken into a custard. Stir rapidly until eggs thicken to consistency you desire. Remove from heat and stir in cream to stop cooking.

Connie Gibbons

Asparagus Quiche

This is a crustless quiche and is low in calories (178 per serving).

May prepare ahead   Serves 5-6

1-10½ ounce can asparagus,   **8 ounces Swiss cheese,**
   drained   **grated**
1 cup skim milk   **1 small onion, finely minced**
5 eggs   **½ teaspoon basil**
½ teaspoon pepper   **1 teaspoon salt**

Place asparagus spears in bottom of quiche pan. Beat milk and eggs in a medium bowl. Add remaining ingredients and blend lightly with fork. Bake at 325 degrees, uncovered, for 30 minutes or until knife inserted comes out clean.

Mrs. Susan Sherrill Ownsbey

Breakfast Quiche

Even my kids like this!

Serve immediately   Serves 6
Freezes well

1-9 inch pie shell, unbaked   6 ounces bulk sausage,
4 eggs, beaten   cooked, crumbled, and
¾ cup milk   drained
⅛ teaspoon pepper   4 ounces mozzarella cheese,
¼ teaspoon salt   shredded

Combine eggs, milk, salt and pepper. Layer in pie shell: half of mozzarella, sausage, and remainder of mozzarella. Pour egg mixture over top. Bake at 350 degrees for 30 minutes.

Gail Hardin

Broccoli and Ham Quiche

May prepare ahead   Serves 6-8

1 cup ham, chopped   ½ cup milk
1 package broccoli, cooked   ½ cup mayonnaise
  and drained   ½ cup onion, chopped
2 cups Swiss cheese, grated   1-9 inch pie shell
2 eggs

Mix all ingredients together and pour into a 9-inch pie shell. Bake at 350 degrees for 1 hour.

Margie Kircus

Chicken Spinach Quiche

May prepare ahead
Freezes well

Serves 4-6

2 pounds cooked chicken,
  cubed
1½ cups sharp cheese, grated
3 eggs, beaten
¾ can evaporated milk
½ teaspoon salt
½ teaspoon garlic
¼ cup chopped onion,
  sauteed

1-10 ounce package frozen
  spinach, thawed and
  drained
½ teaspoon pepper
½ teaspoon paprika
1 deep-dish frozen pie shell

Preheat oven to 425 degrees. Bake pie shell for 5 minutes. Mix all ingredients and pour into pie shell. Bake on a cookie sheet for 25 minutes or until golden brown. Let stand for 20 to 30 minutes before serving.

Mrs. Mary Lewis Bryant

Crab Quiche

May partially prepare ahead
Serve immediately after cooking

Serves 8

1-9 inch pie shell
4 eggs
2 cups light cream
2 tablespoons instant
  minced onion
1-17 ounce can cream corn
1 teaspoon salt
⅛ teaspoon cayenne
  pepper

1-7½ ounce can crab meat,
  drained
1 cup Swiss or mozzarella
  cheese, shredded
Parsley flakes
Croutons

In a bowl beat eggs, cream, onion, corn, salt, and pepper. Cover and refrigerate. About 1 hour before serving heat oven to 425 degrees. Pat crab meat dry. Sprinkle crab meat and cheese in pie shell. Pour egg mixture over crab meat and cheese. Sprinkle with parsley. Bake for 15 minutes. Reduce oven temperature to 300 degrees and bake for 30 minutes more. Let stand for 10 minutes.

Mrs. Holt Harris

Quiche Lorraine

May prepare ahead   Serves 8

¾ pound bacon
2-9 inch frozen pie shells
4 ounces Grueyere cheese
1 pound sharp Cheddar
  cheese
4 eggs

Pinch red pepper
Pinch black pepper
1¾ cups half-n-half
½ teaspoon salt (optional)

Fry bacon until crisp; crumble and sprinkle in thawed pie shells. Grate cheese and put on top of bacon. Combine eggs, salt, peppers, and half-n-half. Pour mixture over cheeses. Bake at 400 degrees for 25 to 35 minutes. Let set before serving.

Jan P. Gray

Ham and Cheese Sandwich Souffle

Serve immediately   Serves as many as desired

Sliced bread, twice as much
  as ham and cheese
Butter
Sliced ham (thin)
Sliced Cheddar cheese

2 cups milk
2 eggs
½ teaspoon dry mustard
Salt and pepper to taste

Remove crusts from bread. Butter both sides. Make sandwiches and place in a casserole dish (size of dish depends on number of sandwiches). Beat together milk, eggs, and spices. Pour over sandwiches and soak at least 1 hour. Bake at 400 degrees for 40 to 50 minutes.

Candy Grooms

Mock Cheese Souffle I

Must prepare ahead   Serves 8

8 slices buttered bread, cut in   **2½ cups milk**
thirds, crusts removed   **4 eggs**
½ pound medium Cheddar   **1 teaspoon dry mustard**
cheese, grated   **1 teaspoon salt**

Place half of bread strips in a greased 2-quart casserole to form one layer.
Cover this with half of the cheese. Repeat with another layer of bread
and then cheese. Beat remaining ingredients together and pour over
bread mixture. Cover and let stand in refrigerator for 12 to 24 hours.
Set casserole in pan containing small amount of water. Bake at 350
degrees for 1 hour.

Jennie Stultz

Mock Cheese Souffle II

Serve immediately   Serves 6-8

6 slices of bread   **½ tablespoon Worcestershire**
½ pound sharp cheese   **sauce**
4 eggs   **Salt and pepper to taste**
2½ cups milk   **Butter or margarine**

Grease a 9 x 13-inch glass baking dish. Cut crust off bread and line bottom of casserole. Cover with cheese. Mix 4 eggs slightly beaten with milk,
Worcestershire sauce, salt, and pepper. Pour over bread and cheese. Dot
with butter. Put in pan of hot water and bake for 45 minutes at 350
degrees.

Mrs. Paul Quinn

Deviled Eggs

May prepare ahead   Serves 20

10 hard-boiled eggs   **Salt and freshly ground**
½ cup mayonnaise   **black pepper to taste**
4 tablespoons unsalted butter,
  melted

Peel the eggs and cut in half. Carefully scoop out the yolks, and arrange the whites on a tray. With an electric mixer or a food processor blend the egg yolks, mayonnaise, and melted butter until smooth. Season with salt and pepper to taste.

Put the egg mixture in a pastry bag filled with a large star tip. Pipe the mixture carefully and very neatly into the egg whites halves. Cover with plastic wrap and refrigerate until ready to serve.

Variation: Deviled egg may be topped with a spoonful of red, black, or golden caviar.

Jennifer Davis

Curried Eggs and Mushrooms

This is a delicious and different side dish.

May prepare day ahead   Serves 4

5 hard-boiled eggs   **1 teaspoon paprika**
½ pound mushrooms, fresh   **¼ cup cheese (Swiss or**
6 tablespoons butter, divided   **Cheddar), grated**
2 tablespoons flour   **Curry powder to taste**
1 cup milk   **Bread crumbs**
½ teaspoon salt   **2 tablespoons butter, cut up**
½ teaspoon pepper

Chill eggs and cut into quarters. Sauté sliced mushrooms in 4 table-spoons butter. Prepare a cream sauce from the remaining 2 tablespoons butter, flour, and milk. Add salt, pepper, and paprika to sauce. Add cheese and curry powder to sauce. Mix eggs, mushrooms, and sauce in a 1½-quart casserole dish. Top with bread crumbs and butter. Broil until browned.

Mrs. Sam Howe (Cherry)

Breads

Angel Biscuits

May prepare ahead   Makes 4 to 5 dozen

1 package yeast
2 to 3 tablespoons warm water
5 cups flour
⅓ cup sugar
2 cups buttermilk

1 tablespoon baking powder
1 teaspoon salt
1 teaspoon soda
1 cup shortening

Dissolve yeast in water. Sift dry ingredients together. Cut in shortening. Stir in yeast mixture and buttermilk. Roll out onto a floured board and cut into biscuits. Brush top with beaten egg, if desired. Bake at 400 degrees for 10 to 20 minutes until brown. Dough keeps well in refrigerator for several days, but allow to warm before baking.

To make ham biscuits cut biscuits open while still warm and butter with very thin pat of butter and fill with sliced ham or lightly-browned country ham. These can be made ahead and refrigerated or frozen and heated just before serving.

Jennifer Davis

Hint: When working with fresh garlic - to remove garlic odor from fingers, rub with a spoon (silver-plated). The metal removes the odor.

Susan's Biscuits

May prepare ahead   Yields: 12-15
Freezes well after cooking

2 cups Bisquick
1 stick margarine or butter,
  melted

1 cup sour cream

Mix all ingredients and bake in greased muffin pans at 350 degrees about 20 to 25 minutes. May be baked in small muffin pans for a daintier biscuit, about 18 to 20 minutes. This should make 24 to 36 small biscuits.

Biscuits should be cooked before freezing. To reheat, wrap in foil and warm in a 250 to 300-degree oven.

Mrs. Anne Neal

The Best Biscuits

My advice to my children and others setting out on their own:
If the bread is outstanding, the meal will be memorable! Learn to
make these biscuits, pick up prepared meats and trimmings from your local
deli, and you'll impress the world.

May prepare ahead   Serves 15-20

4 cups flour
1 cup wheat germ (or cracked wheat)
1 teaspoon soda
1 package yeast (dissolved in 2 tablespoons lukewarm water)

¼ cup sugar
1 tablespoon baking powder
1 teaspoon salt
1 cup shortening
2 cups buttermilk

Mix dry ingredients. Cut in shortening. Stir in yeast and buttermilk. Roll out on floured cloth. Cut biscuits and bake on cookie sheet at 400 degrees for 10 minutes.

Note: Mix up this biscuit dough and keep in refrigerator. Just pinch off the quantity of dough needed for each meal. Keeps for one week in covered container in refrigerator.

Mrs. Kay K. Moss

Broccoli Bread

This recipe was given to me by my aunt, Mrs. E. S. Ballard.

Serve immediately   Serves 8-10

1 package chopped broccoli, thawed and drained
1 large onion, chopped
4 eggs, beaten

1 stick margarine, melted
¾ cup cottage cheese
1 teaspoon salt
1 box Jiffy muffin mix

Combine all ingredients in the order listed. Mix well. Pour batter into a 9 x 13-inch dish. Bake at 400 degrees for 15 to 20 minutes.

Mrs. Robert S. Pearson

Cheese Biscuits

*This recipe is truly a biscuit as opposed to a
cheese wafer or cheese straw.*

May freeze after cooking*   Yields: 16-20

2 cups flour
3 teaspoons baking powder
½ teaspoon soda
1 teaspoon salt

2 teaspoons sugar
½ cup shortening
½ cup sharp Cheddar
  cheese, grated
⅔ cup buttermilk

Combine dry ingredients in a bowl and cut in the shortening until like
coarse crumbs. Mix in cheese. Make a well and add milk at once. Quickly
stir with fork just until dough follows fork around bowl. Turn onto lightly
floured surface. Knead gently 10 to 12 strokes and roll thin. Cut into
small biscuits. Place on greased baking sheet and bake at 425 degrees
for 8 minutes.

**Note: To freeze: cook only until biscuits start to brown; remove from oven. To serve
after freezing: thaw and bake at 425 degrees for 4 to 5 minutes.*

Mrs. Joe B. Maynard

Breakaway Bread

May prepare ahead   Yields: 1 loaf

3 cans biscuits, quartered
1 stick margarine, melted
1 large bell pepper, finely
  chopped

1 onion, finely chopped
½ pound bacon, fried and
  crumbled
Parmesan cheese

Dip quartered biscuits in margarine and layer one can in bottom of bundt
pan. Sprinkle ½ of pepper, onion, bacon, and Parmesan cheese on top.
Repeat with one more can of biscuits, green peppers, onion, bacon, and
cheese. Top with third can of biscuits. Bake at 350 degrees for 45
minutes. Invert pan onto serving platter (I put a lot of Parmesan cheese
on each layer).

Mrs. Don Barringer (Tina)

Cranberry Bread

Beautiful, delicious and a worthy gift at Christmas.

May prepare ahead   Yields: 1 loaf

2 cups flour, sifted
1½ teaspoons baking powder
½ teaspoon baking soda
1 teaspoon salt
1 cup sugar
¼ cup butter

1 egg, beaten
1 teaspoon orange peel
¾ cup orange juice
1½ cups light raisins
1½ cups fresh or frozen
  cranberries, chopped

Sift flour, sugar, baking powder, salt, and soda into bowl. Cut in butter until mixture is crumbly. Add egg, orange peel, and orange juice all at once. Stir just until mixture is evenly moist. Fold in raisins and cranberries. Spoon in greased 9 x 5 x 5-inch loaf pan and bake at 350 degrees for 1 hour and 10 minutes.

Hope Parks

Dill Bread

Must prepare ahead   Yields: 1 loaf

1 package yeast
½ cup lukewarm water
1 cup cottage cheese
1 tablespoon butter, melted
1 egg
2 tablespoons onion, chopped

2 tablespoons dill seed
2 tablespoons sugar
1 teaspoon salt
¼ teaspoon soda
2½ cups flour

Sprinkle yeast over water. Heat cottage cheese to lukewarm. Combine all ingredients except flour; add flour gradually. Cover. Let rise until double. Stir down. Put in greased 1½-quart casserole. Let rise until light - about 40 minutes. Bake at 350 degrees for 50 minutes. Brush with additional melted butter. Sprinkle with salt.

Mrs. Joseph Philip Coyle

Filled Cheese Bread

*This is Marsha Howe's recipe. Don't be afraid
to try it even though it LOOKS complicated.*

Prepare one day ahead or same day   Yields: 1 large loaf

1⅓ cups lukewarm water	½ teaspoon oregano
1 envelope dry yeast	¾ pound thinly sliced
1 teaspoon sugar	Monterey Jack, Cheddar,
3½ to 3¾ cups flour, divided	or provolone cheese
1 teaspoon salt	½ teaspoon basil
¼ cup mayonnaise	2 tablespoons olive oil
½ cup scallions, chopped	1 egg, beaten

Combine water, yeast, and sugar in a large bowl. Stir briefly and let
stand until the yeast dissolves and begins to foam (5 to 10 minutes). Stir
1½ cups of the flour and the salt into the yeast mixture. Beat well until
smooth and bubbly. Gradually add enough of the remaining flour to
make a fairly soft dough. Do NOT add more flour than the dough can
absorb. Turn out onto a lightly floured surface and knead lightly until
the dough is just barely non-sticky (approximately 2 minutes). Place in
an oiled bowl and turn to coat with a light film of oil. Cover and let rise
in a warm, draft-free place until doubled in bulk (approximately 30
minutes). *Note: I use a cold oven with the light on.*

Punch down the dough and turn out onto a lightly floured surface. Let
relax for 10 minutes. Preheat oven to 425 degrees. Roll dough into an
even 16 x 12-inch rectangle about ⅛-inch thick. Spread a 4-inch bank
of mayonnaise down the center of the dough leaving a 1 ½-inch border
on the two short sides. Sprinkle mayonnaise with scallions and cover
with overlapping slices of cheese. Sprinkle all with oregano and basil.
Drizzle with olive oil. Fold the two short ends of the dough up and over
the filling. Dampen the long edges of the dough with cold water. Pull
them up to completely enclose the filling, overlapping by about 1 inch
on top. Press gently to seal. Flip loaf over, seam side down, onto a greased
baking sheet.

Slash the top in several places to let steam escape. Brush with beaten
egg and bake at once for 35 minutes. Transfer to a rack and let cool for
20 minutes. Cut into thick slices to serve.

Mrs. Sam Howe (Cherry)

Grecian Lemon Nut Bread

May prepare ahead   Yields: 1 loaf

¾ cup butter or margarine,   ¼ teaspoon baking soda
  softened   ⅛ teaspoon salt
1½ cups sugar   Rind of 1 lemon, grated
3 eggs   ¾ cup pecans, chopped
¾ cup buttermilk   Juice of 2 lemons
2¼ cups flour   ¾ cup powdered sugar

Cream butter and sugar until light and fluffy. Add eggs and beat well.
Combine dry ingredients. Add buttermilk and dry ingredients to sugar
mixture, beginning and ending with buttermilk. Stir just until all ingredients are moistened. Stir in lemon rind and pecans. Spoon batter into
a greased 9 x 5 x 3-inch loaf pan. Bake at 325 degrees for 1¼ hours or
until bread tests done. Combine lemon juice and powdered sugar and
stir well. Punch holes in top of warm bread and pour on glaze.

Ginny Ratchford

Honey Orange Bread

Can be served at a wedding breakfast.

May prepare ahead   Serves 12

¼ cup (½ stick) butter,   ¾ cup whole wheat flour
  softened   ½ cup unprocessed bran
1 cup honey   1 tablespoon baking powder
1 egg   ½ teaspoon baking soda
1½ tablespoons grated   ½ teaspoon salt
  orange rind   ¾ cup orange juice
1 cup flour   ¾ cup walnuts, chopped

Heat oven to 325 degrees. Cream butter with honey; add egg and orange
rind. Mix dry ingredients and add to creamed mixture alternately with
orange juice. When batter is fairly smooth, stir in nuts. Pour into
buttered 9 x 5 x 3-inch loaf pan and bake for 60 to 70 minutes until
skewer inserted in center comes out clean. Turn bread out and cool on
rack.

Mrs. Paulette H. Elmore

Oatmeal Bread

Freezes well after cooking   Yields: 1 loaf

3 cups flour (half may be   2 teaspoons salt
   whole wheat)   1 egg
1¼ cups rolled oats   ¼ cup honey
1½ tablespoons baking   1½ cups milk
   powder

Mix dry ingredients in a large bowl. Mix egg, honey, and milk in medium bowl. Pour wet mixture into dry mixture. Stir until moistened (mixture will not be smooth). Spoon batter into greased loaf pan. Bake 1 hour and 15 minutes at 350 degrees.

Mrs. Kay Kincaid Moss

Quick Poppy Seed Loaf

You may divide this into two loaves and freeze one and eat the other hot from the oven. The frozen one bakes in less time - about 45 minutes.

May prepare ahead   Yields: 1 loaf

1-18 ounce butterpecan cake mix   ½ cup vegetable oil
1-3¾ ounce package French   4 eggs
   vanilla pudding mix   1 cup pecans, chopped
1 cup hot water   1 tablespoon poppy seeds

Combine cake mix, pudding mix, water, vegetable oil, and eggs in a large mixing bowl. Beat well. Stir in pecans and poppy seeds. Pour batter in greased 9 x 5 x 3-inch loaf pan. Bake at 350 degrees for 1 hour and 5 minutes. Check with wooden pick. Cool for 10 minutes in pan. Remove and cool on a rack.

Hope Parks

Vorte Limpe

Traditional Swedish bread

May prepare ahead

Yields: 2 loaves

2½ cups medium rye flour
2 packages dry yeast
⅓ cup packed brown sugar
1 tablespoon salt
2 cups water
¼ cup molasses
¼ cup margarine

2 tablespoons grated orange
  peel
1 tablespoon anise seeds
1 tablespoon fennel seeds
3½ to 4 cups flour
½ to 1½ cups flour
1 egg, beaten

Combine rye flour, yeast, sugar, and salt. Blend. Heat water, molasses, and margarine in saucepan until very warm (120 to 130 degrees). Add to rye flour mixture. Blend with electric mixer at low speed until moist. Beat 2 minutes at medium speed. Add orange peel, anise, and fennel seeds. Stir in 3½ to 4 cups of flour to form a sticky dough. Knead dough, adding additional flour until dough is smooth, pliable and no longer sticky (about 5 minutes). Place dough in greased bowl. Cover and let rise in warm place until light and not quite double in size, about 45 to 60 minutes. Punch dough down and divide into 2 parts. Shape into round loaves and place on greased cookie sheet. Cover and let rise in warm place until light but not quite double in size, 30 to 35 minutes. Brush loaves with beaten egg. Bake at 375 degrees for 25 to 35 minutes until loaf sounds hollow when lightly tapped. Remove from cookie sheet and cool.

Connie Gibbons

Beer Bread

Serve immediately

Serves 6-8

3 cups self-rising flour
3 tablespoons sugar

12 ounces beer, at room
  temperature

Put flour and sugar into bowl. Pour beer slowly into bowl. Gently mix. Grease loaf pan. Pour batter into pan and bake at 350 degrees for 40 to 50 minutes.

Mary Jane Stewart

Monkey Bread

This is a breakfast-like Danish that is great for brunch.

May prepare ahead   Yields: 1 loaf

3 cans biscuits, cut into   1 cup sugar
  4 pieces each   1 stick butter, melted
1 tablespoon cinnamon   1 cup brown sugar

Put cinnamon and sugar in plastic bag and coat biscuit pieces well.
Grease bundt pan. Mix butter and brown sugar, pour over top and bake
at 350 degrees for 30 minutes.

Mrs. Penny White

Moravian Sugar Bread

May prepare ahead   Yields: 2-12 x 15-inch
Freezes well   or 4-8-inch round or square cakes

1 cup sugar   1 cup mashed potatoes
1 cup lard   4 cups (approximately) flour
1 teaspoon salt   ½ cup cream
3 eggs, beaten   Brown sugar, as needed
2 packages yeast, dissolved in   Cinnamon, as needed
  lukewarm water   Butter, as needed

Cream sugar, lard, and salt. Add eggs and mashed potatoes. Add yeast
and water and stir in flour until dough is stiff. Let dough rise until double bulk (about 3 to 4 hours). Work out into 2 thin cakes (each 12 x
15-inches) on oiled, flat pans. Let rise again. Then punch holes in dough
with finger, 1½ inches apart. Sprinkle with cream. Then heavily sprinkle
with brown sugar as needed. Sprinkle with cinnamon and dot with small
pats of butter. The holes will catch some of the sugar and butter
mixture and hold it on the cake. Bake at 425 degrees until top is golden
and cake tests as done.

Eat warm or cold. To reheat, wrap in foil and place in a 250- degree oven
for about 10 minutes.

Mrs. T. Dale Ward (Ann)

Hot Roll Moravian Sugar Cake

May prepare ahead   Serves 15
Freezes well

1 package Pillsbury hot roll mix   ¾ cup warm water
⅓ cup instant non-fat dry milk   (105 to 115 degrees)
⅓ cup Hungry Jack mashed   ½ cup sugar
   potato flakes   ⅓ cup margarine or butter,
2 eggs   melted

Topping:
⅔ cup light brown sugar,   1 teaspoon cinnamon
   packed   ½ cup margarine or butter,
½ cup nuts, chopped   melted

Grease a 13 x 9-inch pan. In large bowl dissolve yeast from hot roll mix in warm water. Stir in half of flour from hot roll mix and remaining ingredients, beat two minutes at medium speed. Add remaining flour from mix and beat well. Cover loosely with plastic wrap and cloth towel. Let rise in warm place (80 to 85 degrees) until light and doubled in size, about 45 minutes. Stir down dough and spread in prepared pan. Cover and let rise in a warm place until light and doubled in size, about 45 minutes.

Heat oven to 375 degrees. Make small pockets in dough by pressing lightly with floured fingertips. Sprinkle brown sugar/cinnamon mixture over dough. Drizzle with melted margarine and sprinkle with nuts. Bake at 375 degrees for 15 to 20 minutes or until golden brown.

Tillie Hall

Phyllis Cannon's Cream Cheese Braids

Must prepare ahead
Freezes well after cooking

Yields: 4 loaves

Dough:
1-8 ounce carton sour cream, scalded
½ cup sugar
½ cup butter, melted
1 teaspoon salt

2 envelopes dry yeast
½ cup warm water
2 eggs, beaten
4 cups flour

Filling:
2-8 ounce packages cream cheese, softened
¾ cup sugar

1 egg, beaten
2 teaspoons vanilla
⅛ teaspoon salt

Glaze:
2 cups powdered sugar
2 teaspoons vanilla

¼ cup milk

Scald sour cream in pot and mix in sugar, butter, and salt. Cool to lukewarm. In a large mixing bowl dissolve yeast in warm water. Stir in sour cream mixture and eggs. Gradually stir in flour with a spoon. Cover tightly and chill overnight. Dough will be very soft.

Divide soft dough into 4 equal portions. Turn each portion onto a heavily floured surface and knead 4 or 5 times. Roll each into a 12 x 8-inch rectangle.

Combine ingredients for filling with an electric mixer until blended. Spread ¼ of filling mixture over each rectangle leaving a ½-inch margin. Carefully roll up jelly-roll fashion, firmly pinch edge and ends to seal. Place seam side down on greased baking sheets. Make 6 X-shaped cuts down the top of each loaf. Cover and let rise in warm place for 1 hour.

Bake at 375 degrees for 15 to 20 minutes. Combine ingredients for glaze and spread on warm loaves. Cut into 12 slices to serve.

Mrs. Dale Brittain (Beth)

Christmas Coffee Cake I

May prepare ahead   Serves 8-10
Freezes well

2 cups flour   ½ teaspoon soda
2 cups brown sugar   ½ cup butter
½ teaspoon salt   1 egg, beaten
1 cup sour cream   ½ cup pecans, chopped

Combine flour, sugar, salt and then cut the butter into the mixture. Spread 2½ cups of this on the bottom of a well-greased 11 x 2 x 7-inch pan. Blend soda, sour cream, and egg into remaining mixture. Spoon on top of mixture. Sprinkle on nuts. Bake at 350 degrees for 35 minutes.

Allison Decker Sonier
Mrs. Joye S. Rankin

Christmas Coffee Cake II

This is my traditional Christmas coffee cake which I bake and give to special friends for their Christmas breakfast.

May prepare ahead   Serves 8-10
Freezes well

1 stick margarine or butter   1 teaspoon soda
1 cup sugar   1 teaspoon baking powder
2 eggs   1-8 ounce carton sour cream
2 cups flour   1 teaspoon vanilla

Filling:
½ cup light brown sugar   1 teaspoon flour
1 teaspoon cinnamon   ½ cup pecans, chopped

Cream margarine and sugar. Add eggs, one at a time. Sift together flour, soda, and baking powder. Mix flour mixture alternately with sour cream and add vanilla. Alternate cake mixture and filling in a greased tube pan beginning with batter and ending with filling on top. Bake at 350 degrees for 30 minutes.

Mrs. Mary Lewis Bryant

Blueberry Coffee Cake

Great when topped with Cool Whip or vanilla ice cream.

Serve immediately   Serves 6-8

1 quart blueberries   ½ cup oil
½ cup pecans, chopped   1 cup sugar
½ cup sugar   1 cup flour
1 stick margarine or butter   2 eggs

Grease a 10-inch pie plate and pour blueberries into plate. Combine pecans and ½ cup sugar and spread over blueberries. Melt butter; add oil, 1 cup sugar, flour, and eggs. Beat these ingredients together and pour over berry mixture. Bake at 325 degrees for 1 hour.

Ginny Hall (Mrs. Alex)

Buttermilk Coffeecake

Freezes well   Makes one 9-inch cake

1 teaspoon unsalted butter,   ⅔ cup buttermilk
  softened plus 12 tablespoons   1 egg, lightly beaten
  unsalted butter, cut into bits   ½ cup pecans or almonds,
2 cups plus 1 tablespoon   finely chopped
  flour, sifted   1 teaspoon ground cinnamon
1½ teaspoons baking powder   ½ cup currants
1 cup light brown sugar

Preheat the oven to 425 degrees. With a pastry brush, brush the bottom and sides of a 9-inch layer cake pan with the teaspoon of softened butter. Use the 1 tablespoon flour to flour pan evenly.

In a large mixing bowl combine 2 cups flour, baking powder, brown sugar, and butter bits and rub them together with your fingertips until they look like fine crumbs. Set aside ½ cup of this mixture to use for the topping.

Into mixture remaining in bowl gradually stir buttermilk, egg, nuts, cinnamon, and currants. When ingredients are well combined and batter is smooth, pour it into floured pan and sprinkle top evenly with reserved crumb mixture. Bake in center of oven for 15 minutes and reduce heat to 375 degrees for remaining 20 to 25 mintues. Serve coffee cake warm or at room temperature.

Lin Lineberger

Sour Cream Coffee Cake

Freezes well after cooking

Makes 1 tube cake or
6 mini loaves

1 stick margarine
1 cup sugar
2 eggs
2 cups flour
1 teaspoon baking powder

1 teaspoon baking soda
1 teaspoon salt
1 cup sour cream
1 tablespoon vanilla

Topping:
⅓ cup sugar
1 tablespoon cinnamon

⅓ cup brown sugar
1 cup pecans, chopped

Cream together margarine, sugar, and eggs. Add flour, baking powder, soda, and salt. Add sour cream and vanilla. Mix all ingredients well. Spread ⅓ batter in bottom of greased bundt or tube pan and add ⅓ of topping ingredients that have been mixed together, alternating batter and topping and ending with nut topping. (For mini-loaf pans, use only 2 layers per pan.) Bake for 30 minutes at 350 degrees for mini loaves or 45 minutes at 350 degrees for a bundt or tube pan.

Mrs. Karen L. Staker

Strawberry Gems

May prepare ahead

Makes 1 dozen

1 egg, beaten
¼ cup oil
¼ cup milk
¾ cup sugar
1 cup self-rising flour

½ cup sliced strawberries
(frozen are best)
¼ cup sugar, optional
¼ teaspoon cinnamon,
optional

Mix egg, oil, and milk together. Blend sugar and flour; add to liquid mixture. Stir lightly and add strawberries last. Bake at 375 degrees for 25 minutes in 1½-inch muffin tins.

Optional topping: Mix together ¼ cup sugar and ¼ teaspoon cinnamon and sprinkle over muffins before baking.

Marilyn Price

Crescent Caramel Swirl Coffee Cake

This is best when served warm.

Serve immediately   Serves 6-8

½ cup butter or margarine   2 tablespoons water
½ cup nuts, chopped   2-8 ounce cans refrigerated
1 cup brown sugar   crescent dinner rolls

Preheat oven to 375 degrees or 350 degrees for colored tube pan.

In small saucepan melt butter. Coat bottom and sides of a 12-cup fluted tube pan with 2 tablespoons of melted butter and sprinkle pan with 3 tablespoons of nuts. Add remaining nuts, brown sugar, and water to butter; heat to boiling while stirring occasionally.

Remove crescents from cans in rolled sections but DO NOT UNROLL. Cut each section into four slices. Arrange eight slices in prepared pan, separating each pinwheel slightly to allow sauce to penetrate. Spoon half the caramel sauce over dough. Repeat with remaining dough and pour remaining caramel sauce over dough. Bake for 25 to 30 minutes (30 to 35 minutes for colored pan) until deep golden brown. Cool for 3 minutes and turn onto serving platter to serve.

Mrs. J. Caswell Taylor, Jr.

Quick Sally Lunn

Serve immediately   Yields: 1 loaf

⅓ cup butter   ½ teaspoon salt
⅓ cup sugar   2 cups flour
3 eggs   1 cup milk
2 teaspoons baking powder

Cream butter and sugar. Add eggs, one at a time. Mix dry ingredients and add alternately with milk. Pour in greased bread pan and bake at 425 degrees for 30 to 45 minutes.

Anne Decker

Applesauce Muffins

Batter may be stored in the refrigerator for up to 8 weeks.

May prepare ahead   Yields: 12 large

2 sticks soft margarine
1½ cups sugar
2 eggs
1 teaspoon vanilla
4 cups flour
3 teaspoons cinnamon

1 teaspoon cloves
2 teaspoons allspice
1 cup pecans, chopped
1-1 pound can applesauce
2 teaspoons soda

Mix together margarine, sugar, eggs, and vanilla. Sift together flour, cinnamon, cloves, and allspice and add these two mixtures together. Add pecans. Mix together applesauce and soda and add to other mixture. Bake at 400 degrees for 10 to 15 minutes.

Mrs. John Guglielmetti

Betty Beall's Breakfast Muffins

These can be stored in the freezer or they will keep in the refrigerator about one week. Good warm or cold.

May prepare ahead   Yields: 1 dozen

4 large shredded wheat
   biscuits
1 cup skim milk or
   2 percent milk
1 cup package baking mix
1 teaspoon baking powder
½ to ¾ cup white sugar
   substitute that measures
   like sugar

¼ cup honey
1 teaspoon vanilla
1 cup ground raw cranberries
   or blackberries or raisins
1 teaspoon cinnamon
2 eggs, separated

Spray a muffin pan with a non-stick spray. Preheat oven to 375 degrees. Mix milk with broken shredded wheat biscuits. Add baking mix and stir to moisten. Add all other ingredients except egg whites and beat by hand until smooth. Fold in stiffly beaten egg whites. Spoon into muffin pan and bake for about 40 minutes at 375 degrees or until the muffins test done. Cool on rack.

Lin Lineberger

Merry Christmas Wreath

May prepare ahead   Serves 10-12

1 package active dry yeast   1 teaspoon salt
¼ cup warm water   1 egg, well beaten
1 cup milk, scalded   3½ cups flour, sifted
¼ cup sugar   Candied cherries, halved
¼ cup shortening   Slivered almonds

Soften active dry yeast in warm water. Combine milk, sugar, shortening, and salt. Cool pan in lukewarm water and add yeast and egg. Gradually stir in flour to form soft dough; beat vigorously. Cover and let rise in a warm place until double, about 2 hours.

Grease a 10-inch ring mold and spread bottom with sugar/fruit topping made by mixing the following ingredients:

2 tablespoons light corn   2 tablespoons butter or
   syrup   margarine, melted
½ cup brown sugar

Place halved candied cherries, cut side up, and slivered almonds on sugar mixture. Shape dough in almond-sized balls; roll in melted butter. Place two rows deep in pan. Let rise until double. Bake at 400 degrees for 20 to 25 minutes in a preheated oven. Loosen and turn out quickly. Serve with whipped butter.

Mrs. Terry Ratchford (Trish)

Beer Muffins

Serve immediately   Yields: 8

2 cups Bisquick   1½ teaspoons sugar
¾ cup beer, at room   Dash of salt
   temperature

Combine all ingredients, mixing well. Spoon batter into greased muffin tins about ⅔ full. Bake at 425 degrees for 10 to 12 minutes.

Lynn Hancock

Refrigerator-Gingerbread Muffins

This is a great brunch recipe!

Batter keeps in
refrigerator for several weeks

Yields: 2 dozen

1 cup Crisco
1 cup sugar
1 cup dark molasses
5 eggs
2 teaspoons soda
1 cup buttermilk
4 cups flour

2 teaspoons ground ginger
½ teaspoon ground allspice
½ teaspoon ground cloves
½ teaspoon ground cinnamon
1 cup pecans, chopped
1 cup golden raisins

Combine shortening and sugar, creaming until light and fluffy. Stir in molasses and add eggs one at a time, beating well after each addition. Dissolve soda in buttermilk. Combine flour and spices; add to creamed mixture alternately with buttermilk, beating well after each addition. Stir in pecans and raisins. Store batter in covered container for several weeks.

When ready to bake, preheat oven to 350 degrees and fill greased (or lined) muffin cups 2/3 full. Bake for about 20 minutes or until muffins test done.

Note: unchilled batter takes slightly less baking time.

Becca Mitchell

Parmesan Toasts

*This is wonderful with spaghetti or lasagna and
is different from plain garlic bread.*

May prepare ahead

Serves 8-10

1 loaf Italian bread,
   cut in ½-inch slices
1 garlic clove, halved crosswise

Olive oil for brushing
   slices
1 cup Parmesan cheese

Bake slices at 350 degrees for 7 to 8 minutes until crisp but not golden. Rub slices with cut side of garlic. Brush generously with oil and sprinkle with Parmesan cheese. Bake 7 to 8 minutes or until cheese is melted.

Mrs. Frank P. Cooke, Jr.

Blueberry Muffins

Serve immediately   Yields: 1 dozen

1½ cups flour   1 egg
½ cup sugar   ½ cup milk
2 teaspoons baking powder   ¼ cup shortening, melted
½ teaspoon salt   1 cup fresh blueberries

Sift dry ingredients, then moisten with the combined egg, milk, and shortening. Stir enough to thoroughly blend; then fold in blueberries. Bake in well-greased muffin tins in a 400-degree oven for 20 to 25 minutes.

Mrs. Donald R. Thrower

Icebox Bran Muffins

Store batter in covered container in refrigerator. It will keep for 4 to 5 weeks.

May prepare ahead   Yields: 6 dozen

4 eggs   1½ teaspoons salt
2 cups sugar   5 teaspoons soda
2 cups corn oil   1 quart buttermilk
2 cups Nabisco 100% Bran   2 cups Kellogg's All-Bran
5 cups flour, sifted

Beat eggs, sugar, and oil together. Beat in Nabisco 100% Bran. Sift together flour, salt, and soda. Mix in alternately the flour mixture and buttermilk, beginning and ending with flour. Last, stir in by hand the Kellogg's All-Bran so it will not be chopped up. Bake in greased muffin tins at 400 degrees about 20 minutes (for miniatures, bake for 15 minutes at 350 degrees).

Mrs. Eva Ann McLean

Zucchini Cornbread

Serve immediately   Serves 6-8

6 eggs
1 box Ballard cornbread mix
1-12 ounce carton cottage
   cheese
½ pound feta cheese

6 to 8 cups zucchini,
   peeled, seeded, grated,
   and water squeezed out
½ pound butter, melted

Mix together eggs, cornbread mix, cottage cheese, feta cheese, and zucchini. Pour melted butter into batter and bake at 350 degrees for 45 minutes or until golden brown. Use a 12 x 18-inch pan.

Katherine T. Currence

Gourmet Corn Sticks

May prepare ahead   Yields: 10 sticks

½ cup yellow cornmeal
½ cup flour
2 tablespoons sugar
1¼ teaspoons baking powder
1 teaspoon salt
½ cup corn kernels (cut from
   a large ear of corn)

5 tablespoons unsalted
   butter, melted and
   cooled
1 cup less 2 tablespoons
   heavy cream
1 large egg, separated (at
   room temperature)
1 tablespoon vegetable oil

Heat two well-seasoned 5-stick corn stick molds in a preheated 425-degree oven. In a bowl combine the cornmeal, the flour, the sugar, baking powder, salt, and corn. In another bowl combine well the butter, cream, and egg yolk; stir the mixture into the cornmeal mixture, and stir the batter until it is combined.

In a small bowl beat the egg white until it just holds stiff peaks and fold it gently into the batter. Brush the molds with the oil and spoon the batter into them filling them completely, and bake the corn sticks in the 425-degree oven for 15 to 20 minutes, or until they are golden. Invert the corn sticks onto a rack and let them cool for 10 minutes before serving.

Mrs. J. Caswell Taylor, Jr.

Crust Cornbread

Serve immediately   Serves 6-8

1⅓ cups cornmeal   1 egg, beaten
⅓ cup flour   1 cup buttermilk
1 teaspoon baking powder   2 tablespoons shortening,
½ teaspoon soda   melted
½ teaspoon salt

Blend cornmeal, flour, baking powder, soda, and salt in a bowl. Mix egg, buttermilk, and shortening; stir into dry ingredients. Pour into a well-greased, heated 10-inch skillet. Bake in a preheated 375-degree oven for 20 to 25 minutes.

Tillie Hall

Gritty Cornbread

Serve immediately   Serves 6-8

1 cup self-rising cornmeal   2 eggs
¼ cup oil   1-8 ounce carton sour cream
1-16 ounce can cream corn

Mix ingredients together in bowl and blend with hands to work out bubbles. Pour in greased iron frying pan and bake in oven at 425 degrees until golden brown (approximately 20 to 25 minutes).

Mrs. Rebecca B. Greene

Corn Bread

Freezes well   Serves 6-8

3 eggs   1 teaspoon salt
½ cup Mazola oil   1 box Flako cornbread mix or
1 cup sour cream   1 cup self-rising cornmeal
1 small can creamed corn

Mix eggs, oil, sour cream, corn, and salt. Then add cornbread mix and pour mixture into a greased 9-inch square pan. Bake at 375 degrees for 35 minutes.

Lin Lineberger

Crunchy Cornbread Dressing

I prepare cornbread and chop celery and parsley the day before.

Must prepare ahead   Serves 12

1-9 x 13-inch pan of cooked   2 cups parsley, chopped
  cornbread   1 can cream of chicken soup
½ stick butter   2 cups chicken broth
1 large onion, chopped   Salt and pepper to taste
6 cups celery, chopped   Paprika

Sauté onion in butter and add to crumbled cornbread. Add celery, parsley, and chicken soup to mixture. Mix well. Add broth until well moistened. Add salt, pepper, and paprika to taste. Spray two 9 x 9-inch pans with Pam. Divide mixture. Sprinkle with paprika. Cook at 350 degrees for about 45 minutes or until brown. Cut into squares and garnish with parsley.

Claire Kincaid

Turkey Dressing

May prepare ahead   Serves 12
Freezes well

3 cups bread crumbs (biscuit   1 teaspoon baking powder
  or toasted bread)   1 tablespoon sage
2 cups corn bread   ½ medium onion, chopped
2 to 3 hard-boiled eggs   (optional)
¾ to 1 cup celery, chopped   Turkey broth
½ stick margarine or butter

Mix all the above ingredients together and add enough turkey broth to make a soft batter. Cook uncovered at 400 degrees until brown.

Mrs. Bud Anthony

Jalapeno Cornbread

*The amount of green chili-peppers used will determine
just how hot this cornbread will be.*

May prepare ahead

Serves 8-10

1 cup cornmeal
½ teaspoon soda
2 eggs, slightly beaten
1 cup cream style
  yellow corn
⅓ cup oil or melted shortening

½ teaspoon salt
⅔ cup buttermilk
1-4 ounce can green chili-
  peppers, chopped
1 cup sharp Cheddar
  cheese, grated

Combine all ingredients, except cheese, in a bowl. Mix well and pour ½ batter into hot, greased 9-inch square baking pan. Sprinkle cheese and cover with remaining batter. Bake at 375 degrees for 30 to 40 minutes.

Cathy McCosh

My Mother's Cornbread

Serve immediately

Serves 6

1¼ cups plain or self-rising
  flour
1 tablespoon baking powder
  (use this amount with either
  plain or self-rising flour or
  cornmeal)
1 teaspoon sugar

1½ cups plain or self-
  rising white cornmeal
1 heaping teaspoon salt
1 egg
1⅔ to 2 cups milk
¾ cup Crisco shortening

In a large bowl measure all dry ingredients. Make a well in center and put Crisco into this well. Break an egg over the Crisco. With your fingers break the egg and work the mixture. Add the milk and work gently. Do not overmix or beat. Pour into greased pan (I use an iron frying pan) and bake in a preheated 400-degree oven for 25 minutes or until done.

Mary Jane Stewart

Miracle Rolls

These are the easiest and best rolls I have ever tried.
Once served, everyone wants the recipe.

Must prepare ahead   Yields: 1 dozen

1 package yeast   2½ cups flour
1 cup warm buttermilk   1 teaspoon baking powder
¼ teaspoon soda   1 teaspoon salt
3 tablespoons sugar   1 stick butter, melted
3 tablespoons butter-flavored
  Crisco, melted

Place yeast in large bowl. Add warm buttermilk, soda, sugar, and Crisco; stir until yeast is dissolved. Add flour, baking powder, and salt. Stir until dough is of proper consistency. Add more flour if needed. Knead well, roll out, and cut with a biscuit cutter. Brush with melted butter and fold in half. Cover and put in a draft-free place; let rise until double (approximately 1 hour). Bake for 10 to 12 minutes at 400 degrees.

Sharron Davis

Hazel Robinson's Sour Cream Rolls

Must prepare 1 day ahead   Yields: 6 dozen
Freezes well

1 cup sour cream   ½ cup warm water
½ cup plus 1 tablespoon sugar   2 packages yeast
1 teaspoon salt   2 eggs
½ cup margarine   4 cups flour

Melt sour cream in double boiler. Add ½ cup sugar, salt, and margarine. Stir until margarine is melted. Cool to room temperature. Put yeast in large warm bowl; add water and sprinkle with 1 tablespoon sugar. Add sour cream mixture, eggs, and flour to yeast. Stir until blended. Cover and refrigerate overnight. Next day: Bring dough to room temperature. Divide into 3 parts. Roll each part ¼-inch thin. Cut with biscuit cutter. Brush with butter. Fold over and press together lightly. Allow to rise until double. Bake at 375 degrees for 15 minutes.

Mrs. H. Garrett Rhyne

Spoon Bread

This recipe can be doubled but cannot be halved.

May prepare ahead and cook later   Serves 4-6

**½ cup cornmeal mix or   ¼ to ½ teaspoon salt
  cornmeal   2 eggs, lightly beaten
2 cups milk, scalded   Butter**

Mix cornmeal with 2 cups scalded milk in top of double boiler. Cook until thick and then add salt to taste. Cool slightly and add lightly beaten eggs. Place a walnut-size piece of butter in bottom of casserole (or souffle dish) and melt. Pour mixture into dish and keep until ready to cook. When ready to serve, bake in a 400-degree oven for 30 to 45 minutes or until golden brown.

Lin Lineberger

Sausage and Apple Stuffing

This makes enough to stuff a 12-pound turkey.

May prepare ahead   Yields: 10 cups

**8 cups cubed white bread   1 pound bulk sausage
  (about 16 slices)   1 large onion, chopped
2 large apples, pared,   ½ cup water
  cored, and chopped   1 teaspoon salt**

Slightly dry the bread; either toast or put in a 250-degree oven for 10 minutes. Cook and crumble sausage. Pour off drippings, return 2 tablespoons to skillet. Add onion and saute until tender. Stir in apples, salt, and water; bring to a boil. Pour over sausage and bread. Toss until entire mixture is evenly moistened.

Mrs. Donald D. Howe (Fran)

Swedish Pancakes (Platter)

Must prepare ahead   Serves 4

3 eggs, separated   ⅛ teaspoon salt
½ cup flour   2 tablespoons sugar
1½ cups half-n-half   3 tablespoons butter, melted

Beat egg yolks with sugar, salt, and melted butter. Stir in flour and milk.
When ready to use, add the stiffly beaten egg whites. Cook in traditional
Swedish platter pan or make silver dollar-size pancakes on conventional
griddle.

Serve with lingonberries (a Swedish berry available in gourmet shops,
similar to cranberries, but smaller and sweeter) or whole berry cranberry
sauce, topped with a dollop of sour cream.

Connie Gibbons

German Pancakes

Serve immediately   Serves 2

2 eggs   Powdered sugar
⅓ cup flour   2 tablespoons almonds,
⅓ cup milk   sliced and toasted
¼ teaspoon salt   ½ cup currant jelly
1 tablespoon butter

Preheat oven to 450 degrees. In a medium bowl beat eggs with an electric mixer on high speed until frothy. Slowly add flour, beating on
medium speed until blended. Stir in milk and salt. Melt butter in a
10-inch oven proof skillet. Pour egg mixture into skillet. Bake for 15 to
16 minutes or until pancake is browned and puffed. Remove from oven.
Sprinkle with powdered sugar and almonds. Serve with currant jelly.

Mrs. Greg Bobo

Old Fashioned Hot Cakes

Serve immediately   Serves 4-6

1¼ cups flour   1 egg, beaten
2½ teaspoons baking powder   ¾ cup milk
3 tablespoons sugar   3 tablespoons oil
¾ teaspoon salt

Mix together all ingredients and cook on hot skillet until done. Serve
with butter and your favorite syrup.

Marjorie Kircus

Oven Baked French Toast

Serve immediately   Serves 4-6

¼ cup butter, melted   ½ cup orange juice
2 tablespoons honey   ⅛ teaspoon salt
½ teaspoon ground cinnamon   6 slices bread
3 eggs

Combine butter and honey in a 9 x 13-inch pan. Spread to cover bottom
of pan and sprinkle with cinnamon. Combine eggs and juice with salt
and mix well. Dip bread in this mixture, drain, and place in pan. Bake
at 400 degrees for 15 minutes. Invert to serve.

Mrs. Robert S. Pearson (Jane)

Waffles

Serve immediately   Makes 4 to 5 waffles

2 eggs, well beaten   1½ teaspoons salt
2 cups flour, sifted   2 cups buttermilk
3 rounded teaspoons baking   4 heaping tablespoons lard,
  powder   melted
1 teaspoon soda   1 rounded tablespoon sugar

Mix all of the above ingredients together. If batter is soggy, add more
flour. Pour into hot, greased waffle iron and cook accordingly. If you wish
to use left-over batter the next day, add 1 teaspoon baking powder.

Cookbook Committee

This 'n That
Pickles, Relishes and Sundries

Barbeque Sauce

May prepare ahead   Yields: 2 cups

3 tablespoons onion flakes   3 tablespoons brown sugar
3 tablespoons butter   1 teaspoon dry mustard
1 cup hot catsup   1 teaspoon garlic salt
¾ cup water   ¼ teaspoon red pepper
2 tablespoons Worcestershire
  sauce

Mix above ingredients and heat thoroughly.

Marjorie Kircus

Barbeque Sauce For Chicken or Pork

*I use this with pork barbeque, mixing it with the meat the second half of
the cooking time, or over chicken as it bakes. This also makes delicious barbeque
when the meat is cooked in the crock pot; then it can be
prepared in the morning and ready for supper.*

May prepare ahead   Yields: 2 cups

1 large onion, chopped   1½ tablespoons brown
1½ tablespoons margarine   sugar
Approximately 10 ounces   2 tablespoons salad oil
  tomato sauce   2 tablespoons vinegar
1 tablespoon Worcestershire   ⅔ cup catsup
  sauce   Juice of one lemon
1 tablespoon mustard   Dash of salt and pepper

Use regular-size frying pan (approximately 9-inch) to brown onion in
margarine. Add tomato sauce; cover and cook for 5 minutes. Add remaining ingredients. Simmer uncovered for 10 minutes. May be used over
meat right away or refrigerated for later use.

Mrs. John Dalton

Tom's All-Purpose Industrial Strength Barbeque Sauce and Marinade

May prepare ahead

Yields: Approximately 1 quart

3 tablespoons Worcestershire sauce
1 tablespoon white Worcestershire sauce
2 tablespoons Heinz 57 sauce
½ cup Paul Newman's Own Salad Dressing
½ tablespoon lemon juice
½ cup honey

1 pint vinegar
½ teaspoon black pepper
¼ teaspoon red pepper
½ teaspoon Mrs. Dash
1 teaspoon garlic powder
2 dashes of ginger
1 teaspoon mustard

Combine all ingredients in a medium saucepan and bring to a boil. Let boil for 3 to 5 minutes; then let cool before pouring over the meat.

To use as a dipping or "mop" sauce, add 1 cup catsup and 2 tablespoons brown sugar. However DO NOT USE the recipe with these ingredients if cooking on the grill because catsup or brown sugar will burn and turn the meat black.

Mrs. Tom Avery

Tenderloin Marinade

Must prepare ahead

Enough for 1 tenderloin

2 cloves garlic, crushed
½ cup soy sauce
1 tablespoon cooking oil
½ teaspoon salt

¼ teaspoon pepper
¼ teaspoon ginger
¼ teaspoon sugar
1 beef tenderloin

Prepare marinade by mixing all ingredients above (except tenderloin) together. Then add tenderloin and let sit for at least 1 hour (the longer the better). Have beef at room temperature when ready to cook. Remove beef from marinade and cook at 325 degrees for 20 to 25 minutes per pound. Saute fresh mushrooms in butter. Add marinade and drippings from beef to mushrooms. Pour over tenderloin before serving. Serve with wild rice.

Mrs. Giles B. Beal, III

Ka-Bob Marinade

*This is an excellent mixture to marinate all ka-bob ingredients,
bell peppers, cherry tomatoes, onion, meat, or seafood.*

May prepare ahead   Serves 6

¼ cup soy sauce   1 cup oil
⅓ cup lemon juice   1 cup red wine vinegar
Pepper   Garlic juice to taste

Mix all ingredients together thoroughly. Marinate all day before grilling.

Margie Kircus

Meat Marinade
(For Beef or Poultry)

Must prepare ahead   Makes 3 to 4 cups

1 large bottle Kikoman steak   ⅔ cup honey
  sauce   2 tablespoons basil
¼ cup wine vinegar (tarragon)   1 teaspoon oregano
4 tablespoons Worcestershire   ¼ cup red wine
  sauce
3 to 4 cloves garlic

Mix together all ingredients. Marinate meat at least several hours - best
if done overnight.

Mrs. John N. Glenn (Pam)

Lemon Herbed Sauce for Grilled Chicken

May prepare ahead   Makes 2½ cups

½ cup Wesson oil   ¼ cup lemon juice
1 teaspoon basil leaves   1 teaspoon oregano leaves
2 teaspoons Worcestershire   Dash of pepper
  sauce

Put all ingredients in blender and blend well. Pour over one whole
chicken, cut-up, or 6 to 8 selected pieces of chicken for several hours.
Grill or broil the chicken as needed.

Mrs. Frank Mayes (Marion)

Cranberry-Burgundy Sauce (For Ham)

May prepare ahead   Yields: 2 ½ cups

1 pound can whole cranberry
  sauce
½ cup burgundy
5 or 6 whole cloves

1 cup brown sugar
2½ teaspoons prepared
  mustard

Mix all ingredients together in a saucepan. Simmer uncovered for 5 minutes.

May be used as a glaze for baked ham: during the last 30 minutes of baking time. Spoon half of the sauce over ham and pass the remainder.

Mrs. Barbara McCarthy

Remoulade Sauce

Serve as a cocktail sauce for boiled shrimp.

May prepare ahead   Yields: 1 cup

⅔ cup catsup
2 tablespoons prepared
  horseradish
1 tablespoon Worcestershire
  sauce
1 tablespoon celery, minced
1 tablespoon parsley, minced

½ teaspoon dry mustard
½ teaspoon Tabasco sauce
1 tablespoon green onion,
  minced

Combine all ingredients and chill before serving with fresh boiled shrimp.

Mrs. Anne Neal

Blender Hollandaise Sauce

Serve immediately   Serves 12

3 egg yolks   **Pinch cayenne pepper**
2 tablespoons lemon juice   **4 tablespoons butter**

Put egg yolks, lemon juice, and cayenne pepper in blender. Blend for
3 seconds on high. While continuing to blend; melt butter to bubbling
and add in a steady stream. Keep warm over hot water.

Connie Gibbons

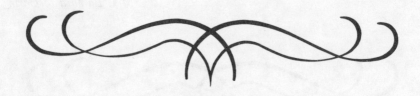

Giblet Gravy

Excellent served over dressing at Thanksgiving and Christmas.

May prepare ahead   Serves 10-12

Giblets from turkey cavity   **Salt and pepper to taste**
4 to 5 hard-boiled eggs   **½ cup celery, chopped**
2 cups turkey stock or chicken   **(optional)**
** bouillon**   **½ cup onion, chopped**
1 to 2 cups turkey dressing   **(optional)**

Boil giblets in 2 to 3 cups of water until tender. Remove, chop finely,
and return to water. Add chopped boiled eggs, 2 to 3 cups turkey stock
or chicken bouillon (I prefer the stock), and cooked turkey dressing to
thicken to your taste. Add salt and pepper to taste. Simmer over low heat
until ready to serve. (You may add chopped celery and chopped onion
if not already in your dressing.)

Patti Hunter

Cucumber Pickles

This recipe is for enough pickles to fill one 1-gallon jar.

Must start 6 weeks ahead   Makes a bunch

Whole cucumbers, enough to   **⅓ box mixed pickling spice**
   fill a 1-gallon jar   **7 cups sugar**
White vinegar, to fill jar   **½ to 1 tablespoon celery**
5 teaspoons powdered alum   **seed**
5 teaspoons salt

Put whole cucumbers in gallon glass jars. Fill with white vinegar; add powdered alum, salt, and mixed pickling spice. Close jar for 6 weeks. This does NOT have to be refrigerated.

Six weeks later - Take pickles out of jar and place in a large bowl. Cut pickles cross ways, add sugar and celery seed, and let sit while you rinse the jar with water. Put finished pickles back in jar and let sit. When ready to eat, put into smaller jars, refrigerate, and serve.

Mrs. Nan Anthony

Grandma's Pickled Beets

This is a recipe that I got from my grandmother,
Mrs. Irene Blanton, of Shelby, North Carolina.

May prepare ahead   Yields: 1 jar

1-16 ounce can of beets   **3 tablespoons sugar**
Vinegar   **3 whole cloves**

Place can of beets in saucepan. Add vinegar to half-way point with beets in saucepan. Begin to bring to a boil. Add 3 tablespoons of sugar and bring to a full boil. Take off heat and cool. Pack in jar with 3 cloves. Refrigerate until ready to serve.

Rebecca B. Greene

Okra Pickles

Must prepare ahead   Makes 5 quarts

2 pounds okra   **½ cup water**
5 pods hot red or green pepper   **6 tablespoons salt**
5 garlic cloves, peeled   **1 tablespoon celery or**
4 cups white vinegar   **mustard seed**

Wash okra and pack in hot sterilized jars. Put 1 pepper pod and 1 garlic clove in each jar. Bring remaining ingredients to a boil and pour over okra and seal. Set jars down into water (180 degrees) to cover and process for 10 minutes.

Marjorie Kircus

Frosted Grapes

Must prepare ahead   Makes as many as you wish

Egg whites   **Granulated sugar**
Small bunches of grapes

Beat egg whites until stiff and dip small bunches of grapes into the egg whites. Let grapes stand until nearly dry on wax paper. Sprinkle with granulated sugar. Refrigerate until dry in closed container. May serve as a garnish on any meat, cheese, or vegetable tray.

Cookbook Committee

Herb Butter

Makes a nice gift at Christmas.

May prepare ahead   Makes 1½ cups

1 stick REAL butter   **2 spring onions**
1 teaspoon fresh parsley   **½ teaspoon dill**

Soften butter. Chop parsley and onions including the tops very fine. Add parsley, onion, and dill to softened butter. Cream together and pack in glass jar. Use on French bread, steaks, seafood, or vegetables.

Mrs. Marilyn Johnson

Snail (Garlic) Butter

Serve with snails, on French bread, or on steaks (just before cooking).

May prepare ahead   Makes 1 cup

½ cup butter, at   Freshly ground pepper
  room temperature   to taste
Salt to taste   2 cloves garlic
                                     ¼ cup parsley

In a processor place butter, seasonings, garlic, and parsley. Cream together.

Lin Lineberger

Sweetened Condensed Milk

Use in place of 1 can of Eagle Brand. Originally printed in Southern Living.

May prepare ahead   Yields: 1 ¼ cups

1 cup instant nonfat dry   ⅔ cup sugar
  milk solids   3 tablespoons margarine
⅓ cup boiling water   butter blend, melted

Combine all of the above in a blender. Process until smooth (about 20 seconds). Store in refrigerator.

Candy Grooms

Do-Ahead Broiled Bacon For A Crowd

Serve immediately   Serves 8-10
Freezes well

2 pounds bacon

Preheat broiler. Place bacon in batches on rack in broiler pan. Broil for 1 to 2 minutes per side or until desired crispness. Drain well. Pack in freezer bags and freeze. Remove desired number of slices and heat slowly in conventional oven or microwave.

Connie Gibbons

Christmas Jam

Delicious and unique to serve at a Christmas brunch or to give as a gift.

Must prepare ahead   Yields: 8 half pints

1-11 ounce package dried   1-8 ounce jar maraschino
  apricots   cherries
1-30 ounce can pineapple   6 cups sugar
  chunks (in heavy syrup)
3½ cups water

In a large saucepan combine apricots, pineapple and syrup, water, and
cherry syrup. Let stand for 1 hour. Cook slowly until apricots are tender.
Add sugar and cook, with frequent stirring, until thick and clear (216
degrees on candy-jelly thermometer). Cut cherries into quarters and add
to the mixture. Cook a few minutes longer at 220 degrees. Pour into hot
sterilized jars; seal.

Mrs. Kay K. Moss

Spiced Fresh Cranberry Relish

May prepare ahead   Yields: 1 pint

1 pound (4 cups) fresh   ½ teaspoon allspice
  cranberries   ⅛ teaspoon ground cloves
2 cups sugar   ½ teaspoon cinnamon
½ cup water   ⅛ teaspoon salt
½ cup fresh oranges, diced
½ teaspoon ground ginger

Wash cranberries and place in a saucepan with sugar and water. Cover
and bring to the boiling point. Cook only until the skins burst - about
8 to 10 minutes. Add oranges, spices, and salt; cook one minute. Cool
and serve with meat or poultry.

Mrs. J. Caswell Taylor, Jr.

Cranberry Chutney

May prepare ahead   Yields: 9-10 cups

3-4 small oranges
1 cup unpeeled apples,
  chopped
½ cup seedless raisins
½ cup orange juice or water
½ teaspoon cinnamon

4 cups cranberries
2 cups sugar
¼ cup pecans, chopped
½ teaspoon ginger
1 tablespoon vinegar

Cut oranges and scoop them out. Fold in everything else with orange pulp. Heat to boil; simmer until cranberries pop open. Chill until serving time.

Lin Lineberger
Mrs. Philip Coyle

Pomander Spice Mixture

Great smelling during the holiday season.

Use anytime, anywhere   Yields: Fillings
                                                   for 6-8 pomanders

¼ cup ground cinnamon
  cloves
2 tablespoons nutmeg
½ cup orrisroot (preservative
  found at drug stores)

2 tablespoons allspice
¼ teaspoon ginger
½ pound of whole cloves

Mix the above ingredients. Place in pomander, a shallow bowl, or an ashtray to make any room smell wonderful.

Susie Phelps-Sikes

293

Christmas Essence

May prepare ahead   Smell fills the whole house

½ orange peel   ½ lemon peel
¼ cup cloves   2 bay leaves
1 cinnamon stick

Simmer in water in an uncovered pan and a lovely aroma prevails.

Mrs. Penny White

Holiday Essence

May prepare ahead   Smell fills the whole house

1 grapefruit peel   2 orange peels
2 lemon peels   2 cinnamon sticks
1 tablespoon cloves   1 tablespoon allspice

Mix together all ingredients. Put in pot of water. Bring to a boil. Reduce heat and simmer to give your home a festive scent.

Mrs. Joye S. Rankin

Sweets

Fresh Apple Cake

May prepare ahead   Makes 1 tube cake
Freezes well

1¼ sticks butter or margarine   ¼ teaspoon salt
2 cups sugar   1 teaspoon baking powder
2 eggs   1 cup nuts, chopped
2 cups flour   2 cups apples, chopped
¼ teaspoon cinnamon   1 cup raisins
1 teaspoon soda

Cream together butter and sugar. Add eggs one at a time and beat well.
Add flour which has been sifted with the other dry ingredients. (Batter
is very stiff.) Add apples, nuts, and raisins. Bake in a greased and floured
tube pan at 350 degrees for 1 hour.

Mrs. Rick Hodges (Vicki)

Blueberry-Peach Batter Cake

Freezes well   Serves 8

2 cups blueberries   1 teaspoon baking powder
4 ripe peaches, peeled and   ¼ teaspoon salt
  sliced   ¾ cup milk
Juice of ½ lemon   ½ cup sugar
¾ cup sugar   1 tablespoon cornstarch
1 cup flour, sifted   ¼ teaspoon salt
¼ cup butter, softened   1 cup boiling water

Line a greased 8-inch square pan with berries and peaches. Sprinkle
lemon juice on top. Cream ¾ cup sugar and butter together. Sift flour,
baking powder, and ¼ teaspoon salt together; add alternately with milk,
creamed sugar, and butter, beating well. Spread batter OVER fruit. Combine ½ cup sugar, cornstarch, and ¼ teaspoon salt; sprinkle over batter.
Pour boiling water over all. Bake in preheated 350 degree oven for 1
hour. Serve plain or with cream topping.

Mrs. James B. Garland (Betsy)

Austrian Chocolate Ecstasy Cake

Best made 1 day ahead   Makes one 2-layer cake

4 ounces semi-sweet chocolate   1½ cups flour
¼ cup butter   1 teaspoon vanilla
2 eggs   ½ teaspoon salt
2 cups sugar   1 teaspoon baking powder
1½ cups milk   1 cup pecans, finely chopped

Preheat oven to 350 degrees. Grease two 9-inch round cake pans and line them with waxed paper; grease paper. In a 3-quart saucepan melt chocolate and butter; remove from heat. With wooden spoon beat in eggs. Stir in sugar, milk, vanilla, and salt. Add flour and baking powder; stir until smooth. Add nuts. Pour in pans and bake for 30 to 35 minutes. Cool in pans for 5 minutes. Remove from pans; remove paper. Cool on wire racks.

Fudge filling: *(make 1 hour before assembling)*
4 ounces semi-sweet chocolate   ½ cup powdered sugar
¼ cup butter   ⅓ cup milk

Melt chocolate and butter in small saucepan over low heat. Remove. Stir in powdered sugar, then milk. Chill 60 minutes or until spreading consistency.

Chocolate cream: *(make 35 minutes before assembling)*
2 cups whipping cream   1 cup powdered sugar
1 teaspoon vanilla extract   ⅔ cup unsweetened cocoa

In a large mixer bowl place cream, powdered sugar, and vanilla. Sift cocoa over cream; stir in. Refrigerate for 30 minutes. At high speed, beat mixture until stiff peaks form.

Assemble:
Place 1 layer of cake crust side up and top with fudge filling. Place second layer crust side down over filling. Cover top and sides with chocolate whipping cream. Chill thoroughly before serving.

Mrs. J. Phillip Coyle

Perfect Chocolate Cake

May prepare ahead   Makes one 3-layer cake

1 cup cocoa   2¾ cups flour
2 cups boiling water   2 teaspoons baking soda
1 cup butter, softened   ½ teaspoon baking powder
2½ cups sugar   ½ teaspoon salt
1½ teaspoons vanilla extract   4 eggs

Combine cocoa and boiling water, stirring until smooth; set aside to cool. Combine butter, sugar, eggs, and vanilla; beat until light and fluffy (about 5 minutes). Combine dry ingredients; add to sugar mixture alternately with cocoa mixture; beginning and ending with flour mixture. Do not overbeat! Pour batter into 3 greased and floured 9-inch round cake pans. Bake at 350 degrees for 25 to 30 minutes or until toothpick comes out of the center clean. Cool in pans for 10 minutes; remove and cool completely.

Filling:
1 cup whipping cream   1 teaspoon vanilla extract
¼ cup powdered sugar

Beat whipping cream and vanilla until foamy; gradually add powdered sugar, beating until peaks form.

Frosting:
1-6 ounce package semi-sweet   ½ cup half-n-half
   chocolate morsels   ¾ cup butter
2½ cups powdered sugar,
   sifted

Combine chocolate morsels, ½ cup half-n-half, and butter in a saucepan; cook over medium heat, stirring until chocolate melts. Remove from heat; add powdered sugar, mixing well.

Set saucepan in ice and beat until frosting holds its shape and loses its gloss. Add a few more drops of half-n-half, if needed. Spread filling between layers and spread frosting over top and sides of cake.

Refrigerate until ready to serve.

Mrs. Mona L. Fulton

Coconut Cake

Must prepare 1 day ahead   Makes one 2-layer cake

1 box yellow pudding cake mix   **1-8 ounce carton sour cream**
1½ cups sugar   **2 packages frozen coconut**
1½ teaspoons almond flavoring   **1½ cups Cool Whip**

Prepare cake mix according to directions for two 9-inch round cake pans. Be careful to remove from oven as soon as cake tests done rather than depend on time. DO NOT OVERCOOK! Cool layers and slice each layer in two.

Icing: Mix sugar, sour cream, and almond flavoring together. Add 1½ packages coconut to sugar mixture. Place filling between layers only. Mix remaining coconut with Cool Whip and ice top and sides of cake. Allow cake to stand for 24 hours in refrigerator before serving.

Mrs. John D. Bridgeman (Nan)

Miniature Cupcakes

May prepare ahead   Makes 7 dozen

Combine and set aside:
1-8 ounce package cream   **1 egg, beaten**
** cheese, softened**   **⅓ cup sugar**
1-6 ounce package chocolate   **⅛ teaspoon salt**
** chips**

Mix together:
1½ cups flour, sifted   **1 cup water**
1 cup sugar   **⅓ cup oil**
¼ cup cocoa   **1 teaspoon vanilla**
1 teaspoon baking soda   **1 tablespoon vinegar**
½ teaspoon salt

Fill petit liners ½ full with chocolate mixture; drop about ½ teaspoon cream cheese mixture on top. Bake at 350 degrees for 20 minutes.

Cookbook Committee

Hospitality Fruit Cakes

*While my family does not especially enjoy fruit cake, they really seem
to enjoy these mini cakes. They are especially nice to have on hand during
the Christmas season. I enjoy opening a tin of these bite-size snacks
in January and having them with hot spiced tea for a special treat.*

Best preserved in tins
A few days allows flavor to mellow

Makes 12 to 13 dozen
miniature cakes

1 cup butter, not margarine
1 cup sugar
5 eggs
2 cups white raisins
2 cups shredded, packaged
   coconut
½ pound mixed red and green
   candied cherries (for topping)
1 to 1½ pounds mixed candied
   fruit

2 cups flour
2 cups pecans, chopped
1½ teaspoons baking
   powder
1 teaspoon salt
½ cup unsweetened
   pineapple juice
1 teaspoon rum extract
   (optional)

Cream butter until soft, then add sugar and cream until light and
fluffy. Add eggs, one at a time, mixing well after each addition. Put fruits,
nuts, raisins and coconut into large bowl. Toss with ½ cup of flour and
set aside.

Sift remaining 1½ cups flour, baking powder, and salt and add to butter
mixture with pineapple juice, beginning and ending with flour. Add
floured fruits, nuts, and rum. Stir until well blended.

Lightly grease and flour or Pam your miniature muffin tins. Fill pans
⅔ full and top with ½ of a red or green cherry, pressed down slightly.
Bake approximately 20 minutes in a 300-degree oven until lightly
browned.

When cool, store in layers of waxed paper in airtight tins. May dip
bottoms of cakes in rum after one week, if so desired.

Mrs. John D. Bridgeman (Nan)

Italian Cream Cake

This recipe came from relatives in Texas.

Freezes well   Makes one 3-layer cake

1 stick margarine   1 cup buttermilk
½ cup Crisco   1 teaspoon soda
2 cups sugar   1 teaspoon vanilla
5 egg yolks   1 cup coconut
2 cups flour   1 cup pecans, chopped
                              5 egg whites

Cream together margarine, Crisco, sugar, and egg yolks. Mix and add
to creamed mixture, flour, buttermilk, soda, vanilla, coconut and pecans.
(*Note:* I add 1 teaspoon of soda to 1 cup buttermilk and give it time to
work; then stir it. Alternate flour and buttermilk to the creamed mixture.) Add 5 egg whites that have been beaten stiff and fold these in last.
Bake at 350 degrees for 30 minutes in three 9-inch greased and floured
round cake pans. (This makes a LARGE cake!)

Icing:
1-8 ounce package cream
    cheese   1 teaspoon vanilla
1 stick margarine   1 box powdered sugar

Cream cream cheese, softened margarine, and vanilla together. Beat in
powdered sugar to form icing. Ice cake between layers, on top and on
sides after cake has cooled.

Mrs. Nan Anthony

Poppy Seed Cake

Freezes well   Serves 12

1¼ cups vegetable oil
2⅓ cups sugar
3 eggs
1½ tablespoons poppy seeds
1½ teaspoons vanilla
1½ teaspoons almond extract

1½ teaspoons imitation
butter flavoring
3 cups flour
1½ teaspoons salt
1 teaspoon soda
1½ cups buttermilk

Beat together oil and sugar. Add eggs, poppy seeds, and flavorings. Combine dry ingredients and add alternately with buttermilk. Pour into a greased tube pan, bundt pan, or 2 loaf pans. Bake at 350 degrees for approximately 1 hour. Cool in pan for 10 minutes. Remove from pan and cool completely.

Glaze:
¾ cup sugar
¼ cup orange juice
½ teaspoon vanilla
½ teaspoon almond extract

3 tablespoons margarine or
½ teaspoon imitation
butter

Bring all ingredients to a boil. Cook for 2 minutes. Pour over cake and let sit for 10 minutes.

Mrs. Emelyne C. Wellons
Mrs. David W. Smith, III (Tracey)

Bessie's Pound Cake

Freezes well   Makes 1 tube cake

2 sticks butter
½ cup Crisco
3 cups sugar
5 eggs
3 cups flour (plain or cake)

½ teaspoon baking powder
¼ teaspoon salt
1 cup milk
1 tablespoon vanilla
4 tablespoons cocoa (if
making chocolate cake)

Cream butter, Crisco, and sugar together. Add eggs one at a time. Sift flour, baking powder, and salt. Add alternately with milk ending with flour. Add vanilla. Bake at 300 degrees for 2 hours.

Leslie Dale

Apricot Brandy Pound Cake

May prepare ahead   Makes 1 tube cake

2 sticks butter, not margarine   ½ teaspoon lemon extract
3 cups sugar   1 teaspoon orange extract
3 cups flour   ¼ teaspoon almond extract
¼ teaspoon soda   ½ teaspoon rum flavoring
Pinch of salt   1 teaspoon vanilla extract
6 eggs   ½ cup apricot brandy
1 cup sour cream

Cream butter and sugar. Mix flour, soda, and salt. Set aside flour mixture. Add eggs to butter and sugar, one at a time, mixing well after each. Add flour mixture to creamed mixture alternately with sour cream. Mix in flavorings. Bake at 325 degrees for 1 hour and 20 minutes in a greased and floured 10-inch tube pan.

Mrs. Ronald W. Digby (Sandra)

Mother's Brown Sugar Pound Cake

This recipe came from my mother, Mrs. Russell McConnell, who was a marvelous cook. I do not know where she got the recipe, but it is an unusual brown sugar pound cake in that it has the maple flavoring which gives it a very distinctive taste.

Freezes well   Serves 20-24

1 cup Crisco   1 teaspoon baking powder
1 stick regular margarine   ½ teaspoon salt
1 box dark brown sugar   1 cup milk
5 eggs   2 teaspoons maple flavoring
3 cups flour

Beat together Crisco and margarine and gradually add brown sugar, beating together until creamy. Add eggs one at a time, beating well after each. Sift flour and sift again with addition of baking powder and salt. Add dry ingredients alternately with milk, beginning and ending with dry ingredients. Add maple flavoring. Pour into greased and floured tube pan and put into a cold oven. Turn temperature to 300 degrees and bake for 1 hour or until done.

Mrs. Ralph S. Robinson, Jr.

Chocolate Pound Cake

Freezes well   Makes 1 tube cake

3 sticks butter
3 cups sugar
5 large eggs
3 cups flour, sifted

4 tablespoons cocoa
½ teaspoon baking powder
1 cup milk
2 teaspoons vanilla

Frosting:
1 stick butter
½ bar of German chocolate
1 egg, well beaten

1 tablespoon lemon juice
3 cups powdered sugar
1 teaspoon vanilla
1 cup nuts, chopped

Cream butter and sugar. Add eggs one at a time. Mix the flour, cocoa, and baking powder together. Add alternately with milk. Add vanilla. Bake in a greased and floured tube pan at 350 degrees for 1 hour and 15 minutes. Cool.

Frosting directions:
Melt butter and chocolate together. Cool. Add egg, lemon juice, sugar and vanilla. Mix well. Add nuts and frost cake.

Claire Kincaid

Sour Cream Pound Cake

May prepare ahead   Serves 8-10

½ pound butter
2½ cups sugar
6 eggs
3 cups flour

8 ounces sour cream mixed
  with ¼ teaspoon soda
1 teaspoon vanilla, almond,
  or cinnamon flavoring

Cream butter, add sugar, and add eggs one at a time, beating well after each addition. Add flour slowly, alternating with sour cream and soda; starting and ending with flour. Add flavoring. Bake in a greased and floured bundt pan at 300 degrees for 1 hour and increase to 325 degrees for another 25 to 30 minutes. Cool in oven for 5 minutes before inverting on rack or plate.

Cookbook Committee

Plum Cake

This recipe may be doubled if you would like to make several to give at Christmas.

Freezes well   Makes 1 tube cake, 2 large loaves, or 3 small loaves

2 cups self-rising flour
2 cups sugar
1 teaspoon cinnamon
1 teaspoon nutmeg

2 small jars plums with
   tapioca baby food
1 cup oil
3 eggs, beaten
2 cups nuts, chopped

Mix dry ingredients. Add plums, oil, and eggs; mix. Add nuts and bake at 350 degrees for 1 hour in a bundt cake pan; 45 minutes in large loaf pan; 35 minutes in small loaf pans or until toothpick inserted in center comes out clean.

Icing:
½ stick margarine
1 cup powdered sugar

Juice and rind of 1 lemon

Melt margarine. Add sugar and juice. Pour ½ of mixture over cake while hot. After removing cake from pan, pour remaining mixture over cake.

Mrs. J. Ben Morrow (Katie)

Sara's Whiskey Cake

May prepare ahead   Serves 8-10

1 box butter recipe yellow
   cake mix
4 eggs
1 cup milk
1 cup pecans, chopped

1-4 ounce box instant
   vanilla pudding
½ cup vegetable oil
1-2 ounce shot whiskey
   or bourbon

Syrup:
¼ pound butter
½ cup whiskey or bourbon

1 cup sugar

Combine all ingredients for cake except pecans and mix at medium speed for 3 minutes. Stir in pecans. Pour into a greased and floured tube pan. Bake for 50 to 60 minutes at 350 degrees. Five minutes before cake is done, make the syrup by combining the syrup ingredients. Stir over low heat in a saucepan until sugar dissolves. Remove cake from oven and pour half of syrup over top of cake. Let stand for 15 to 20 minutes. Remove from pan and pour remaining syrup over bottom of cake.

Mrs. Barbara McCarthy

Red Velvet Cake

May prepare ahead   Yield: 1 layer cake

½ cup Crisco   1½ cups sugar
2 eggs   1 teaspoon vanilla
¼ teaspoon red food coloring   2¼ cups flour
1 tablespoon vinegar   1 teaspoon soda
2 tablespoons cocoa   1 teaspoon salt
1 cup buttermilk

Cream Crisco and sugar well. Add eggs. Make a paste of cocoa and coloring and add to sugar mixture. Add salt. Put the vanilla in the buttermilk and add slowly to the mixture along with the flour. Mix soda and vinegar and add to batter. Preheat oven to 350 degrees. Bake for 20 to 25 minutes. Make 4 thin layers or 3 medium layers. When making 4 layers, use 1½ times of every thing for frosting (below).

Frosting:
3 tablespoons flour   1 cup sugar
1 cup butter   ½ cup nuts, chopped - to
1 teaspoon vanilla   sprinkle on top (optional)
1 cup milk

Cream butter. Add flour and sugar. Beat well. Slowly add the vanilla and milk. Beat well. Ice the cake and sprinkle the top with chopped nuts if desired.

Marjorie Kircus

Sheath Cake

May prepare ahead

Serves 16-20

1 stick margarine
3 tablespoons cocoa
½ cup shortening
1 cup water
2 cups flour
2 cups sugar

2 eggs
1 teaspoon vanilla
½ cup buttermilk
1 teaspoon soda
1 teaspoon cinnamon

Frosting:
1 stick margarine
2 tablespoons cocoa
6 tablespoons milk

1 box powdered sugar
1 cup pecans, chopped
1 teaspoon vanilla

Mix first four ingredients together in a saucepan. Melt, bring to a boil, and pour over flour and sugar. Mix well and add eggs, vanilla, buttermilk, soda, and cinnamon. Mix well (batter will be very thin). Bake in a 400-degree oven for 25 minutes in a greased and floured 11 x 14-inch pan.

Frosting: Start 5 minutes before cake is to come out of oven. Bring to a boil margarine, cocoa, and milk. Then add powdered sugar, pecans, and vanilla. Ice the cake immediately. Let cool and cut into squares to serve.

Mrs. Linda T. Ratchford

Cheesecake

This recipe appeared in the Chapel Hill Cookbook several years ago.

Must prepare ahead   Serves 12

Crust:
2 cups graham cracker crumbs   4 tablespoons margarine,
3 tablespoons sugar   melted

Filling:
3-8 ounce packages cream   4 eggs
  cheese, softened   1 teaspoon vanilla
¾ cup sugar

Topping:
8 ounces sour cream   ¾ cup sugar

Combine crust ingredients and press into bottom of a 9-inch springform
pan. Combine filling ingredients with an electric mixer. Whip at high
speed for 5 to 10 minutes. Pour into crust. Bake at 350 degrees for about
35 minutes. (Edge should be slightly brown.) Combine topping ingredients and pour over top. Bake for another 7 to 8 minutes. Chill for at
least 6 hours before serving.

Mrs. Eva Ann McLean
Mrs. James Love, III

Fox's Cheesecake

Must prepare ahead   Serves 16
Freezes well

1¾ cups graham cracker   1½ cups sugar
  crumbs   4 eggs, slightly beaten
⅓ cup butter, melted   ⅓ cup cornstarch
¼ cup sugar   2 tablespoons lemon juice
1 pound small curd cream   1 teaspoon vanilla
  style cottage cheese   ½ cup butter, melted
2-8 ounce packages cream   1 pint sour cream
  cheese, softened

Combine graham cracker crumbs, melted butter, and sugar. Press firmly against bottom and 2 inches up sides of a 10-inch springform pan. Sieve cottage cheese into a large mixing bowl; add cream cheese. Beat at high speed of electric mixer until well blended and creamy. At high speed blend in remaining sugar, then eggs. At low speed, add cornstarch, lemon juice, and vanilla. Blend well, then add butter and sour cream. Mix well and pour into pan. Bake at 325 degrees for 1 hour and 10 minutes, or until firm around the edges. Turn off oven and let stand in oven for 2 hours. Remove and cool completely (6 to 8 hours). Chill and remove sides of pan.

Mrs. David W. Smith, III (Tracey)

Praline Cheesecake

Must prepare ahead   Serves 16

1⅓ cups graham cracker crumbs

4 tablespoons sugar

4 tablespoons butter, melted

4-8 ounce packages cream cheese

1⅔ cups dark brown sugar

4 eggs

2⅔ tablespoons flour

⅔ cup pecans, finely chopped

2 teaspoons vanilla

2 teaspoons maple syrup

Additional finely chopped pecans, for garnish

In a large bowl combine crumbs, sugar, and melted butter. Press into the bottom of a 10-inch springform pan. Bake crust in 350-degree oven for 10 minutes and let cool in pan. Beat softened cream cheese and brown sugar until fluffy. Beat in eggs, one at a time, and sift in flour. Add pecans and vanilla. Pour mixture into pan. Bake at 350 degrees for 55 minutes or until it is set. Cool in pan.

Remove sides of pan and transfer with spatula to plate. Brush top with maple syrup and garnish with finely chopped pecans. Chill for at least 3 hours before serving.

Cathy McCosh

Apricot Preserves Pie

Must prepare 1 day ahead

Makes 1 pie

3 egg whites
¼ cup cream of tartar
1 cup sugar

16 Ritz crackers or Waverly
   crackers, crushed
1 teaspoon vanilla
½ cup nuts, chopped

Topping:
½ pint whipping cream

1-6 ounce jar apricot
   preserves

Beat egg whites until foamy; add cream of tartar. Beat until stiff, add sugar and beat until dissolved. Fold in crackers; add vanilla and nuts. Pour into a well greased and floured pie pan.

Bake for 30 minutes in a 325-degree oven. Remove and cool. Mix whipped cream and preserves and spread on cooled pie. Let stand in refrigerator overnight.

Margaret Shive

Mamie's Banana Pie

This is a very old family recipe.

May prepare ahead

Makes 1 pie

½ cup sugar
1 tablespoon butter
2 eggs, separated
⅛ teaspoon salt
⅓ cup flour

¾ cup boiling water
½ teaspoon vanilla
3 bananas, sliced
1-9 inch pie shell, baked

Cream sugar and butter; add slightly beaten egg yolks, salt, flour, and boiling water. Cook in double boiler, stirring constantly until thickened. Cool and add vanilla. Put sliced bananas in baked pie shell, then cream mixture, then more bananas, and top with a meringue. (You may use egg whites to make meringue by adding them to cream of tartar and sugar to taste.) Bake at 325 degrees for 30 minutes.

Delores J. Thornton

Commissary Heart Tarts

This makes a very pretty Valentine dessert.

Must prepare ahead   Serves 8

8 tart shells, homemade or
  frozen
2 ounces semi-sweet chocolate
¾ cup cream cheese
1 cup powdered sugar
⅓ cup whipping cream

1 tablespoon Amaretto
  liqueur
½ teaspoon vanilla
2 pints fresh strawberries
½ cup seedless raspberry
  jam

Melt chocolate over low heat and spread over cooked shells. Beat cream cheese and powdered sugar until smooth and creamy. Add whipping cream, Amaretto, and vanilla. Spoon over chocolate. Chill at least 30 minutes. Combine strawberries and jam, tossing berries gently to coat. Arrange berries over filling.

Mrs. Alex Hall (Ginny)

Chess Pie

Freezes well   Serves 6-8

1 cup brown sugar
½ cup white sugar
1 tablespoon flour
2 eggs
2 tablespoons milk

1 stick butter, melted
1 teaspoon vanilla
1-8 inch pie shell,
  unbaked

Mix sugars and flour together thoroughly; beat in eggs. Add rest of ingredients and mix. Pour into a shallow pie shell. Bake at 350 degrees for 35 to 45 minutes—until set. (I usually make 2 at a time and freeze one for later.)

Ruth Day Michael Dickson

Chocolate Chess Pie

Freezes well   Serves 6-8

1 cup white sugar
½ cup brown sugar
1 teaspoon flour
Dash of salt
2 eggs
2 tablespoons milk

1 teaspoon vanilla
1 stick margarine
1½ squares unsweetened
  chocolate
1 unbaked pie shell

Mix together sugars, flour, salt, eggs, milk, and vanilla. Then melt margarine and chocolate together. Add to sugar and flour mixture. Pour into unbaked pie shell. Bake at 325 degrees for 35 to 40 minutes.

Mrs. Frank Mayes (Marion)

Aunt Pearl's Chess Pie

This recipe is the creation of a great aunt who was as gritty as the sugar but not nearly as sweet. I was lucky enough to be a favorite of hers and, therefore, was allowed to copy her recipe. Most of the quantities were not written down. I have added those through the years.

May prepare ahead   Makes 2 pies

4 eggs
1 cup brown sugar, packed
1 cup granulated sugar
4 tablespoons whole milk

3 tablespoons butter, melted
2 tablespoons cornmeal
½ teaspoon vanilla
2 unbaked pie shells

Beat eggs well. Add remaining ingredients and mix. Pour into the 2 pie shells and bake at 350 degrees until crusts are light brown and tops are a little crusty. (Start watching it after 30 minutes.)

Anne Neal

Chocolate Chip Cookie Pie

Freezes well after cooking   Makes 1 pie

2 eggs
½ cup flour
½ cup sugar
½ cup brown sugar, packed
1 cup butter, melted

1 cup chocolate chips
½ cup walnuts or pecans,
   chopped
1 9-inch pie shell, unbaked

Beat eggs until foamy. Add flour and sugars; beat well. Add butter and stir in chocolate chips and nuts. Pour into pie shell and bake at 325 degrees for 1 hour.

Mrs. Barbara McCarthy

German Chocolate Pie

Freezes well   Makes 4 pies

4 frozen pie shells
6 eggs
1 stick margarine, melted
4 cups sugar
4 tablespoons flour

½ cup cocoa
1 tablespoon vanilla
1 medium can coconut
¾ cup nuts, chopped
1-13 ounce can evaporated milk

Mix all ingredients together and pour equal parts into the 4 pie shells. Bake at 325 degrees for 50 minutes.

Mrs. John B. Garrett, Jr. (Nancy)

French Silk Chocolate Pie

Freezes well   Makes 1 pie

Ritz cracker pie shell:
20 Ritz crackers, crushed   1 cup sugar
3 egg whites, beaten   ½ cup nuts, chopped
1 teaspoon vanilla

Filling ingredients:
½ cup butter or margarine   2 squares unsweetened
¾ cup sugar   chocolate, melted and
1 teaspoon vanilla   cooled
                              2 eggs

Mix pie shell ingredients together and place into pie pan. Bake at 300 degrees for 40 minutes and let cool. Cream margarine or butter. Gradually add sugar, creaming until light. Blend in vanilla and chocolate. Add eggs, one at a time, beating 3 or 4 minutes after each addition on medium speed. Turn into Ritz cracker pie shell and chill several hours before serving. Garnish with Cool Whip, chocolate curls, and toasted pecans.

Mrs. John Guglielmetti (Bonnie)

Chocolate Pie

Quick and very easy!

Must prepare ahead   Makes 1 pie

3 ounces cream cheese   1-8 inch graham cracker
2 tablespoons sugar   pie or regular pie shell,
4 ounces Baker's sweet   cooked and cooled
   chocolate   Additional Cool Whip
1 tablespoon milk   Chocolate shavings
1-8 ounce carton
   Cool Whip

Beat softened cream cheese with sugar until smooth. Melt chocolate with milk over low heat. Add chocolate mixture to cream cheese. Fold in softened Cool Whip. Pour mixture in pie shell and chill. Garnish with additional Cool Whip and chocolate shavings.

Kathy Linker Jenkins

Paper Bag Apple Pie

This is apple pie with a baking twist. It's actually baked inside a brown paper bag—no juice bubbles into the oven.

May prepare ahead   Makes 1 deep dish pie

1 unbaked 9-inch deep dish   2 tablespoons flour
  pie shell   ½ teaspoon nutmeg
6 or 7 tart apples   2 tablespoons lemon juice
½ cup sugar

Topping:
½ cup brown sugar   ½ cup butter or margarine
½ cup flour

Pare, core, and slice apples and place in large bowl. Combine ½ cup sugar, 2 tablespoons flour and nutmeg in cup; sprinkle over apples; toss to coat well; spoon into pastry shell; drizzle with lemon juice.

Combine ½ cup sugar and ½ cup flour for topping; cut in butter and sprinkle over apples. Slide pie into brown bag; fold the open end twice, fasten with paper clip, and place on cookie sheet. Bake in a 425-degree oven for 1 hour (apples will be tender and top bubbly and golden brown); split bag open, remove pie and cool on wire rack. Serve plain or with cheese or ice cream.

Mrs. L. Neale Patrick (Mary Ann)

Nana's Coconut Pie

This is my mother-in-law's recipe and is WONDERFUL!

May prepare ahead   Makes 1 pie

2 eggs, separated   2 heaping tablespoons flour
1½ to 1¾ cups milk   1 can Baker's coconut
¾ cup sugar   1 pie shell, baked

Beat yolks; add some milk to yolks and pour into sugar and flour mixture. Then pour rest of milk in and boil until thickened. Add coconut and pour into baked pie shell. Top with meringue. Bake at 325 degrees until brown.

Delores J. Thornton

315

Colonial Innkeeper's Pie

*This was a recipe that originated in one of the wonderful
inns in New England. It is a combination cake and pie and I have
never seen this recipe or any similar to it anywhere.*

May prepare ahead   Makes 1 pie

Pastry:

1 cup flour, sifted   ½ teaspoon salt
⅓ cup plus 1 tablespoon   2 tablespoons water
  shortening

Sauce:

1½ squares unsweetened   ¼ cup butter
  chocolate   1½ teaspoons vanilla
½ cup water
⅔ cup sugar

Batter:

1 cup flour   ¼ cup shortening
¾ cup sugar   ½ cup milk
1 teaspoon baking powder   ½ teaspoon vanilla
½ teaspoon salt   1 egg

Garnishes:

½ cup pecans, chopped   Chocolate shavings
Whipped cream

Combine PASTRY ingredients. Put into a 9-inch pie plate, flute edges
high, cover and set aside. To make SAUCE, melt chocolate with water;
add sugar and bring to a boil, stirring constantly. Remove from heat;
stir in butter and vanilla until butter melts. Set aside. To make
BATTER, sift together flour, sugar, baking powder, and salt. Add shortening, milk, and vanilla. Beat 2 minutes on medium speed. Add egg and
beat 2 more minutes or until well blended. Pour batter
into prepared pie shell. Stir sauce and pour carefully over batter. Sprinkle
top with pecans, and bake for 55 to 60 minutes or until toothpick comes
out clean. Garnish with whipped cream and chocolate shavings; serve
warm.

Mrs. Charles C. Elliott (Carol)

Coffee Ice Cream Pie

Must prepare ahead

Makes 1 pie

18 Oreo cookies
½ cup butter
1 quart coffee ice cream
1-6 ounce package semi-sweet
  chocolate chips

⅔ cup evaporated milk
1 cup whipping cream
1 ounce Kahlua
1 teaspoon sugar
½ cup pecans, chopped

Crush cookies in blender and mix with melted butter to form crust. Press into a 10-inch pan and freeze. Spread soft ice cream on crust and freeze. Combine chocolate and milk in a sauce pan, stir until smooth and thick. Cool. Pour over ice cream and freeze. Whip cream, add Kahlua and sugar; spread on top of chocolate mixture and sprinkle with pecans.

Ann Roberts

Strawberry Ice Cream Pie

Must prepare ahead

Makes 1 pie

1 cup chocolate wafer crumbs
¼ cup margarine, softened
½ cup pecans, finely chopped

½ gallon vanilla ice cream,
  slightly softened
1 package frozen
  strawberries, slightly thawed

Mix together chocolate wafer crumbs, margarine, and pecans; press into a 9-inch pie pan. Bake at 375 degrees for 7 minutes. Refrigerate until cooled. Spoon a layer of vanilla ice cream into crust, then ½ of the berries. Repeat, topping with berries, and freeze.

Mrs. Sam Howe (Cherry)

Florida Key Lime Pie

Must prepare ahead   Makes 1 pie

1 graham cracker crust
1 pint heavy cream
1 can Eagle Brand sweetened
  condensed milk

½ cup Key Lime juice
1 to 2 tablespoons powdered
  sugar

Whip ½ pint cream until stiff. Fold in milk; then fold in juice. Put into pie shell. Whip remaining ½ pint of cream with sugar. Spread on top of pie. Refrigerate AT LEAST 2 hours before serving. Top with a sprig of mint or red cherry.

Mrs. Paul Quinn

Chocolate Chip Pie

May prepare ahead   Makes 2 pies

1 cup sugar
1 tablespoon flour
5 eggs, well beaten
1 cup white corn syrup
1 stick butter, melted

1 teaspoon vanilla
2 tablespoons bourbon
1 cup chocolate chips
1 cup pecans and walnuts,
  mixed
2-9 inch pie shells, unbaked

Mix flour and sugar. Add to beaten eggs. Add syrup, butter, chips, nuts, and flavorings. Pour into chilled, unbaked pie shells. Bake at 350 degrees for 1 hour.

Becca Mitchell

Old-Fashioned Peach Custard Pie

Must prepare ahead   Makes 1 pie

4 fresh large peaches   1 tablespoon butter or
1 cup sugar   margarine
3 eggs   1 unbaked pie shell
1 teaspoon vanilla

Peel and slice peaches. Add sugar. Beat eggs, and add to peaches; add vanilla. Pour into pie shell. Cut butter thinly over top and bake at 325 degrees for 1 hour or until set.

Sara M. Gray

Lemon Souffle Pie

May prepare ahead   Makes 1 pie

3 egg yolks   1 teaspoon lemon rind
¼ cup lemon juice   3 egg whites, beaten
½ cup sugar   ½ cup sugar
⅛ teaspoon salt   1-8 inch pie shell, baked

Beat yolks until thick. Add lemon juice, ½ cup sugar, salt, and rind. Cook over hot water stirring until thickened. Beat whites until thick and gradually add ½ cup sugar. Fold into yolk mixture. Pour in shell. Bake at 400 degrees until a delicate brown - about 5 minutes.

Anne Decker

Lemon Curd Pie or Tarts

Must prepare ahead   Makes 1 pie or 8 tarts

6 egg yolks, beaten
1 cup sugar
½ cup fresh lemon juice
½ cup unsalted butter,
  cut into pieces

1 tablespoon lemon rind,
  grated
1 pie shell or 8 tart
  shells, baked

To make the lemon curd, strain the beaten egg yolks through a sieve into a medium-size heavy saucepan. Add the sugar and lemon juice; cook over low heat, stirring constantly for about 10 to 12 minutes until the mixture thickens and coats the back of a wooden spoon. Remove from the heat and stir until the mixture cools just slightly. Stir in the butter, a piece at a time, until fully incorporated. Add the rind. Let cool completely. Pour the cooled lemon curd into baked shell(s) and chill until set.

Meringue:
6 to 8 egg whites
½ teaspoon cream of tartar
½ teaspoon vanilla

Pinch of salt
6 tablespoons sugar

Beat egg whites until fluffy. Add cream of tartar, vanilla, and salt. Continue beating and add sugar, one tablespoon at a time. When mixture forms stiff peaks, mound the meringue over the filling, sealing edges. Bake in a preheated 375-degree oven for about 10 minutes or until meringue is golden brown.

Mary Jane Stewart

Hackie's Lemon Pie

Must prepare ahead   Serves 8

1-6 ounce can frozen lemonade
1 pint vanilla ice cream

1-8 ounce carton Cool Whip
1 graham cracker crust

Soften all ingredients; mix together until smooth. Put in pie shell and freeze.

Mrs. Gordon Lipscomb

Mrs. J.H. Matthews' Frozen Lemon Pie

May prepare ahead
Freezes well

Makes 1 pie

3 egg yolks, beaten
½ cup sugar
¼ cup lemon juice
1 teaspoon lemon rind,
  grated
Dash of salt

3 egg whites, stiffly
  beaten
1 cup whipping cream,
  stiffly beaten
Vanilla wafers, crushed

Combine egg yolks, sugar, juice, rind, and salt; cook in a double boiler until thick. Remove from heat and cool completely. Mix stiffly beaten egg whites and stiffly beaten cream; fold this into cooled custard mixture. Line pie pan with crumbs; pour in custard mixture, cover with crumbs and freeze.

Mrs. Frank Matthews (Betty)

Meringue Pie

Must prepare ahead

Makes 1 pie

5 egg whites
¼ teaspoon cream of tartar
1 cup plus 2 tablespoons sugar
2 teaspoons vanilla

1 cup heavy cream
1 tablespoon rum
3 to 4 tablespoons
  unsweetened chocolate, grated

Preheat oven to 400 degrees. Beat whites briefly and add cream of tartar; beat until stiff and dry. Gradually beat in 1 cup sugar and 1 teaspoon vanilla. Spread into greased 9-inch pie plate. Put meringue in oven, turn off heat, leave in oven for 4 hours or overnight. Whip cream; add 2 tablespoons sugar, 1 teaspoon vanilla and 1 tablespoon rum. Pour into baked meringue shell; sprinkle with grated chocolate. Chill thoroughly before serving.

Mary Lou Norcross

Chocolate Pecan Pie

May prepare ahead   Makes 2 pies
Freezes well

3 cups sugar   1 large can evaporated milk
Pinch of salt   1 stick margarine
7 tablespoons cocoa   1 cup pecans
4 eggs   2 unbaked deep-dish pie
1 tablespoon vanilla   shells

Mix sugar, salt, and cocoa together. Add eggs, mix well. Stir in vanilla
and milk. Add melted margarine. Pour into 2 unbaked pie shells.
Sprinkle nuts on top. Bake at 350 degrees for 40 to 45 minutes.

Mrs. J. Ben Morrow (Katie)

Silver Springs Pecan Pie

*This is Margie Foy's recipe and it has been
a favorite of my family for many years.*

May prepare ahead   Makes 1 pie
Freezes well

½ stick butter   2 eggs
1 cup sugar   1 cup pecans, chopped
1 cup white Karo syrup   1-8 inch pie shell
¼ teaspoon salt

Cream butter and sugar. Add Karo syrup, salt, well beaten eggs, and
nuts. Mix well. Pour into unbaked pie shell. Bake for 1 hour at 300
degrees.

Mary Jane Stewart

Mother's Pecan Pie

Freezes well   Makes 2 pies

1 stick butter or margarine   1½ teaspoons vanilla
1 box light brown sugar   2 cups pecans, chopped
4 eggs   3 tablespoons flour
8 tablespoons milk   2 unbaked pie shells

Melt butter or margarine. Beat sugar and butter together. Beat in eggs; add remaining ingredients; mix well. Pour equal amounts into the pie shells and bake at 350 degrees for 35 to 45 minutes.

Mrs. Pamela Mayo
Cathy McCosh

Old English Pie

This makes a wonderful Thanksgiving dessert.

Must prepare ahead   Makes 2 pies

2 cups sugar   1 teaspoon cinnamon
½ stick butter   1 teaspoon nutmeg
4 eggs, separated   1 cup nuts, chopped
1½ tablespoons wine   1 cup raisins
1 teaspoon allspice   2-8 inch pie shells

Combine sugar, butter, and egg yolks. Combine wine, allspice, cinnamon, nutmeg, nuts, and raisins and add to sugar mixture. Fold in 4 stiffly beaten egg whites. Pour into pie shells. Cook slowly at 325 degrees for about 1 hour. Serve with whipped cream. This recipe makes filling for 2 pies, but it can not be halved.

Mrs. J. Philip Coyle

Willie Rosemond's
Danish Mon (Apple) Tart

May prepare ahead   Serves 4-6

½ cup butter, softened
¾ cup sugar
2 eggs
Grated rind of 1 lemon
4 teaspoons lemon juice
1 cup flour, sifted
⅛ teaspoon salt

5 tart cooking apples,
   cored, peeled, and cut
   into thin slices
2 tablespoons butter, melted
1 cup heavy cream, whipped
Cinnamon

Beat together butter and ½ cup sugar until thoroughly creamed and
light. Add eggs, one at a time, and beat well. Add lemon rind and 1 teaspoon lemon juice. Sift together flour and salt and gradually add to butter; mix well. Turn batter into a buttered springform pan or cake pan
with removable sides. Toss apple slices gently with remaining lemon juice
and arrange evenly over batter. Drizzle with melted butter. Sprinkle with
remaining ¼ cup sugar. Bake at 350 degrees for 1 hour and 5 minutes
or until apples are golden brown and cake pulls away from pan. Allow
cake to cool on rack. Serve with whipped cream and cinnamon, if desired.

Debbie Brake

Yummy Pie

May prepare ahead   Makes 1 pie

4 large egg whites, beaten
   stiffly
1¼ cups sugar
Pinch of salt
24 Ritz crackers, broken
   coarsely
1¼ cups pecans, chopped

1¼ teaspoons vanilla
1 deep dish pie shell, baked
Cool Whip or whipped cream
Grated chocolate

Bake pie shell at 325 degrees for 45 minutes; cool. Blend in sugar into
stiffly beaten egg whites. Add salt, crackers, pecans, vanilla, and mix
thoroughly. Pour into baked pie crust and chill for at least 2 hours. Top
with Cool Whip or whipped cream and grated chocolate before serving.

Cathy McCosh

Never-Fail Pie Crusts

May prepare ahead
Freezes well

Makes 2 pie crusts

1¼ cups shortening
3 cups flour
1 teaspoon salt

1 egg, well beaten
5 tablespoons water
1 tablespoon vinegar

Cut shortening into flour and salt. Mix egg, water, and vinegar. Pour liquid into flour mixture and stir until well blended. Roll out to ⅛-inch thickness and line pie pans. Variations: Before rolling out add 1 teaspoon poppy seeds OR 1 teaspoon finely chopped pecans.

Sharron Davis

Apricot Balls

These were served by Mrs. J. H. Matthews to all ladies who attended her parties, meetings, etc. These apricot balls were always devoured with accolades!

May prepare ahead
Freezes well

Yields: 40 balls

10 ounces dried apricots,
  ground
Grated rind and juice of
  1 orange
2 cups sugar

1 cup pecans, finely
  chopped
Powdered sugar

Mix apricots, orange rind and juice, and sugar in a double boiler. Cook over boiling water for 10 to 12 minutes (after water is boiling, stir until thickened). Remove from heat and cool. Add nuts and mix well. Form into small balls and roll in powdered sugar when ready to serve. Store in cool place in a covered container.

Mrs. Frank Matthews (Betty)

Chess Squares

May prepare ahead   Yields: 40 squares

First layer:
1 box yellow Duncan Hines butter cake mix - use dry	1 egg 1 stick butter, melted

Mix dry cake mix in processor with egg and butter. Pour into a 3-quart rectangular GLASS dish.

Second layer:
8 ounces cream cheese, softened 2 eggs	1 box powdered sugar

Soften cream cheese in microwave oven. Add two eggs and 1 box of sugar. Mix in processor and pour onto first layer. Bake at 350 degrees for 50 minutes.

Mrs. Tom Efird (Ann)

Chocolate-Caramel Brownies

For the serious chocoholic!

May prepare ahead   Yields: 35-48 squares
Freezes well

1-14 ounce bag caramels ⅔ cup evaporated milk, divided 1-18½ ounce package German chocolate cake mix	¾ cup butter or margarine, softened 1 cup nuts, chopped 1-6 ounce package semi-sweet chocolate chips

Preheat oven to 350 degrees. Combine caramels with ⅓ cup of milk in top of double boiler. Heat, stirring constantly until caramels are melted. Remove from heat and put aside. Combine cake mix, ⅓ cup milk, and butter. Beat with mixer until firm. Stir in nuts. Press half of cake mix into well-greased 9 x 13-inch pan and bake for 6 minutes. Sprinkle chocolate chips over baked portion. Cover chips evenly with caramel mixture. Sprinkle remaining cake mixture on top. Bake for 15 to 20 minutes. Cool and chill for 30 minutes before cutting into squares.

Mrs. Joanna Woods Owen

Creme De Menthe Brownies

May prepare ahead   Makes 3 to 4 dozen

First layer:
4 eggs   2 teaspoons salt
1 cup sugar   1-16 ounce can chocolate
½ cup flour   syrup

Mix the above ingredients and bake at 350 degrees for 35 to 40 minutes in an ungreased and unfloured 9 x 13-inch pan. Refrigerate to cool.

Second layer:
2 cups powdered sugar   4 tablespoons creme de
½ cup butter, softened   menthe

Mix the above ingredients and beat until smooth. Cover the first layer with this mixture when the first layer had cooled.

Top layer:
6 tablespoons butter, melted   1 cup semi-sweet chocolate
                                      bits, melted

Spread this over the second layer. Let cool before cutting into squares.

Mrs. Neale Patrick (Mary Ann)
Mrs. Dan Page (Ibby)

Hundred Dollar Brownies

May prepare ahead   Makes 1 to 2 dozen

Brownies:

½ cup butter
4 squares unsweetened
  chocolate
2 cups sugar
4 eggs

1 cup flour, sifted
½ teaspoon salt
1 teaspoon vanilla

Over low heat melt butter and chocolate; let cool. Add to sugar and mix well. Add eggs one at a time; mix well. Add flour, salt, and vanilla; mix well. Grease and flour a 10 x 15-inch pan. Pour in batter. Bake in a 350-degree oven for 20 to 25 minutes. DO NOT OVERCOOK! (They are done when they pull away from the pan.)

Frosting:

4 tablespoons butter
1 square unsweetened
  chocolate
1 cup powdered sugar
1 egg

1½ teaspoons vanilla
1½ teaspoons lemon juice
1 cup pecans, chopped

Melt butter and chocolate over low heat. Add powdered sugar. Mix well and remove from stove. Add egg and mix well. Add vanilla and lemon juice, then pecans. This should have a good consistency; if not, add more powdered sugar. Put on brownies while still warm. This acts as a chocolate pecan glaze, and will have a nice sheen.

Mrs. Robin Bean

Pecan Pie Brownies

May prepare ahead   Yields: 24 bars

Filling:
¼ cup margarine or butter   2 eggs
2 tablespoons flour   1 teaspoon vanilla
¾ cup brown sugar, packed   2 cups pecans, chopped

Brownies:
1-21½ ounce package fudge   ¼ cup oil
  brownie mix   1 egg
½ cup very hot water

Grease the bottom of a 13 x 9-inch pan. In a saucepan melt margarine; stir in flour until smooth. Add brown sugar and 2 eggs; mix well. Cook over medium-low heat for 5 minutes, stirring constantly. Remove from heat; stir in vanilla and pecans. Set aside.

In a large bowl combine brownie ingredients and beat with a spoon. Spread in prepared pan. Spoon filling over top. Bake at 350 degrees for 30 to 35 minutes or until set. DO NOT OVERBAKE. Cool and cut into bars.

Mrs. Carole Fuller

Lemon or Coconut Cookies

This recipe was given to me by Mrs. Plato Pearson, Sr., my husband's grandmother.

May prepare ahead   Yields: 3 dozen

1 stick butter, melted   1 small package buttermilk
1 cup sugar   biscuit mix
1 egg, slightly beaten   1 small package instant
1 teaspoon lemon OR coconut   mashed potato flakes
  flavoring

Mix all ingredients and shape in a ball. Chill in refrigerator. Roll into small balls and place on greased cookie sheet. Press down with fork. Bake at 350 degrees for 10 minutes.

Jane Pearson
Kathy Linker Jenkins

Chocolate Meltaways

This is a great holiday pick-up.

May prepare ahead   Yields: 3 to 4 dozen

1 stick butter or margarine
1 ounce unsweetened
 chocolate
¼ cup sugar
1 teaspoon vanilla
1 egg
2 cups graham crackers,
 crushed

1 cup coconut, shredded
½ cup nuts, chopped
¼ cup butter or margarine
1 tablespoon milk or cream
2 cups powdered sugar
1 teaspoon vanilla
2 squares unsweetened
 chocolate

Melt 1 stick butter or margarine and chocolate together, and add to mixture of ¼ cup sugar, vanilla, egg, and graham crackers. Spread in a 9 x 13-inch pan and press down. Top with coconut and nuts; refrigerate for several hours.

Make icing mixture by mixing ¼ cup butter or margarine, 1 tablespoon milk or cream, 2 cups powdered sugar, and 1 teaspoon vanilla. Spread over mixture in pan. Melt 2 squares chocolate and brush/pour over top. Refrigerate for several hours. Take out 30 minutes before slicing so that chocolate top does not crack. Cut into 1½-inch squares to serve.

Mrs. Richard L. Voorhees (Barbara)

"Surprize" Kiss Cookies

May prepare ahead   Makes 3-4 dozen

1⅓ sticks butter
4 tablespoons powdered sugar
1 tablespoon ice water
1 tablespoon vanilla

2 cups flour
1 cup pecans, finely chopped
1-7 ounce bag Hershey's
 Kisses
Powdered sugar

Cream together butter, 4 tablespoons powdered sugar, and ice water. Blend in flour, then vanilla and nuts. Wrap one tablespoon of dough around each Kiss. Bake at 350 degrees for 40 to 45 minutes or until dough is set, but only lightly browned. Roll each cookie in powdered sugar while warm.

Mrs. Dale Brittain (Beth)

Rebecca's Refrigerator Cookies

Garrett's mom always has a cookie jar full of these when the family visits.
The cookie jar is always empty when they leave.

May prepare ahead   Makes 4 rolls

2 cups brown sugar
1 cup Crisco
2 eggs, beaten
1 teaspoon soda
1 teaspoon cream of tartar

4 cups flour
1 cup pecans, chopped
1 teaspoon vanilla
½ teaspoon salt

Cream Crisco. Add beaten eggs. Mix soda, cream of tartar and salt with 1 cup of flour. Mix well. Add nuts and vanilla. Pour onto floured board and knead in rest of flour. Form into 4 long rolls. Slice and bake at 375 degrees for 8 to 10 minutes (not too brown).

Mrs. H. Garrett Rhyne

Fruit Cake Cookies

May prepare ahead   Makes 3 dozen

½ cup butter
1 cup dark brown sugar
4 eggs
3 tablespoons milk
2½ cups flour (reserve
   ½ cup for fruit)
2 teaspoons soda
1 teaspoon cloves
1 teaspoon cinnamon

1 teaspoon nutmeg
1 jigger whiskey
½ pound candied cherries,
   chopped
½ pound candied pineapple,
   chopped
1½ pounds pecans, chopped
2¼ cups white raisins

Cream butter and sugar. Add eggs, one at a time, beating after each. Add milk, flour, soda, cloves, cinnamon, nutmeg, and whiskey; mix well. Flour fruit with ½ cup of reserved flour. Pour batter over fruit and mix. Drop by teaspoon on greased cookie sheet. Bake at 250 degrees for 35 minutes.

Susie Phelps-Sikes

Kahlua Dip and Wafers

May prepare ahead   Yields: 5 dozen

Wafers:

2¼ cups flour
¾ cup sugar
½ teaspoon salt
¼ teaspoon baking powder

¾ cup butter, softened
3 tablespoons Kahlua
½ teaspoon instant coffee
   crystals
1 teaspoon vanilla

Resift flour with sugar, salt, and baking powder. Blend in butter. Mix Kahlua, instant coffee, and vanilla; let stand a minute to soften coffee crystals. Add to flour mixture and blend to a moderately stiff dough. Chill for ½ hour or longer. Roll on a lightly floured board to ⅛-inch thickness. Cut with a floured cutter. Bake at 375 degrees for 5 to 7 minutes until edges are very lightly browned. Cool and store in an airtight container.

Dip:

1-8 ounce package cream cheese
¼ cup Kahlua
2 tablespoons light cream

2 tablespoons almonds,
   chopped, toasted, and
   blanched

Soften cream cheese. Gradually beat in Kahlua and cream until mixture is smooth. Stir in almonds. Serve with Kahlua wafers and fruit such as strawberries, apples, pineapples, and bananas for dipping.

Peggy Cooke

Mother's Date Balls

May prepare ahead   Yields: 4 dozen

1 pound dates, chopped
1 stick butter
2 egg yolks, beaten
⅔ cup sugar

1 teaspoon vanilla
2 cups Rice Krispies
1 cup pecans, chopped
Powdered sugar

Cook dates, butter, egg yolks, and sugar in a skillet, stirring constantly until the mixture bubbles. Continue to stir for 3 minutes. Remove from heat and add the remaining ingredients. Stir until cool. Roll into balls and sprinkle with powdered sugar.

Claire Kincaid

Peanut Butter Squares

May prepare ahead   *Yields: 36 squares*

2 sticks margarine, melted
1½ cups crushed graham
  cracker crumbs
1½ cups (1-12 ounce jar) peanut
  butter

1-1 pound box powdered
  sugar
1-12 ounce package semi-
  sweet chocolate (or
  butterscotch) morsels

Mix margarine, cracker crumbs, peanut butter, and sugar into a
11 x 15-inch pan. Melt chocolate morsels in top of a double boiler. Spread
over crumbs. Cut into squares when chocolate (or butterscotch) hardens.

Mrs. Tom D. Efird (Ann)

Persimmon Cookies

May prepare ahead   Makes 2 to 3 dozen
Freezes well after cooking

1 cup butter
1 cup brown sugar
1 egg
1 cup persimmon pulp
1 teaspoon vanilla

1 teaspoon baking powder
1 teaspoon soda
½ teaspoon salt
2 cups flour

Cream together softened butter and brown sugar. Mix in egg, persimmon
pulp, and vanilla. Add dry ingredients. Drop the batter by teaspoonsful
on an ungreased cookie sheet. Bake at 350 degrees for 12 minutes.

Hint: Use either wild persimmons or the large "tame" persimmons from
the grocery store.

Another note on persimmons: Have you heard that persimmons may not be
picked until after the first frost? That is simply an old wives tale! Some
trees have ripe fruit as early as September, while other persimmons may
not ripen until Thanksgiving. Look for VERY soft persimmons - those
are the sweet, delicious fruits.

Mrs. Kay Kincaid Moss

Linzer Hearts

Must prepare ahead   Makes 4 to 5 dozen

3 sticks sweet butter
1¾ cups powdered sugar,
  softened
1 egg
2 cups unbleached flour

1 cup cornstarch
2 cups walnuts, finely
  chopped
½ cup red raspberry
  preserves

Cream butter and 1 cup of the sugar until light and fluffy. Add egg and mix well. Sift together the flour and cornstarch; add to creamed mixture and blend well. Mix walnuts in thoroughly. Gather dough into a ball. Wrap in plastic wrap and chill for 4 to 6 hours or overnight.

On a well-floured surface roll dough out to ¼-inch thickness. Using a small heart-shaped cookie cutter about 1½-inches long, cut out cookies and place on a cookie sheet lined with parchment paper. Chill cookies for 45 minutes.

Preheat oven to 325 degrees. Bake cookies for 10 to 15 minutes or until they are very lightly browned around the edges. While they are still warm, spread half of the cookies with raspberry preserves, using ¼ teaspoon of jam for each. Top each with one of the remaining cookies. Sift the remaining ¾ cups powdered sugar into a bowl and press tops, bottoms, and sides of the cookies into sugar to cool.

Jennifer Davis

Mom's Butter Cookies

May prepare ahead   Yields: 3 to 4 dozen
Freezes well

½ pound butter
1 cup sugar
3 cups minus 1 tablespoon
  flour

2 egg yolks
1 teaspoon vanilla
Jelly or preserves

Cream butter and sugar, add yolks and flour. Shape into marble-size balls. Make cavity in center and fill with jelly. Bake at 325 degrees until bottom of cookies is slightly browned.

Cathy Foster

Ruthie's Gingerbread Men

These stay good for a long time.
Make at Thanksgiving and they are still good in February.

May prepare ahead   Makes a bunch

1½ cups water   3 cups sugar
2 tablespoons dark corn syrup   1 pound butter
2 tablespoons cloves   10 cups flour
2 tablespoons ginger   1 tablespoon soda
2 tablespoons cinnamon

Mix the 1½ cups of water with the spices and syrup. Bring to a full rolling boil. Meanwhile, cream sugar and butter. Add the spice mixture to
the creamed mixture. Add the flour and soda one cup at a time. Chill
overnight in the refrigerator. Roll on a well-floured board. Cut into
gingerbread men. Make a hole at the top if you wish to hang them on
the tree. Add raisins for decoration, if desired. Bake on an ungreased
cookie sheet at 375 degrees for 6 to 10 minutes. You may also decorate
with icing.

Allison Decker Sonier

Nell's Gingersnaps

May prepare ahead   Makes 2 to 3 dozen

1½ cups butter   1 tablespoon ginger
1 cup sugar   1 teaspoon cinnamon
1 egg   ½ teaspoon salt
¼ cup molasses   ½ teaspoon soda
2 cups flour

Cream butter. Add sugar, egg, and molasses. Add spices to flour and add
to creamed mixture. Roll into small balls and roll in sugar. Bake at 325
degrees for 6 to 10 minutes.

Allison Decker Sonier

Shrewsbury Cakes (Cookies)

*Shrewsbury cakes were popular in early America. This particular
recipe is an adaptation of "To Make Shrewsbury Cakes" from a pre-1715
manuscript that belonged to Martha Washington. These wonderful delicate
shortbread cookies are perfect for 20th century parties as well!
(I research eighteenth century foods and experiment with early methods
of open hearth cookery. This recipe is my absolute favorite!)*

May prepare ahead   Makes 3-4 dozen

1½ cups butter
¾ cup sugar
1 egg white
1 tablespoon rosewater
1 teaspoon sherry

4 cups flour
½ tablespoon cinnamon
1 pinch each-cloves and mace
A little heavy cream (enough
   to make a light dough)

Cream butter and sugar. Add egg white, rosewater, and sherry. Mix
together flour, cinnamon, cloves, and mace. Add these dry ingredients
to wet ingredients. Add heavy cream, a little at a time, to make a light
dough (approximately 1 tablespoon). Roll dough and cut into shapes.
Bake at 375 degrees until lightly browned (approximately 10 minutes).

Hint: Rosewater is available from fancy food stores and pharmacies (be
sure to tell your pharmacist you plan to use the rosewater for flavoring
in foods).

Mrs. Kay Kincaid Moss

Popcorn Trees

Fun for kids and nice for grade mothers to do.

May prepare ahead   Makes 12-16 cones

12-16 ice cream cones
2½ cups powdered sugar
Popped popcorn
Green colored sugar

1 egg white
1 tablespoon water
Red cinnamon candies

Fill cones with popcorn. Cover filled cones with frosting made by mixing together powdered sugar, unbeaten egg white, and water. Decorate
with red cinnamon candies or green colored sugar.

Ginny Hall

Helen's Fudge

May be made weeks ahead
and stored in refrigerator

Makes 5 pounds

5½ cups sugar
1 tall can evaporated milk

¾ pound margarine

Mix the above ingredients and bring to a boil. Boil exactly 8 minutes, stirring constantly. Remove from stove and stir in the following ingredients in order as listed: (Make sure that you add the marshmallow creme last and after all other ingredients are well blended.)

6 squares unsweetened
  chocolate, melted
12 ounces chocolate chips

1 tablespoon vanilla
Pinch salt
1 large jar marshmallow
  creme

Pour into a buttered 9 x 13-inch pan and let set up. When hardened, cut into small squares.

Mary Lou Norcross

English Toffee

May prepare ahead

Makes one 10 x 13-inch slab

½ pound butter
1 cup sugar
1 tablespoon white corn
  syrup

3 tablespoons water
1½ cups nuts, chopped
6 ounces chocolate chips

In a medium-size saucepan melt butter and add sugar. When blended, add corn syrup and water. Stir constantly over moderate heat until mixture reaches hard crack, 290 degrees on a candy thermometer. Add 1 cup chopped nuts and continue cooking and stirring 3 more minutes. Remove from heat and pour immediately onto foil lined cookie sheet. Spread out.

When cooled, ice with half the chocolate chips, melted, and sprinkle with half the remaining nuts. Let first side cool and set, then turn and repeat chocolate and nuts on the other side. When cooled, candy can be broken into pieces.

Mrs. Robert Clements ("Tuga")

Peanut Brittle

Must prepare ahead   Serves 8-10

3 cups sugar   3 teaspoons butter
¼ cup water   1 teaspoon salt
1 cup light corn syrup   1 teaspoon soda
3 cups raw peanuts

Combine first three ingredients. Bring to a soft boil and add peanuts, stirring constantly until brownish-gold. Remove from heat; add butter, soda, and salt. Pour very quickly onto sheet of aluminum foil. Spread and let cool. Break into pieces to serve.

Marjorie Kircus

Peanut Butter Balls

May prepare ahead   Makes 3 to 4 dozen
Freezes well

2 sticks butter   2 cans Angel Flake coconut
1-16 ounce box powdered sugar   1-12 ounce jar crunchy
2½ cups graham cracker   peanut butter
  crumbs   2 teaspoons vanilla
1 cup pecans, chopped

Melt butter in saucepan. Add sugar, graham cracker crumbs, nuts, coconut, peanut butter, and vanilla. Knead well (this takes time and strength to mix all this together). Roll into balls about the size of walnuts. Refrigerate on cookie sheets covered with wax paper. Dip in chocolate mixture (below) and keep in refrigerator in covered container.

Chocolate mixture:
1 large bag Nestle semi-sweet   ½ bar parafin wax
  chocolate chips

Melt chocolate chips and wax in double boiler over low heat, stirring constantly.

Mrs. Donald D. Howe

Ambrosia

This is best when prepared ahead and allowed to stand overnight for the flavors to mix. Serve as a dessert with fruit cake, Lane Cake, etc...at Thanksgiving and Christmas. An old family favorite at our house!

May prepare ahead   Serves 10-12

1 dozen oranges	**1 cup sugar**
1 coconut	

Peel, seed, and section oranges. Open and grate coconut, saving the coconut milk. Add coconut, coconut milk, and sugar to the orange sections and mix well. Maraschino cherries may be added for color. Serve in a glass bowl.

Patti Hunter

Apple Crisp

This is great served warm with ice cream.

May prepare ahead   Serves 4

4 apples	**1 teaspoon salt**
¼ cup water	**1 teaspoon cinnamon**

Topping:

1 cup sugar	**¾ cup flour**
1 stick margarine, softened	

Peel and pare apples; arrange in baking dish. Mix water, salt, and cinnamon; pour over apples. Top with topping (which may be combined in food processor, but is better if you mix by hand). Bake at 350 degrees for 30 to 45 minutes.

Mrs. William P. Adams (Becky)

Boston Creme Dessert

This is also called Chocolate Eclair Cake. It is excellent.

Must prepare ahead   Serves 8-10

2 boxes instant Jello French   1-12 ounce carton Cool Whip
  vanilla pudding   1 box graham crackers
3 cups milk   1 can Pillsbury chocolate
                                    fudge frosting

Mix 2 boxes of pudding with 3 cups of milk. Add Cool Whip and stir until smooth. Line a 9 x 12-inch glass pan with graham crackers. Pour ½ of pudding on top. Place another layer of graham crackers on top of pudding. Pour other half of pudding on top. Frost the top layer with frosting. Refrigerate. Better if sits for 24 hours.

Mrs. Fred Ridgeway Jones, Jr. (Vicki)
Lin Lineberger

Chocolate and White Fondues

Serve immediately   Serves 8

12 ounces milk chocolate or   2 tablespoons kirsch or
  sweet cooking chocolate   brandy or, if desired, 2
¾ cup light cream   teaspoons instant coffee

Assorted fruits and cakes for dipping:
Mandarin orange sections   Pineapple chunks
Maraschino cherries   Seedless green grapes
Apple wedges   Cubes of pound cake
Strawberries   Cubes of angel food cake
Bananas   Marshmallows

Heat chocolate in cream over low heat, stirring until chocolate is melted. Remove from heat and stir in liqueur. Pour into fondue pot or chafing dish to keep warm.

White Fondue:
Follow directions for Chocolate Fondue except substitute white almond bark coating for milk chocolate and decrease light cream to ⅓ cup.

Golden Delicious Apple Cobbler

This is great served warm with vanilla ice cream on top.

May prepare ahead   Serves 4-6

½ cup water
1¼ cups sugar
Juice of one lemon
5 medium Golden Delicious
  apples, peeled and sliced

2 ready-made pie crusts or
  equivalent recipe, at
  room temperature
1¼ cups butter or
  margarine

Bring to boil in medium saucepan over medium heat water, sugar, and lemon juice. Add apples and cook until apples are soft. If using frozen pie crusts, make sure they are thawed enough to be pliable. Press one pie crust into a 1½-quart deep dish. Pour in apple mixture. Dot with butter. Put remaining crust on top, trimming to fit. Bake at 350 degrees for 40 minutes.

Mrs. Anne Neal

Baked Apple-Pumpkin Pudding

Serve immediately   Serves 6-8

1½ cups applesauce
1 cup canned pumpkin
¾ cup dark brown sugar,
  packed
½ teaspoon salt

⅛ teaspoon ground cloves
1 teaspoon cinnamon
¼ teaspoon ground nutmeg
4 eggs, thoroughly beaten
1 cup light cream

Combine applesauce, pumpkin, sugar, salt, and spices. Mix well; stir in well-beaten eggs; cream; blend thoroughly. Pour into a buttered 2-quart baking dish. Bake in a preheated 350-degree oven for 1 hour and 15 minutes or until mixture is firm. Serve warm, if desired, with whipped cream into which grated orange rind has been folded; or if you prefer, serve with extra applesauce.

Ellen K. Widmer

Apple Strudel

Serve immediately   Serves 6-8

2 cups plus 2 tablespoons
  flour
½ teaspoon salt
⅔ cup shortening
½ cup half-n-half
½ to 1 cup sugar
Dash of salt

1 tablespoon lemon juice
2 tablespoons butter, melted
1 tablespoon cinnamon
1 teaspoon ginger
2 cups apples, peeled and
  sliced

Combine 2 cups flour and ½ teaspoon salt; cut in shortening. Add half-n-half and stir until moistened. Shape into a ball and chill.

Combine sugar, dash of salt, lemon juice, butter, cinnamon, ginger, and apples. Mix well.

Roll pastry into 12 x 8-inch rectangle on a lightly floured surface. Spread with apple mixture. Roll up jellyroll fashion, beginning at long side; moisten edges and ends with water to seal. Transfer roll to a greased 15 x 10 x 1-inch jellyroll pan. Bake at 425 degrees for 40 minutes. Cool for 5 minutes and transfer to a serving platter.

Sprinkle with powdered sugar and cinnamon. Serve with whipped cream.

Allison Decker Sonier

Banana Pudding

Must prepare day before   Serves 12

Vanilla wafers
10 bananas, sliced
1-small container Cool Whip
1-8 ounce carton sour cream

1 package instant vanilla
  pudding, prepared with
  2 cups milk

Place vanilla wafers in bottom of Pyrex dish. Slice bananas and place on top of vanilla wafers. Mix Cool Whip, sour cream, and vanilla pudding. Pour over bananas and wafers. Cover and refrigerate overnight.

Mrs. Donald R. Thrower

Smokey Mountain Blackberry Pudding

This "pudding" is actually a moist cake.

May prepare ahead   Serves 6
Freezes well

1½ cups flour	½ cup shortening
1 cup brown sugar	⅓ cup buttermilk
½ teaspoon soda	1 egg
¼ teaspoon salt	2 cups blackberries

Mix all dry ingredients. Rub in shortening. Stir in buttermilk and egg or mix at low speed. Stir in blackberries. Bake in well-greased 8-inch square pan in a 350-degree oven until lightly browned, approximately 1 hour.

Mrs. Kay Kincaid Moss

Blueberry Pudding

Delicious served with whipped cream topping or ice cream.

Serve immediately   Serves 4-6

1 quart blueberries, washed	1 cup flour
1 cup butter, melted	1 cup sugar
½ teaspoon cinnamon	Juice of ½ lemon

Place blueberries in bottom of casserole dish. Mix all other ingredients and toss lightly with blueberries. Bake in preheated 350-degree oven for 45 minutes.

Mrs. James B. Garland (Betsy)

Bread Pudding and Whiskey Sauce

Must prepare ahead   Serves 8-10

2 cups milk	1 teaspoon cinnamon
1 stick butter	½ teaspoon nutmeg
3 eggs	½ cup raisins
Sugar to desired sweetness	5 cups French bread cubes,
1 teaspoon vanilla extract	day-old (about 1 loaf)

Whiskey sauce:
1 stick butter   ½ cup bourbon, divided
1 cup sugar

To prepare pudding:
Scald milk; remove from heat; stir in butter to melt. Beat eggs on high until pale and frothy. Add sugar, vanilla, cinnamon, and nutmeg. Beat until well blended. Beat in milk to blend. Stir in raisins. Grease a 1½-quart dish. Place bread in pan, pour egg-milk mixture over bread, and stir until bread is soaked. Let stand for 30 minutes patting down bread occasionally.

Preheat oven to 350 degrees. Place pudding in oven and lower to 300 degrees, bake for 40 minutes. Increase temperature to 425 degrees and continue baking until browned and puffy, about 15 to 20 minutes. Serve warm with sauce spooned over top.

To prepare Whiskey Sauce:
Heat butter, sugar, and ¼ cup bourbon until hot and steamy, and sugar is dissolved. Stir occasionally. Add remaining ¼ cup bourbon and serve over pudding.

Mrs. Barbara McCarthy

Rice Pudding

Serve immediately   Serves 4-6

½ cup rice, uncooked	3 eggs
4 cups milk	¾ cup sugar
¼ cup butter	

Combine rice and milk and cook until rice is tender. Add butter and mix. Beat eggs; mix in sugar. Add to hot rice mixture, mixing well. Pour into a 2-quart baking dish and bake for 50 minutes at 350 degrees.

Cookbook Committee

Sherry Pudding

May prepare ahead   Serves 12

6 egg yolks   ½ cup water
1 cup sugar   6 egg whites, stiffly beaten
1 cup sherry   1 cup vanilla wafer crumbs
1 tablespoon gelatin   1 cup pecans, finely chopped
                                   ½ pint whipping cream

Beat egg yolks; add 1 cup sugar and 1 cup sherry. Cook in double boiler until thick. Stir in 1 tablespoon gelatin which has been dissolved in ½ cup water. Let stand until it begins to congeal. Fold in 6 stiffly beaten egg whites. Place thin layer of custard in greased Pyrex loaf pan, followed by layer of crumbs and nuts which has been mixed. Repeat layers until all is used. Pat down each layer well. Congeal in refrigerator, unmold, and ice with whipped cream. Slice as you would a loaf cake.

Mrs. William A. Current

Chocolate Layer Dessert

May prepare ahead   Serves 8-10

1 cup flour   1-3½ ounce package
1 stick butter or margarine,   instant chocolate
   softened   pudding
1 cup pecans, chopped   2 cups milk
1 cup powdered sugar   1 semi-sweet chocolate bar,
1-8 ounce package cream   grated or ½ cup
   cheese   pecans, chopped
1 cup Cool Whip from a large
   carton
1-3½ ounce package instant
   vanilla pudding

Crust: Mix flour, butter, and 1 cup chopped pecans; spread in a 9 x 13-inch baking dish. Press down mixture with a fork. Bake at 350 degrees for 20 minutes. Let cool. 1st layer: Mix sugar, cream cheese, and Cool Whip; spread on crust.

2nd layer: Whip pudding mixes with milk. Spread on 1st layer. Spread the remaining Cool Whip from the large carton on the 2nd layer and top with grated candy bar or nuts. Refrigerate until ready to serve.

Variation: Butterscotch pudding may be substituted.

Mrs. Elizabeth Neisler Sumner
Mrs. Carol G. Matthews

345

Chocolate Mousse

Must prepare ahead   Serves 8-10

6 ounces unsweetened
  chocolate, broken into pieces
1 cup sugar, divided
⅓ cup water
6 large eggs, at room
  temperature
¼ teaspoon cream of tartar

2 tablespoons strong coffee
  (or 1 teaspoon instant
  coffee dissolved in 2
  tablespoons hot water)
1 tablespoon vanilla extract

Cut chocolate pieces in half and add to work bowl of food processor fitted with metal blade. Turn machine on and off a few times, then process 1 minute or more until chocolate is very finely chopped. Dissolve ½ cup sugar in water and bring to a rolling boil. With the machine running, pour boiling mixture through feed tube and process until smooth. Let mixture stand in processor. Separate eggs. With an electric mixer beat egg whites with cream of tartar until firm. Then add remaining ½ cup sugar gradually, beating until stiff peaks form.

Add egg yolks, coffee, and vanilla to cooled chocolate mixture. Turn machine on and off. Scrape down sides. Let machine run 3 to 4 seconds. Add ¼ of the egg whites and process, turning machine on and off, until well mixed. Add remaining egg whites all at once. Turn machine on and off only until the chocolate mixture starts to cover the egg whites. Do not overprocess. If large clumps of egg white remain, gently fold them in with a spatula. It does not matter if mixture has streaks of egg white. Spoon mixture into 9 individual ½ cup serving dishes or a 1½-quart serving dish. Refrigerate several hours until firm.

For a baked version of this mousse, spoon mixture into 10 individual 6-ounce custard cups, filling them ⅔ full. Place filled cups on an aluminum baking sheet which has been preheated in a 425-degree oven. Bake for 12 to 15 minutes or until well puffed.

Lin Lineberger

Kahlua Mousse

This is my original recipe.

May prepare ahead   Serves 4

¼ cup brewed coffee
20 large marshmallows, cut
  into pieces
3 tablespoons Kahlua (or
  coffee liqueur)

1 cup non-dairy whipped
  topping
Unsweetened chocolate

Combine coffee and marshmallows over low heat, stirring frequently until marshmallows are melted. Stir in Kahlua. Chill until thick (for about 1 hour). Beat in topping until well-blended. Spoon into individual dishes. Chill at least 1 hour before serving. Top with dollop of whipped topping and shavings of unsweetened chocolate.

Candy Grooms

Lemon Mousse With Blueberries

Must prepare ahead   Serves 6

1 quart blueberries
1 cup sugar, divided
5 eggs, separated

Juice of 2 large lemons
1 cup cream, whipped stiffly
2½ teaspoons lemon zest,
  grated

Wash berries and put in serving bowl. Sprinkle with ¼ cup sugar. In a double boiler beat egg yolks with the rest of the sugar over heat until mixture is a light lemon color. Add lemon juice and cook, stirring until mixture coats a spoon. DO NOT BOIL. Remove from heat and cool. Beat egg whites until stiff. Fold gently into cooled lemon mixture. Fold in cream and lemon zest. Chill. Just before serving, spoon the cold mousse over the berries.

Serving: Dessert looks very light and pretty in a clear glass serving dish such as a souffle dish or glass brioche mold. Garnish with sprigs of mint.

Hint: When grated lemon zest is called for, I use a vegetable peeler to peel strips of lemon rind without any bitter white pith. Then I mince them with a sharp knife. I find this much easier and less messy than trying to grate the lemon (especially since I always scrape the ends of my finger on the grater!)

Mrs. Barbara McCarthy

Austrian Chocolate Mousse

May prepare ahead   Serves 6

1 cup chocolate bits
1 ounce unsweetened chocolate
Boiling water
¾ cup XXXX powdered sugar
2 teaspoons vanilla

4 eggs, separated
4 tablespoons sweet butter,
    softened (Land O Lakes)
½ cup heavy cream
2 tablespoons powdered
    sugar

Put chocolate bits and broken unsweetened chocolate in bowl. Pour boiling water over to cover. Cover bowl tightly and let stand for 5 minutes. Uncover and carefully pour off as much water as possible. Add ¾ cup powdered sugar, vanilla, egg yolks, and butter. Beat until smooth. In separate bowl beat egg whites until stiff but not dry. Fold into chocolate mixture and place in pretty glass bowl. Chill several hours until set. Whip cream with 2 tablespoons powdered sugar and garnish top of mousse.

Peggy Hall

Swedish Cream

*This recipe was sent to me from my mother, from The Junior
League of Knoxville, Tennessee, Cookbook, The Pear Tree.*

Must prepare ahead   Serves 8-10

1 cup sugar
1 envelope unflavored gelatin
2 cups heavy cream
2-8 ounce cartons sour cream

1 teaspoon vanilla
Frozen raspberries, thawed,
    OR other sweetened
    sliced fruit

Combine sugar, gelatin, and cream in a medium saucepan. Let gelatin soften for 5 minutes. Over medium heat, stir constantly until gelatin is dissolved. Remove from heat and let cool. Stir in sour cream and vanilla. Pour into a glass bowl or pan and refrigerate until set, at least 4 hours (or overnight).

When ready to serve, spoon mixture into stemmed sherbet glasses and top with desired fruit. This is so simple, but very elegant.

Mrs. Samuel L. Howe (Cherry)

Sis Torrence's Chocolate Torte

*The ladies of the bridge club celebrated my engagement with a beautiful
lunch at Scotty Quinn's complete with recipes. This cake, served with
style by Charlie Holmes, was the hit of the party.*

Must prepare ahead   Serves 12

1¾ cups flour	1¾ cups sugar
¼ teaspoon baking powder	1¼ teaspoons soda
1 teaspoon salt	1 teaspoon vanilla
4-1 ounce squares	⅔ cup margarine, softened
unsweetened chocolate,	1¼ cups water
melted	3 eggs

Combine all ingredients except eggs together in a large mixing bowl;
beat for 2 minutes at medium speed with an electric mixer. Add eggs
and beat for an additional 2 minutes. Spoon ¼ of the batter into each
of 4 greased and floured 9-inch cake pans and bake at 350 degrees for
20 to 22 minutes. Let cool in pan for 10 minutes; then remove and allow
to cool completely. (These can be done ahead and frozen.)

Chocolate filling:

1½-4 ounce Hershey bars	¾ cup margarine, softened
½ cup toasted almonds,	
chopped	

Melt chocolate in a double boiler and let cool. Add margarine beating
at low speed of mixer until smooth and thick. Stir in almonds.

Whipped cream:

2 cups whipping cream	1 teaspoon sugar
1 teaspoon vanilla	

Combine ingredients in cooled medium mixing bowl and beat until stiff
peaks form.

To assemble: Place 1 cake layer on plate and spread with ½ chocolate filling. Place another layer on top and spread with ½ whipped cream.
Repeat. Garnish with grated chocolate and refrigerate. Allow to come
to room temperature before serving or chocolate filling layer will be hard.

Mrs. H. Garrett Rhyne

New Year's Eve Charlotte Russe

Prepare 1 day ahead   Serves 8-10

2 eggs, separated
⅓ cup sugar
¼ teaspoon salt
1½ cups milk, scalded
1 envelope gelatin
¼ cup water
1 cup whipping cream
3 tablespoons powdered
  sugar
1 teaspoon vanilla

Cognac
3 tablespoons sherry
Light corn syrup
1½ dozen ladyfingers
Additional cup whipped
  cream slightly sweetened
  with 2 tablespoons
  powdered sugar and
  2 tablespoons cognac
  for garnish

Mix egg yolks, sugar, and salt in a double boiler. Add scalded milk and thicken. Soften gelatin in water and add to thickened custard. Let cool. Beat egg whites and fold into custard mixture. Whip cream and add vanilla, sugar, and cognac. Fold into custard mixture. Grease low crystal bowl with light corn syrup and line with ladyfingers. Sprinkle sherry over ladyfingers. Pour in mixture of custard, egg whites, and cream; refrigerate overnight. Before serving whip additional cream with sugar and cognac; garnish and serve by spoonfuls on dessert plates.

Billie May and Walter Carroll

Charlotte Russe

May prepare ahead   Serves 6-8

2 egg whites
½ cup powdered sugar, sifted
1 tablespoon unflavored
  gelatin
½ cup milk

2 teaspoons vanilla
4 tablespoons of sherry
1 pint whipping cream
Ladyfingers

Beat egg whites until stiff. Add sugar slowly and beat well. Soften gelatin in milk and place over very low heat until gelatin is dissolved. Cool this mixture a little and pour it over the egg whites, mixing well. Add vanilla and sherry. Then fold in cream which has been whipped. Arrange ladyfingers in bowl, sealing edges together. Pour in mixture; chill and serve.

Mrs. Tom Hunter (Patti)

Peach Cobbler

Makes Own Crust

May prepare ahead   Serves 6-8

1 stick butter or margarine	½ cup milk
¾ cup self-rising flour	1 egg, beaten
1¼ cups sugar	2 (or more) cups peaches

Preheat oven to 425 degrees. Into a 1½-quart casserole dish put stick of butter and put into oven to let butter melt as well as heating the dish. Meanwhile mix flour, sugar, milk, and egg together thoroughly. Pour mixture into hot dish; then spread the peaches evenly on top of the batter. DO NOT MIX. Bake at 425 degrees for 35 minutes, uncovered. (Substitute another fruit for the peaches, if desired, and top with vanilla ice cream.)

Cookbook Committee

Peach Ginger Crunch

This is an original recipe from my mother-in-law, Lois McCosh of Columbus, Georgia. She won the grand prize in the Peach Dish Contest with this recipe, during the 1976 Georgia Peach Festival, in Reynolds, Georgia.

Serve immediately   Serves 6-8

2 tablespoons butter	½ box yellow cake mix
6 large peaches	2 cups pecans, chopped or
¼ cup crystalized ginger,	whole
chopped	½ cup brown sugar
⅔ cup sugar	1 stick butter

Preheat oven to 250 degrees. Grease a deep dish pie plate with the 2 tablespoons of butter. Peel and slice peaches; mix with ginger and place in deep dish. Sprinkle with sugar, then put on the dry cake mix. Put pecans over the cake mix and sprinkle with brown sugar. Melt the 1 stick of butter and drizzle it over the top. Bake for 2 hours. Garnish with whipped cream or ice cream.

Cathy McCosh

Strawberry Chantilly Torte

This is a really fine dessert and well worth the effort. Men love it.

May prepare ahead   Serves 8-10

1 cup cake flour, sifted
1 teaspoon baking powder
¼ teaspoon salt
1 stick butter or margarine
1½ cups sugar, divided into 3
   equal amounts of ½ cup
   each
5 eggs, separated

1 teaspoon vanilla
3 tablespoons milk
¾ teaspoon almond extract
2 pints strawberries
2 cups cream for whipping
½ cup slivered almonds,
   toasted

Butter bottoms of two 9-inch layer cake pans. Dust lightly with flour, tapping out any excess. Sift flour, baking powder, and salt onto waxed paper. In a medium-size bowl cream butter or margarine with ½ cup sugar until fluffy. Beat in egg yolks, one at a time, until blended, then beat in vanilla and milk. Fold in flour mixture until blended; spread evenly in prepared pans.

Beat egg whites with ¼ teaspoon almond extract until foamy-white and double in volume in a large bowl; sprinkle in ¾ cup of the remaining sugar, 1 tablespoon at a time, beating all the time until sugar dissolves completely and meringue stands in firm peaks. Spread evenly over batter in pans; sprinkle with almonds.

Bake in 350-degree oven for 30 minutes or until meringue is delicately browned. Cool layers in pans on wire racks for 5 minutes; loosen around edges with a knife; turn each out onto palm of hand, then place, meringue side up on racks. Cool completely.

Wash strawberries, hull and quarter.

Beat cream with remaining ¼ cup sugar and ½ teaspoon almond extract.

To assemble: put part of strawberries and then cream on one layer of cake. Place cake layer on top of this and top with remaining berries, toasted slivered almonds, and cream.

Ginny Hall

James Forney's Strawberry Roll

Serve immediately   Serves 10-12

5 egg whites
1 cup sugar
5 egg yolks, beaten
Juice and rind of 1 lemon
1 cup flour, sifted

1 quart fresh strawberries
¼ cup sugar
2-½ pint cartons whipping
cream

On high speed of mixer beat egg whites until soft peaks form. Gradually add 1 cup of sugar. Turn mixer to low speed and quickly add the beaten egg yolks, lemon juice, and rind. By hand fold in flour, then pour into a jelly roll pan that has been greased and lined with wax paper. Bake at 350 degrees for 15 minutes or until done.

Turn out cake on a tea towel or cloth that has been sprinkled with 2 tablespoons of sugar. Roll up warm cake, from long side, in the towel and let cool. Wash and cap strawberries. Mix together 2 cups strawberries, cut very fine, with ¼ cup sugar. Unroll the cake and add sweetened strawberry mixture. Cut the remaining strawberries in halves to use for decoration. Reserve. Roll up the cake, beginning from long side. Beat cream until stiff. Frost cake roll with whipped cream. Garnish with reserved strawberries.

Catherine Ann Carstarphen

Strawberry Coconut Nests

May prepare ahead   Serves 8

1-8 ounce package cream
cheese, whipped
½ cup sugar
2 teaspoons milk
1 teaspoon vanilla
2 packages shortcake dessert
cakes

1-3½ ounce can flaked
coconut
1 quart fresh strawberries,
sweetened
Whipped cream

Combine cream cheese, sugar, milk, and vanilla. Beat until smooth. With fork remove small amount of center from each dessert cup. Frost cups with cream cheese mixture; sprinkle with coconut. At serving time, spoon strawberries into centers. Put dollop of sweetened whipped cream on top of each.

Mrs. J. Caswell Taylor, Jr.

Real Strawberry Shortcake

The shortcake layers may be frozen before stacking with berries.

May prepare ahead   Makes 1 dozen

2 cups flour   **¼ cup sugar**
¼ teaspoon salt   **½ cup butter, softened**
1 tablespoon baking powder   **½ cup milk**

Mix all dry ingredients. Work in softened butter with hands or knives. Mix in milk, just until a soft dough forms.

Roll out and cut into circles (use a plate for a pattern to cut circle), 6 to 10-inch diameter.

Bake on cookie sheet in a 400-degree oven for about 15 minutes or until golden. Cool. Assemble shortcake by stacking layers with sliced sugared strawberries. (Or use blackberries, raspberries, or sliced peaches.)

Pour heavy cream over shortcake as it is served on top with real whipped cream.

Mrs. Kay Kincaid Moss

Baked Vanilla Custard

This only has 101 calories per serving.

Serve immediately   Serves 6

3 eggs, slightly beaten   **½ to 1 teaspoon vanilla**
¼ cup sugar   **2 cups skim milk, scalded**
¼ teaspoon salt   **Nutmeg**

Combine eggs, sugar, salt, and vanilla; beat well. Gradually add milk, stirring constantly. Pour into 6-6 ounce custard cups. Sprinkle with nutmeg, if desired. Place cups in a 13 x 9 x 2-inch pan. Pour hot water into pan to a depth of 1 inch. Bake at 325 degrees for 40 to 45 minutes or until knife inserted halfway between center and edge of custard comes out clean. Remove cups from water; cool. Chill thoroughly.

Cookbook Committee

Justines

Must prepare ahead   Serves 10

½ gallon Breyers vanilla   ½ cup brandy
  ice cream   Sliced almonds

Soften ice cream and mix with brandy. Pour into parfaits, cover, and freeze. Remove from freezer 10 minutes before eating. Top with sliced almonds.

Ann Cain

Lemon Snow With Custard Sauce

Must prepare ahead   Serves 6

1 envelope unflavored gelatin   1 cup frozen lemonade or
¾ cup cold water   limeade concentrate
½ cup sugar   2 egg whites
⅛ teaspoon salt

Sprinkle gelatin on cold water in top of double boiler to soften. Place over boiling water and stir until gelatin is dissolved. Remove from heat, add sugar and salt; stir until dissolved. Add frozen lemonade or limeade and stir until melted. Chill until mixture is consistency of beaten egg whites. Add egg whites. Beat until mixture begins to hold its shape. Turn into a 6-cup mold or individual molds. Chill until firm. Unmold and serve with Custard Sauce.

Custard Sauce:
1½ cups milk   3 tablespoons sugar
1 whole egg   ⅛ teaspoon salt
2 egg yolks   1 teaspoon vanilla

Scald milk in top of double boiler. Beat whole egg and egg yolks; stir in sugar and salt. Gradually add small amount of the hot milk, stirring constantly.

Return to double boiler and cook, stirring constantly over hot (not boiling) water until mixture coats the spoon. Remove from heat, cool. Stir in vanilla.

Mrs. W. J. Pharr (Catherine)

Lila's Fruit Ice

May be served as a palate refresher or a wonderful summer dessert.

Must prepare ahead   Serves 6

1 cup sugar	5 tablespoons lemon juice
1½ cups boiling water	½ cup orange juice
1 teaspoon lemon rind	1 cup apricots plus juice
1 teaspoon orange rind	1½ bananas

Dissolve sugar in the water and lemon rind and orange rind. COOL. Rice apricots and bananas. Fold into cooled liquid. Stir in orange juice and lemon juice and freeze in ice cream freezer, stirring occasionally. Serve in scalloped ½ orange shell garnished with fresh mint or candied orange slice.

Sandy Rankin

Homemade Butter Pecan Ice Cream

This recipe originated from Helen Moore's column in
The Charlotte Observer donated by Winnifred Nance.
I am always asked to bring this to our annual church picnic.

Must prepare ahead   Makes 3 quarts

3 tablespoons butter	1-3 ounce box butter pecan
1 cup pecans, chopped	pudding mix
3 large eggs	4 tablespoons Cremora in 1/4
1½ cups sugar	cup hot water
Dash of salt	1 teaspoon vanilla
1 can condensed milk	1 teaspoon maple flavoring
1 can evaporated milk	2 teaspoons butter flavoring
	Whole milk to fill cannister

Preheat oven to 300 degrees. Melt butter. Spread pecans out on a cookie sheet, pour butter over them and stir well. Cook in oven for 15 minutes, stirring often. Do NOT scorch! Set aside. Blend eggs, sugar, and salt. Add all other ingredients and mix together well. Pour into ice cream cylinder. Add milk to bring mixture to fill line. Freeze according to ice cream freezer instructions.

Mrs. Samuel L. Howe (Cherry)

Homemade Vanilla Ice Cream

Must prepare ahead   Serves 10-12

2-16 ounce cans Pet milk   2 cups sugar
½ pint whipping cream   2 teaspoons vanilla
1½ quarts milk

Mix all ingredients and pour into a gallon ice cream freezer. Freeze
according to freezer instructions. Option: You may add fresh strawberries
or peaches to make your favorite fruit ice cream.

Ruth Day Dickson

Vanilla Ice Cream
(with fruit)

Serve immediately   Makes 2 quarts

1 can Eagle Brand sweetened   2 tablespoons vanilla
  condensed milk   2 cups sweetened fruit
2 large eggs   (optional)
                                Milk to fill cannister

Mix condensed milk, eggs, and vanilla with an electric blender or
mixer. Fold in fruit if desired. Pour into freezer can of ice cream maker.
Add milk to fill line. Freeze according to manufacturer's directions.

Mrs. Anne N. Neal

Hot Fudge Sauce

May prepare ahead   Makes 3 cups

½ stick margarine   1¼ cups sugar
2 squares unsweetened   ½ teaspoon vanilla
  chocolate   1 large can evaporated milk

Combine ingredients in heavy saucepan. Simmer until it thickens, about
30 minutes. Serve over cake, vanilla ice cream, or ice cream pie.

Mrs. Mac Thornton

Cinnamon-Blueberry Sauce

This is originally from a Southern Living magazine.

Serve immediately   Yields: 1¼ cups

1-16½ ounce can blueberries,   **2 teaspoons cornstarch**
** undrained**   **½ teaspoon ground cinnamon**
¼ cup sugar   **2 tablespoons lemon juice**

Drain blueberries, reserving ¼ cup juice. Combine sugar, cornstarch and cinnamon in a small saucepan. Stir in reserved blueberry juice and lemon juice; blend well. Bring to a boil over medium heat; reduce heat to low and simmer for 5 minutes, stirring occasionally. Stir in blueberries. Serve sauce warm over ice cream.

Mrs. David Simpson (Emily)

Granola Ice Cream Topping

May prepare ahead   Makes 2 cups

2 cups granola   **1 tablespoon brown sugar**
4 tablespoons butter

Melt butter in frying pan. Stir in brown sugar until completely mixed. Add granola and cook over low heat for 2 to 3 minutes. Cool completely and pack in a glass jar to save.

To serve: Chill oven-proof serving bowls filled with ice cream that is still HARD. Layer granola heavily on top and run under broiler for about 30 seconds just before serving.

Mrs. Marilyn Johnson

Equivalents

Beans, green (cut)	1 pound	3 cups (uncooked)
Beans, dried	1 cup	½ pound
Bread	2 slices	1 cup crumbs
Butter	1 stick	½ cup or 8 tablespoons
Buttermilk	1 cup	1 cup yogurt
Carrots	7 to 9 carrots	2 cups (cooked) or 1 pound
Chocolate	1 square	1 ounce or 4 tablespoons (grated)
Cocoa	4 cups	1 pound
Coffee, ground	5 cups	1 pound or 40 to 50 cups
Cheese, grated	4 cups	1 pound
	1 cup	¼ pound
Crabmeat	2 cups	1 pound
Cream cheese	3-ounce package	6 tablespoons
Cream, heavy	½ pint	2 cups whipped
Cucumbers	2-6 inch cucumbers	1 pound
Dates, pitted	2 cups	1 pound
Eggs	1	¼ cup
Egg white	1	1½ tablespoons
Egg whites	4 to 6	½ cup
Egg yolk	1	1 tablespoon
Egg yolks	6 to 7	½ cup
Flour, sifted	4 cups	1 pound
Flour, cake	4½ to 5 cups	1 pound
Graham cracker crumbs	11 crackers	1 cup
Lemon	1 juiced	2½ tablespoons
Macaroni	1 cup, uncooked	2 cups, cooked
Meat, cooked and diced	2 cups	1 pound
Marshmallows	16	¼ pound
Milk, condensed	1¼ cups	14-ounce can
Milk, evaporated	⅔ cup	6-ounce can
	1⅔ cups	14½-ounce can
Noodles	1 cup, uncooked	1½ cups, cooked
Nuts, shelled	2 cups, chopped	½ pound
Orange	1 juiced	½ cup or 6 to 8 tablespoons

Peas, in pod	1 pound	1 to 1½ cups, shelled or 1 cup, cooked
Potatoes, white	1 pound	2 to 5 medium, or 2 to 3 cups cooked and mashed
Prunes	1 pound	4 cups, cooked
Raisins, seedless	3 cups	1 pound
Rice, uncooked	2¼ cups	1 pound
Rice, uncooked	1 cup	3 cups, cooked
Spinach	1 pound	6 cups raw, or 1½ cups cooked
Sugar, granulated	2 cups	1 pound
Sugar, brown (packed)	2¼ cups	1 pound
Sugar, powdered	3 to 3½ cups	1 pound
Tea, loose	1 pound	5 cups (about 155 tea cups)

Weights and Measures

Dash = Less than ⅛ teaspoon
Pinch = Less that ¼ teaspoon
1 tablespoon = 3 teaspoons = ½ ounce
2 tablespoons = 1 ounce = ⅛ cup
1½ ounces = 3 tablespoons = 1 jigger
4 tablespoons = ¼ cup
5⅓ tablespoons = ⅓ cup
8 tablespoons = ½ cup
16 tablespoons = 1 cup

1 cup = 8 ounces = ½ pint
2 cups = 1 pint = 1 pound
16 fluid ounces = 2 cups = 1 pint
4 cups = 1 quart = 32 ounces
2 pints = 32 ounces = 1 quart = 2 pounds
2 quarts = ½ gallon
4 quarts = 1 gallon = 8 pounds

Can Sizes

Can Size	Weight	Cupfuls
6-ounce can	6 ounces	¾ cup
8-ounce can	8 ounces	1 cup
12-ounce can	12 ounces	1½ cups
No. 1 can	11 ounces	1⅓ cups
No. 1½ or 303 can	16 ounces	2 cups
No. 2 can	20 ounces	2½ cups

Size of Pans and Baking Dishes

Common Kitchen Pans to Use as Casseroles When The Recipe Calls For:

4-cup baking dish:
  9-inch pie plate
  8 x 1¼-inch layer cake pan
  7⅜ x 3⅝ x 2¼-inch loaf pan

6-cup baking dish:
  8 or 9 x 1½-inch layer cake pan
  10-inch pie plate
  8½ x 3⅝ x 2⅝-inch loaf pan

8-cup baking dish:
  8 x 8 x 2-inch square pan
  11 x 7 x 1½-inch baking pan
  9 x 5 x 3-inch loaf pan

10-cup baking dish:
  9 x 9 x 2-inch square pan
  11¾ x 7½ x 1¾-inch baking pan
  15 x 10 x 1-inch jelly-roll pan

12-cup baking dish:
  13½ x 8½ x 2-inch glass baking pan

15-cup baking dish:
  13 x 9 x 2-inch metal baking pan

19-cup baking dish:
  14 x 10½ x 2½-inch roasting pan

Total Volume Of Various Special Baking Pans

Tube Pans:	
7½ x 3-inch bundt tube pan	6 cups
9 x 3½-inch fancy tube or bundt pan	9 cups
9 x 3½-inch angel cake pan	12 cups
10 x 3¾-inch bundt or crownburst pan	12 cups
9 x 3½-inch fancy tube mold	12 cups
10 x 4-inch fancy tube mold (Kugelhupf)	16 cups
10 x 4-inch angel cake pan	18 cups

Substitutions

1 teaspoon allspice	½ teaspoon cinnamon plus ⅛ teaspoon cloves plus ¼ teaspoon nutmeg
1 teaspoon baking powder	¼ teaspoon soda plus ½ teaspoon cream of tartar
1 cup butter	1 cup sweet milk plus 1 tablespoon lemon juice or vinegar
1 square chocolate (unsweetened)	3 tablespoons cocoa plus 1 tablespoon butter
1 6-ounce package chocolate (semi-sweet)	2 squares unsweetened chocolate plus 2 tablespoons shortening plus ½ cup sugar
3 tablespoons cocoa	1 square unsweetened chocolate (omitting 1 tablespoon butter)
1 tablespoon cornstarch	2 tablespoons flour (for thickening) or 4 teaspoons tapioca
¾ cup cracker crumbs	1 cup bread crumbs
1 whole egg	2 yolks plus 1 tablespoon water
1 cup flour, sifted	1 cup plus 2 tablespoons sifted cake flour
1 cup cake flour, sifted	1 cup minus 2 tablespoons flour
1 cup self-rising flour	1 cup flour and 1½ teaspoons baking powder
1 medium clove garlic	½ teaspoon garlic powder plus ⅛ teaspoon instant flakes plus ½ teaspoon salt (omitting other salt in recipe)
1 tablespoon fresh herb	1 teaspoon dried herbs
1 cup honey	3/4 cup sugar plus ¼ cup liquid
1 medium lemon	2 to 3 tablespoon juice or 1½ teaspoon lemon flavoring
1 cup fresh milk	½ cup evaporated milk plus ½ cup water or 4 tablespoons powdered milk dissolved in 1 cup water
1 cup molasses	1 cup honey
1 teaspoon dry mustard	1 tablespoon prepared mustard
1 medium onion	2 tablespoons instant, chopped, or minced onion flakes or 1½ teaspoons onion powder

1 teaspoon poultry
seasoning . . . . ¼ teaspoon thyme plus
¾ teaspoon sage

1 teaspoon pumpkin pie
spices . . . . ½ teaspoon cinnamon plus
½ teaspoon ginger plus
½ teaspoon allspice plus
⅛ teaspoon nutmeg

1 cup sour cream . . . . 1 cup evaporated milk (or 1 cup
heavy cream) plus 1 tablespoon
vinegar or ⅞ cup buttermilk plus
3 tablespoons butter

1 cup granulated sugar . . . 1 cup light brown sugar, well packed

1 cup tomato catsup . . . . . . 1 cup tomato sauce plus
½ cup sugar plus
2 tablespoons vinegar

1 cup tomato juice . . . . ½ cup tomato sauce plus
½ cup water

1 cup whipping cream . . . . ¾ cup whole milk plus
⅓ cup butter (only works if cream is
going into recipe to be cooked; will not
whip)

INDEX

Index

Order Form

Southern Elegance
Junior League of Gaston County, N.C.
P.O. Box 3684
Gastonia, North Carolina 28053

Please send ____ copies of **Southern Elegance**. $15.95 each
North Carolina residents add sales tax. $ .96 each
Postage and handling $ 2.50 each
                          TOTAL ENCLOSED $ _____

Name _____
Address _____
City _____ State _____ Zip _____

Charge to: Acct. # _____ Exp. Date _____

☐ VISA
☐ MASTERCARD _____ Phone (___) _____
                    Signature
Make checks payable to Southern Elegance.

- -

Order Form

Southern Elegance
Junior League of Gaston County, N.C.
P.O. Box 3684
Gastonia, North Carolina 28053

Please send ____ copies of **Southern Elegance**. $15.95 each
North Carolina residents add sales tax. $ .96 each
Postage and handling $ 2.50 each
                          TOTAL ENCLOSED $ _____

Name _____
Address _____
City _____ State _____ Zip _____

Charge to: Acct. # _____ Exp. Date _____

☐ VISA
☐ MASTERCARD _____ Phone (___) _____
                    Signature
Make checks payable to Southern Elegance.

Reorder Additional Copies

Order Form

Southern Elegance
Junior League of Gaston County, N.C.
P.O. Box 3684
Gastonia, North Carolina 28053

Please send _____ copies of **Southern Elegance**. $15.95 each

North Carolina residents add sales tax. $ .96 each

Postage and handling $ 2.50 each

             TOTAL ENCLOSED $ _____

Name _____

Address _____

City _____ State _____ Zip _____

Charge to: Acct. # _____ Exp. Date _____

☐ VISA
☐ MASTERCARD _____ Phone (___) _____
                  Signature

Make checks payable to Southern Elegance.

Order Form

Southern Elegance
Junior League of Gaston County, N.C.
P.O. Box 3684
Gastonia, North Carolina 28053

Please send _____ copies of **Southern Elegance**. $15.95 each

North Carolina residents add sales tax. $ .96 each

Postage and handling $ 2.50 each

             TOTAL ENCLOSED $ _____

Name _____

Address _____

City _____ State _____ Zip _____

Charge to: Acct. # _____ Exp. Date _____

☐ VISA
☐ MASTERCARD _____ Phone (___) _____
                  Signature

Make checks payable to Southern Elegance.

Reorder Additional Copies